Real English
Grammar

Hester Lott

the new pre intermediate grammar
Common European Framework: A2–B1

Marshall Cavendish
Education

© 2006 Marshall Cavendish Education

First published 2006 by Marshall Cavendish Education

Marshall Cavendish is a member of the Times Publishing Group

Marshall Cavendish ELT
119 Wardour Street
London W1F 0UW

www.mcelt.com/grammar

Design and production by Hart McLeod, Cambridge

Illustrations by Kate Charlesworth, Virginia Gray and Sarah Wimperis

Printed and bound by Times Offset (M) Sdn. Bhd. Malaysia

Introduction

To the teacher

This book is a comprehensive grammar and grammar practise book at pre intermediate level. It covers all the essential issues of English grammar in a way which is accessible to a student with limited vocabulary and grammatical knowledge. The book introduces the use of grammatical terminology, while at the same time explaining the meaning of the terms, so the students will gradually become familiar with the concepts and language involved. There are plenty of simple, natural examples of all the grammar explanations.

The underlying principle behind the book is presenting grammar in context. All the units begin with a text exemplifying the use of the grammar item in a real context. There is a CD of these initial texts (which are read in a variety of accents at a natural speed) which will help the students to improve both their comprehension and pronunciation of spoken English. The exercises are also contextualised and cover a wide variety of genres of modern English, from emails and stories, to schedules and quizzes. This should help your students get used to the kind of format they will meet in exams at a later stage, as well as sensitising them to features of grammar in various contexts and at the same time increasing their vocabulary.

The book can be used in a variety of ways:

- as the main text in a course with a grammatical syllabus
- as a grammar text book for remedial work in class on areas which cause problems for the students
- for self-study and revision set as homework
- for the students to keep to hand to check up on any areas of doubt they might have at any time when working in English.

There is an accompanying teacher's book which will give you more detailed instructions as how to best use the book, with sample lesson plans and some suggested extension exercises.

At the end of each group of units covering topics in related fields (for example, different tenses with future meaning, or articles and nouns) there is a Review Unit which revises and practises the topics covered. These could be used as tests.

The answers to the exercises are contained in the answer key booklet which you will find at the back of the book.

To the student

This book will help you move from elementary to intermediate level and should help you understand more complicated grammar. There is a free CD of reading texts to accompany this book. Our website (www.mcelt.com/grammar) has full details of how to receive your copy. You can listen to the CD as you read the texts, before going on to study each relevant grammar point. The book is full of stories, articles and conversations, which I hope you will enjoy reading and listening to.

You can start at the beginning and do all the units, or you can choose any units that you think will be helpful to you. It will be helpful to keep the book with you when you are doing your homework, or reading in English so you can quickly check anything that you are not clear about. There is an answer key which you can take out and use to check your answers.

Maliha

CONTENTS

present simple (I listen)

JIM WINS LBY AWARD

Jim Patterson is the winner of the 'Local Businessman of the Year' award. His company, Gargantuan Games, **designs** and **sells** computer games. It started in 1993 and it now **sells** 20 different games. It **has** a turnover of £2 million a year and **makes** a small profit. The game that people **like** best, and that **is** the biggest seller **is** *Space Rally Seven*. In this game, players **travel** through space in a race against other space ships. The players **have to** be careful not to crash into asteroids and not to get lost in black holes. Jim always **thinks** that his next new game will be the best ever!

[From The *Swenton Times*]

form	infinitive	singular	plural
	talk	I **talk**	we **talk**
		you **talk**	you **talk**
		he / she / it / Mark **talks**	they / Mark and Sarah **talk**

After **I**, **we**, **you** and **they**, we use the infinitive form (e.g. **talk** / **like** / **hope**). After **he**, **she**, and **it**, we add **s** (e.g. **knows** / **likes** / **hopes**). But with **ch**, **o**, **sh**, **ss**, we add **es**:

I teach → she teach**es**   we do → he do**es**
you push → it push**es**   they pass → she pass**es**

if the infinitive ends in <u>***consonant + y***</u>, it changes to ***consonant + ies***:

I stu<u>dy</u> → she stud**ies**   we fl<u>y</u> → it fl**ies**
have changes to **has**:
I have → he ha**s**

states

We use the present simple to talk about *states and situations that we expect to stay the same*:

- I **like** this band a lot. (*I like it now and I will probably like it next month.*)
- Sajjad **wants** to be an engineer.
- Tom **lives** in the centre of town.
- Alex **works** in the accounts department.

repeated events

We also use the present simple say that *something happens again and again*:

- Michael **cycles** to work in the morning. Madeleine **walks** to school.
- The computer shop **opens** at 10 a.m.
- The leaves **go** brown and **fall** from the trees in autumn.

We can also use the present simple to say *how often something happens* – with an *adverb* (e.g. **always**, **often**, **usually**, **sometimes**, **never**):

- Seema **always turns off** her computer in the evening.
- I **usually watch** the news on the TV in the morning.
- I **never look** at my emails at the weekend.

or with an *adverb phrase* (e.g. **every day**, **once a week**, **every weekend**):

- Sanjit **cleans** his car **every weekend**.
- I **pay** all my credit card bills **once a month**.

headlines

Newspapers use the present simple, particularly in headlines, to describe *recent events*:

- Mason **wins** gold!
- Thieves **steal** film star's cat

EXERCISES

A Read the information about Anita and her sister and put the words from the box in the right form into the gaps.

have	share	never	~~live~~	live	work	take	take	see	speak	offer	often	love
			go	phone	buy	finish						

Anita ⁰ _lives_ in Bangalore in the south of India. She has a flat in the north of Bangalore. The flat ¹............................ a sitting room, two bedrooms, a kitchen, and a bathroom. She ²............................ the flat with her sister, Mridul. Her sister is two years older than her. They like each other very much and they ³............................ argue about anything. Their father and mother ⁴............................ in Hyderabad, in the centre of India. Bangalore is a long way from Hyderabad, so the sisters ⁵............................ their parents only three or four times a year. Anita and Mridul both ⁶............................ in a telephone call centre. The telephone call centre is in the south of Bangalore. They ⁷............................ a bus to work every morning. They both ⁸............................ very good English and every day they ⁹............................ people all around the world and sell insurance products. They also ¹⁰............................ loans to people who need to borrow money. Most of the people that they speak to on the phone are friendly, but sometimes people can be quite rude. They ¹¹............................ work at about six in the evening and then they ¹²............................ some things in the local supermarket and ¹³............................ the bus home. In the evenings, Anita ¹⁴............................ does a yoga class and Mridul ¹⁵............................ to a dancing class. Mridul ¹⁶............................ Indian dancing.

B Read the notes in brackets about lightning and make sentences. Put the verbs in the right form.

0 (Lightning / happen / when there is a build up of electrical charge in the sky)
   Lightning happens when there is a build up of electrical charge in the sky.

1 (A positive charge / rise / from the ground through a cloud, and / move / to the top of the cloud)
   ....

2 (A negative charge / increase / at the bottom of the cloud)
   ....

3 (A giant spark / jump / between the charges)
   ....

4 (This spark / cause / lightning to flash within the cloud and from the cloud to the ground)
   ....

5 (Lightning / flash / somewhere in the world about 80 times every second)
   ....

6 (Lightning strikes / usually / occur / at the beginning or end of a storm)
   ....

7 (Lightning / injure / about 1000 people in the USA every year)
   ....

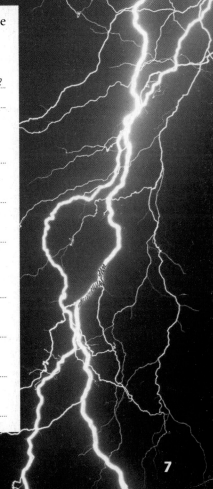

JANICE: Why **do** you **want** to become a pilot, Tom?

TOM: Well, I love flying – I am an airline steward, you see – but I **don't like** serving food all the time.

JANICE: **Do** you **need** perfect eyesight to be a pilot?

TOM: No, you **don't need** perfect eyesight – 20/20 vision, I mean – but I expect you need good eyesight (with or without glasses).

JANICE: Go on! Fill in the application form. You have to put your name in the top right box.

TOM: Which box? Sorry, often I **don't know** which is left and which is right.

JANICE: Oh dear! I **don't think** they will like that!

negatives

To make the negative of the present simple, we use **do not /does not** + *infinitive*:

infinitive	singular	plural
swim	I **do not swim**	we **do not swim**
	you **do not swim**	you **do not swim**
	he / she / it **does not swim**	they **do not swim**

We often use the contractions **don't** and **doesn't**:

do not → **don't**   does not → **doesn't**

We use the negative present simple to talk about –

states and long-term situations now:
- I know Maria but I **don't know** her husband.
- Henry **doesn't like** his school.
- I **don't have** a mobile phone.
- They **don't live** in Ireland – they have a house in Italy now.

things that never happen:
- Ingrid and Sam are vegetarians. They **don't eat** meat. (= *They never eat meat.*)
- Sunita **doesn't buy** anything on the Net. (= *She never buys anything on the Net.*)

Note: after **never** we use a positive verb:
- Sonia **never walks** to work.

questions

To make questions in the present simple, we use **do /does** + *subject* + *infinitive*:

infinitive	singular	plural
swim	**do** I **swim**?	**do** we **swim**?
	do you **swim**?	**do** you **swim**?
	does he / she / it **swim**?	**do** they **swim**?

We can use present simple questions to ask about –

states and long-term situations now:
- **Does** Helga **work** in advertising?
- Why **do** they **want** to buy a new car?
- Where **does** Mary **live**?

things that happen again and again:
- **Do** you **eat** fruit every day?
- Where **does** Ismah **buy** her clothes?

Note this idiom:
- What **do** you **do**? (= *What's your job?*)

Note: in the UK, we don't usually say **Do you have...**? We say **Have you got...?**:
- **Have** you **got** some food?

A Look at the information about Andrew, Peter, and Lucy. Then write the question or the reply.

name:	Andrew	Peter	Lucy
job:	teacher	farmer	dancer
works:	in a university	on a farm	in the theatre
earns:	£32,000 a year	£27,000 a year	£16,000 a year
likes his / her job:	no	yes	yes
wants a new motorbike:	yes	no	no
hobby:	riding motorbikes	knitting	none

questions

0 'Does Peter work in a university?'

1 'What .... do?'

2 'Does Lucy work on a farm?'

3 'What ....?'

4 '...?'

5 '............................. more money than Andrew?'

6 'Where ....?'

7 'Do they all like their jobs?'

8 'Does Peter want to buy a new motorbike?'

9 '...?'

10 'Does Lucy have a hobby?'

11 'What hobbies ....?'

replies

'No, he doesn't work in a university.'

'He works on a farm.'

'No, she doesn't ....'

'She works in the theatre. She's a dancer.'

'No, she doesn't earn a lot of money.'

'No, Peter makes less money than Andrew.'

'He works in a university.'

'Lucy and Peter ...., but Andrew .... his job.'

'No, ... to buy a new motorbike'

'Yes, Andrew wants a new motorbike.'

'No, ... a hobby.'

'Andrew likes riding motorbikes and Peter likes knitting.'

B Look at this questionnaire on Internet use. Put the words in brackets in the right sequence, and use **do** or **does** to write the questions. Circle your answer(s) for each question.

0 (use / you / the Internet / ?) *Do you use the internet?* .... often (sometimes) never

1 (use / your friends / the Internet / ?) .... often sometimes never don't know

2 (you / use / why / the Internet / ?) .... for work for recreation for study

3 (think / you / that the Internet is easy to use / ?) .... yes no sometimes

4 (give you / the Internet / useful information / ?) .... often sometimes never

5 (you / things / buy / on the Internet / ?) .... often sometimes never

6 (sell / things / you or your friends / on the Internet / ?) .... often sometimes never

7 (music / your friends / download / from the Internet / ?) .... often sometimes never don't know

8 (your parents / the Internet / like / ?) .... yes no don't know

9 (the Internet / you / think / is a good thing / ?) .... yes no don't know

3 present simple of be (I am)

Alisha Dearly: Here we **are**, at the Montreal Annual Student fashion awards. There **are** hundreds of people in the room, but I **am** with the famous Maya Bukowski and we**'re** very close to the catwalk! How **are** you, Maya?

Maya Bukowski: I**'m** just divine, darling.

Alisha: That**'s** wonderful. Now, all the designers **are** in the back room, helping the girls and boys to add the perfect final touches to their clothes. And here**'s** the first – oh my goodness! It**'s** an amazing creation – covered in peacock feathers! What do you think, Maya?

Maya: Darling! I think it**'s** just divine!

Alisha: It **is**, isn't it? But then this **is** by Giacomo Stretti, who **is** always superb. And what about this next creation? I think the students this year **are** more courageous than last year.

Maya: Oh absolutely, darling. But it**'s** all divine!

form

infinitive	singular	plural
be	I **am** (I**'m**)	we **are** (we**'re**)
	you **are** (you**'re**)	you **are** (you**'re**)
	he / she / it **is** (he**'s** / she**'s** / it**'s**)	they **are** (they**'re**)

We usually contract **am**, **are** and **is** after *pronouns* and *names*:
- I**'m** ready to begin.
- She**'s** the only girl in the football team.
- I hope you**'re** not afraid of dogs.
- Jack**'s** taller than Paolo.

We also usually contract **is** after **there**, **here**, and **that** (but NOT after **this**):
- **There's** a lot of water on the bathroom floor.
- **Here's** a slice of pizza for you.
- **That's** a lovely hat!

When we write, we don't usually contract **are** after **here**, **there**, **these** and **those**.

use

We use **be** in the present to –

describe *a person or thing*:
- Deven **is** tall and dark.
- Those cars **are** very expensive!
- Jeanne **is** the girl I met in Paris.

talk about *a current situation*:
- Jacob**'s** in the gym.
- Sue and Jamie **are** on holiday.

talk about *something which happens from time to time* (often with an adverb like **often**, **always**, **sometimes**):
- We**'re sometimes** late for our dance class.
- Gavin **is always** happy to see you.

Note: we use **be + a / an** when we are talking about *what job someone does*:
- My sister**'s a** nurse.
- Kevin**'s an** architect.
- I**'m a** teacher.

EXERCISES

A

Read this conversation between Alisha and Maya at the fashion show and put the correct verb in the gap. Use the contracted form if you can.

0 Sasha ..*'s*.... the most famous model in the show.

1 I know. She .... the girl at the front.

2 Most of the clothes .... for women.

3 This year blue .... their favourite colour.

4 We .... really lucky to have seats in the front row!

5 That boy .... incredibly thin!

6 You .... interested in Marie Helene's collection, aren't you?

7 No, I .... more interested in the beach clothes.

8 Those hats .... absolutely beautiful!

9 The models .... all so tall.

10 I don't think it .... as good as last year's show.

B

Look at the picture and add a form of the verb **be** or **and** to the words to make sentences. Use a contracted form of the verb where you can.

0 Don Makeba ..*'s*.... a doctor.

1 He .... the doctor we talked to last week.

2 He .... his friend Matt .... both surgeons.

3 Don .... a specialist in hip .... knee surgery, …

4 … and Matt .... a specialist in heart surgery.

5 Don .... at work now.

6 This afternoon we .... in the hospital, watching an operation.

7 The instruments .... all clean and sterile.

8 I .... a bit nervous about watching an operation.

9 The doctors .... completely calm – they listen to music while they work.

10 The patient .... unconscious, of course!

JAKE: Mum, is our bus coming soon?
TANYA: I don't know, Jake. **Are** you tired?
JAKE: Yes, and I**'m not** very happy. It's cold. My jacket**'s not** warm enough and Freddy**'s not** warm enough.
TANYA : Freddy's fine.
JAKE: No, he**'s not**. We're hungry, Mum.
TANYA : I've got some apples in my bag...
JAKE: We**'re not** hungry for fruit – we're hungry for chocolate!
TANYA : No chocolate! **It isn't** very good for you. Have an apple.
JAKE: Why **is it** cold today? It was sunny yesterday.
TANYA : Because this is England! Thank goodness, the bus is coming!

negatives	To make the negative of the present simple of **be**, we use **not** or **n't**:

singular	plural
I **am not** / **'m not**	we **are not** / **'re not** / **aren't**
you **are not** / **'re not** / **aren't**	you **are not** / **'re not** / **aren't**
he / she / it **is not** / **'s not** / **isn't**	they **are not** / **'re not** / **aren't**

We usually use one of the contracted forms, especially when we speak:

- ▪ **I'm not** ready to go out.
- ▪ You **aren't** too thin!
- ▪ John **isn't** very busy.
- ▪ We**'re not** hungry, thank you.
- ▪ Guo Guifang**'s not** a doctor.

questions

To make questions with **be**, we put **am / is / are** before the <u>subject</u>:

singular	plural
am <u>I</u>?	**are** <u>we</u>?
are <u>you</u>?	**are** <u>you</u>?
is <u>he</u> / <u>she</u> / <u>it</u>?	**are** <u>they</u>?

We don't usually contract the verb in questions, when we write:

- ▪ Where **am** <u>I</u>? NOT ~~Where'm I?~~

We use these questions to ask *if something is true*:

- ▪ **Are** <u>you</u> angry?
- ▪ **Is** <u>your car</u> a Honda?

We use these questions with question words (e.g. **where**, **why**) to ask for *information about people and things*:

- ▪ Why **is** <u>Misha</u> in New York?

with always etc.

In a negative sentence we put a frequency adverb (**always**, **sometimes**, **usually** etc) after **not** or **n't**:

- ▪ Frank isn**'t always** in the office.
- ▪ You aren**'t often** so patient!

In a question we usually put the frequency adverb after the *<u>subject</u>*:

- ▪ Is <u>Gabriella</u> **sometimes** late?
- ▪ Are <u>we</u> **always** the first to arrive?

A Underline the errors in the **be** verbs in the following text, and write the correct verb and subject. Use contractions where possible. Sometimes there is more than one error.

WANG: Excuse me, <u>are I</u> in your class? My name is Wang Shuren.
am I

TINA: I aren't a teacher. I'm the secretary here. Is you from Korea?
....

WANG: No, I're not Korean. I'm Chinese. I'm looking for my English class.
....

TINA: Your English is very good! Is you in an advanced class?
....

WANG: No, it not is very good. I want to do an intermediate class.
....

TINA: Am Karen the intermediate teacher, Tracey?
....

TRACEY: No, she aren't the intermediate teacher. I think she teaches the beginners.
....

TINA: Maybe it's Paul. But he's n't here today. His class is tomorrow morning.
....

TRACEY: But Joe has a pre-intermediate class today. Am it at 2 o'clock today, Tina?
....

TINA: Yes, it is at 2.
....

WANG: Where're his class?
....

TINA: It is n't in this building. It's in the other building, in room 6.
....

B Make questions, or negative answers to complete the conversation. Sometimes more than one form is correct.

Misha:

0 *Are you alright?*

I am, too! 1 ....?

What 2 ....?

Look! I think that's our bus.

4 ....?

I was wondering … Are you the man from the library?

Oh, sorry! I'm so silly!

How amazing! Sorry, I am being rude.

Really! 8 ....?

Of course! Oh look, 9 ....?

Oh dear, it looks completely full!

Tony:

Yes, I'm fine. I'm waiting for the Hampstead bus.

Yes, it's due now.

It's number 28.

No, 3 ....

Yes, I'm quite sure. That's number 128.

No, 5 .... I work in an estate agent's.

No, 6 .... My brother works in the library.

No, 7 .... Everyone makes that mistake. We're twins.

Yes, we're identical – exactly the same. He's the manager of the video library.

Yes, that's definitely a number 28.

10 .... There's room at the back for us! Come on!

5 present continuous (I am listening)

KAREN: Hi Rupert! Yes … I'm fine. … And you? … Good. … No, I'm **sitting** on a train in the middle of Wales! I know! I'm **going** to Carmarthen, or I'm **trying** to … No, the train is delayed. I'm **waiting** for the train to leave Llanelli station. … Yes, Simon's here too; he's **sitting** next to me, **enjoying** the Welsh countryside. Oh, the train **is moving** now, thank goodness! Oh, we're **going** into a tunnel. I'm **losing** you. Sorry Rupert, the connection **is breaking up** …

form

We make the present continuous with the auxiliary verb **be** (**am** / **is** / **are**) and the **ing** *form* of the main verb:

singular	plural
I **am playing** (I'm playing)	we **are playing** (we're playing)
you **are playing** (you're playing)	you **are playing** (you're playing)
he / she / it **is playing** (he's playing)	they **are playing** (they're playing)

We usually use the contracted form (**I'm**, **he's** etc), especially when we speak.
If the main verb ends in *consonant* + **e**, we cut off the **e** and add **ing**:

    make → **making**   move → **moving**
    have → **having**   smile → **smiling**

If the verb ends in **ie**, we change it to **y** + **ing**:
    lie → **lying**   die → **dying**

If the main verb ends with a *single vowel* + *single consonant*, we usually double the consonant and add **ing**:

    put → **putting**   cut → **cutting**
    hit → **hitting**   drum → **drumming**

Exceptions: visit → **visiting**   listen → **listening**   remember → **remembering**
We don't double **w** and **y**:
    know → **knowing**   spray → **spraying**

use

We use the present continuous to talk about –
things happening now:
    ■ I'm **writing** an email at the moment.
    ■ They're **cooking** dinner in the kitchen.
temporary situations:
    ■ Julia's **working** for a solicitor during her summer holiday.
    ■ Deven and I **are taking** the business studies course.
things that people plan to do in the future:
    ■ Rachel's **going** to the rehearsal this evening.
    ■ We're **moving** into a new flat next week.
(See unit 19 for more on the present continuous used for the future.)

EXERCISES

A Write the present continuous of the verb in brackets in the gaps in the following text.

It is election time. I (0 – try) _am trying_ to decide who to vote for. All the political parties (1 – promise) .... different things. The Red Party (2 – offer) .... to give jobs to everyone, and they (3 – say) .... that they will spend less money and reduce taxes. The Blue Party say that the Red Party (4 – lie) .... , and the Red Party won't really reduce taxes, so they (5 – ask) .... us to vote for them, if we want taxes reduced.

The Yellow Party candidate, who (6 – stand) .... outside the supermarket (7 – give) .... free pens to everyone who takes one of their leaflets. She says she (8 – expect) .... to win the election because the majority of people (9 – feel) .... confused about the policies of the other parties.

The Green Party is very small and won't win, but they (10 – work) .... very hard to change the other parties' policies.

B Look at the picture and make sentences about what the people and animals are doing, using the words in brackets.

0 (the boy in the orange T-shirt / read / a book) _The boy in the orange T-shirt is reading a book._

1 (the woman with the white hat / talk / to her dog) ....

2 (the children on the football pitch / play / football) ....

3 (the family by the lake / have / a picnic) ....

4 (the park keeper / pick up / some rubbish) ....

5 (the two girls / talk / on their mobile phones) ....

6 (the pigeons / eat / an old sandwich) ....

7 (the man under the tree / listen to / the radio) ....

8 (the man and woman holding hands / dream / of their future) ....

9 (the two girls / ride / their bikes through the gates) ....

10 (the old woman / enjoy / the roses) ....

RACHEL: Hello Darren. **Is** Gabriella **playing** today?

DARREN: No. She**'s not coming** today.

RACHEL: Oh, what a shame. **Am I playing** first or second violin? I can't remember what the conductor said last week ...

CHRISTINA: Rachel, can you help me with this music stand. **I'm not managing** very well. I cut my hand this afternoon.

RACHEL: Oh, **is** it **bleeding**?

CHRISTINA: No, it **isn't bleeding** now, but it's quite painful.

RACHEL: Give the music stand to me. There. **Are** you **sitting** next to me?

CHRISTINA: I think so. Oh, thank you. Now, I hope I can play my cello!

negatives

We make the present continuous negative by adding **not** after the auxiliary **be**:

singular	plural
I**'m not** singing	we**'re not** / **aren't** singing
you**'re not** / **aren't** singing	you**'re not** / **aren't** singing
he / she / it**'s not** / **isn't** singing	they**'re not** / **aren't** singing

There is no difference in meaning between the two contracted forms.

Note: if there are two verbs close together, we don't need to repeat the subject and the auxiliary **be** (+ **not**):
- Tom **isn't eating** or **drinking** anything.
- The children **aren't swimming** or **playing** tennis.

We use the negative present continuous to say that *something is not happening now or in the future*:
- **I'm not working** at the moment – I'm reading the paper.
- Mario **isn't going** on holiday in August; he has to work all summer.s

We sometimes use this form to say we *refuse to do something*:
- **I'm not speaking** to Jane any more! She's horrible!
- **I'm not cooking** dinner tonight. It's your turn!

questions

To make present continuous questions, we put **am** / **is** / **are** before the subject:

singular	plural
am I winning?	**are** we winning?
are you winning?	**are** you winning?
is he / she / it winning?	**are** they winning?

We also use this form after a question word like **where**, **why**, **how**, **what** etc. and we don't use the contracted form of the verb:
- Where **are** you **calling** from? NOT ~~Where're you~~...
- Why **is** Tom **shivering**? NOT ~~Why's Tom~~....

Note: if there are two verbs close together, we don't need to repeat the subject and the auxiliary **am** / **is** / **are**:
- **Is** Diana **singing** and **dancing** in the show?

EXERCISES

A Paulette and Charlie are rehearsing a scene from a play with Julian (the director). Write the missing words to make a *question* or a *negative answer*, using the words in brackets.

CHARLIE: What (0 – I / do) _am I doing_ at the beginning of this scene, Julian?

JULIAN: Well, (1 – you / not / feel) .... very happy. What do you think? (2 – you / wait) .... by the window for Paulette to come home?

CHARLIE: Probably. (3 – I / look) .... out of the window? Or (4 – I / walk) .... up and down (5 – worry) ....?

JULIAN: No, (6 – you / not / watch) .... from the window, because it says in the script that (7 – you / not / expect) .... her to come home till later.

PAULETTE: (8 – he / sit) .... by the fire, (9 – try) .... to read the paper, but not really (10 – succeed) ....?

CHARLIE: Yes, that's a good idea.

JULIAN: Hey, (11 – I / direct) .... this play, or Paulette?

CHARLIE: Sorry Julian. (12 – She / not / try) .... to tell me what to do. It was just a suggestion.

PAULETTE: Yes. Sorry, Julian. Now, (13 – we / rehearse) .... , or just chatting all evening?!!

JULIAN: Oh! (14 – I / not / work) .... with that woman any more! Goodbye!

B Write the responses in the negative.

0 'Tim is running in the marathon today.' 'No, _Tim isn't running in the marathon today._'

1 'Thousands of people are doing the marathon this year.' 'And millions of people ....!'

2 'Some people are wearing animal costumes.' 'And lots of people ....'

3 'Is Mike wearing a funny costume?' 'No, he ....'

4 'Look, he's running in that duck suit!' 'No, ...'

5 'The man in the bear suit is enjoying the race.' 'No, ...'

6 'That woman is crying!' 'No, ...'

7 'Are they stopping the race?' 'No, ...'

8 'She is asking for some water!' 'No, ...'

9 'She's continuing the race!' 'No, ...'

10 'I'm training to run in the marathon next year.' 'And ....!'

7

To:
Cc:
Bcc:

Subject:

Attachments: none

Font ▽ | Text S... | B I U T | ☰ ☰ ☰

Hi, Ros,
What are you doing these days? I haven't seen you in months. Are you very busy?
I'm still working in the same job, but I am getting a bit bored with it. I want to meet
some new people and have new experiences. I go to Salsa classes twice a
week. I am learning the steps but I often make mistakes. It's a lot of fun, but I
don't meet any gorgeous men!
I see Sidra sometimes. We meet up for lunch or go shopping. She seems really
happy with her life. Did you know she has three kids now! She's on holiday in
Wales at the moment.
I am writing this email at work and I must stop now – my boss is walking towards
my desk!
Let's meet for lunch soon. Give me a ring!
Julie

present simple

We use the present simple to talk about –
permanent situations:

- Hilary **works** in a bank in Edinburgh.
- The Krugers **live** in a big house with a gym and a swimming pool.
- Raoul **speaks** six languages!
- The Statue of Liberty **stands** on an island.

things that happen again and again:

- The sun **rises** in the East.
- I often **study** at night.
- Alam **designs** cars.
- Anna **plays** the violin beautifully.
- People **come** here to fish.

We frequently use <u>*adverbs*</u> before the verb in the present simple to say *how often something happens*:

- I <u>usually</u> **cook** for my family.
- Sam <u>always</u> **seems** very busy.
- We <u>never</u> **go** on holiday in the winter.

Note: we put the adverb after **be**:

- Tom **is** <u>usually</u> late for work.
- We**'re** <u>frequently</u> bored at school.

If we use a <u>time phrase</u> it usually goes at the end of the clause:

- Jeff **buys** a new computer <u>every year</u>.
- Sanjay **walks** his dog <u>every morning</u>.

present continuous

We use the present continuous to talk about –
temporary situations:

- Hilary **is working** in Glasgow this month.
- Joe **is studying** Italian at university.
- Alam **is designing** a sports car at the moment.
- The Krugers **are living** in a flat because the builders are working in their house.

things that are happening now:

- Look, the sun **is rising**.
- Listen! Anna**'s playing** a piece by Mozart.
- Ssh! I**'m speaking** on the phone.
- 'Why **is** that man **standing** in the rain?' 'He**'s waiting** for a taxi, I think.'

We sometimes use **still** with the present continuous to say that *something is continuing to happen*:

- I can't come to the phone right now. I**'m** <u>still</u> **cooking** dinner.

To talk about *something happening in a current period of time* we use the present continuous, with phrases like **this month**, **these days**, **at the moment** at the end of the clause:

- Mae-Ling **is going** to the gym a lot <u>these days</u>.
- Jo **is working** very hard <u>at the moment</u>, because she**'s doing** her exams <u>this week</u>.

We do not usually use the present continuous with *describing verbs*, e.g:

be, have, seem   like, want, need   think, know, understand, remember, mean, notice

We use the present simple with *describing* verbs to talk about *something that is happening now*:

- Sam **is** in his office. He's writing a report. NOT ~~Sam is being in his office~~.
- Suna **doesn't seem** very happy today. NOT ~~Suna isn't seeming very happy today~~.
- What **does** that road sign **mean**? NOT ~~What is that road sign meaning?~~

(See unit 8 on *describing verbs*.)

EXERCISES

A Yumi is on holiday in Borneo. She is on a trip into the jungle to see orang-utans in the wild. Look at what the ranger is saying and complete the gaps. Choose the *present simple* or *present continuous* of the verbs in brackets.

RANGER: Okay, let's wait quietly here on the path for a few minutes. The orang-utans, (0 – often / come) ...*often come*...... out of the jungle to meet human visitors on this path. Orang-utans (1 – live) .... on the ground and in the trees of the forest. Orang-utan (2 – be) .... a Malay word and (3 – mean) .... 'person of the wild' or 'person of the woods'. But people say that the local people here in Borneo (4 – not / call) .... them orang-utan – they (5 – have) .... another word for them.

Look, over there, can you see those two orang-utans? Look, they (6 – walk) .... towards us between the trees. They (7 – be) .... a mother and a young orang. The young one (8 – be) .... about two years old. Oh, the mother (9 – seem) .... a bit nervous, and they (10 – turn) .... away now. Look, the mother (11 – dig) .... in the ground with a stick, and the child (12 – watch) .... her, and now he (13 – have) .... a stick and he (14 – dig) .... in the ground, too. Baby orang-utans (15 – always / learn) .... by watching and then trying to do the same thing. Do you notice how the mother (16 – stare) .... at us? She (17 – wonder) .... if we are safe and not dangerous. I (18 – not / think) .... she is afraid of us now, and yes, they (19 – get up / and / come) .... closer to us now.

Orang-utans (20 – be) .... very thoughtful and clever animals but they can be quite assertive too. Oh no, hold onto your camera, Yumi, she (21 – look) .... at it and I think she (22 – want) .... it!

B Some of the staff at Frisco Stores are having their lunch break. Use the words in brackets to complete the sentences about the people in the pictures. Use the *present simple* or *present continuous*.

0 Charlie *is eating a sandwich* .
  (eat / a sandwich)

1 Kofi ....
  (be / the manager)

2 Kofi ....
  (talk / to a customer)

3 'What is Julian doing?' 'He ....
  ....' (fill / the shelves)

4 Louise ....
  (work / at the checkout)

5 Louise ....
  (drink / a cup of coffee)

6 Charlie ....
  (read / a novel)

7 Charlie ....
  (sell / meat)

8 'Where are Julian and Kofi?' '...........................
  ....' (work / in the shop)

9 'Where are Louise and Charlie?' '...........................
  ....' (be / in the canteen)

10 'What is Julian's job?' 'He ....
  ....' (fill / the shelves)

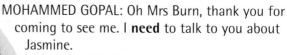

8 verbs not used in the continuous
(I know, I want)

MOHAMMED GOPAL: Oh Mrs Burn, thank you for coming to see me. I **need** to talk to you about Jasmine.

MELISSA BURN: Oh dear, is she being naughty?

MOHAMMED: No, no, she is always very polite and friendly. I **want** to talk to you about her work. She usually works hard at school, and does all her homework, but, at the moment, she isn't doing her homework and she isn't concentrating in lessons. She **seems** a bit restless and unhappy.

MELISSA: Yes, I **think** I **know** what the problem **is**. Her pet hamster Tommy died last week. She **is** very unhappy about that.

MOHAMMED: Oh, I **see**. Poor Jasmine.

MELISSA: Well, I'm going to the pet shop with her today to buy a puppy. She **is** very excited about that.

---

verbs used in the continuous	We use verbs which describe an *action* or *situation* in the present continuous to talk about *something happening now*:

- Donna **is running** round the park.
- Bill, can you help me? I**'m cooking** dinner.
- I**'m** just **sitting** and **watching** TV at the moment.
- I**'m not enjoying** this film. Let's go out and eat.

---

verbs not used in the continuous	We don't use the present continuous with verbs which we use to *describe people* or *things*:

- Amanda**'s** at the cinema. (NOT ~~She's being at the cinema.~~)
- Simon **likes** that painting. (NOT ~~Simon is liking that painting.~~)
- The dog **seems** a bit sad. (NOT ~~The dog is seeming a bit sad.~~)
- I **don't understand** this sentence. (NOT ~~I'm not understanding this sentence.~~)
- **Do** you **love** him? (NOT ~~Are you loving him?~~)

Here is a list of some common *describing verbs*:

state	thinking	feeling
be seem mean	think know believe understand	like want love
contain have	remember notice forget	prefer hate
	see (= *understand*)	need hope

The verbs **be**, **have**, and **think** can be used in the continuous in the following phrases, but the meaning of the verb is different:

She's **being** good / bad / silly etc. (= *behaving in a certain way*)

She's **having** a shower / a meal / a bad day etc ... (= *experiencing something*)

She's **thinking about** / **of** something. (= *considering something*)

---

look and feel	**Look** and **feel** can be used in either the simple or the continuous to talk about *something happening now*:

- Ismah **looks** / **is looking** happy.
- **Do** you **feel** / **Are** you **feeling** tired?

EXERCISES

A

Complete the sentences using the words in brackets in the *present simple* or *continuous*.

GUIDO: It's really nice having dinner together like this.

JACKY: Yes, it is. I'm having a lovely evening.

GUIDO: And the food is wonderful, isn't it?

JACKY: Absolutely delicious. My steak was perfect!

GUIDO: I think I'll have a coffee after the main course – or what about a dessert?

JACKY: No thanks. Nothing more for me.

GUIDO: I'll pay the bill, don't worry! Mmm, I can't find my credit card!

JACKY: Oh dear, I don't think I have enough money in my purse …

WAITER: Excuse me, have you finished your meal?

0 Jacky ......*likes*...... (like) Guido.

1 Guido .... (like) Jacky.

2 They .... (enjoy) their food.

3 They .... (sit) near the fire.

4 Jacky .... (be) really happy.

5 Jacky .... (want) a coffee.

6 Guido .... (want) a coffee.

7 Guido .... (have) his credit card.

8 Jacky .... (have) enough money to pay the bill.

9 The waiter .... (wait) to take their plates.

10 The waiter .... (be) very friendly.

B

Rob is at a meeting in his company. Read the conversation and decide if the underlined verbs are correct or not. Write a tick or the correct form of the *present simple* or *continuous* in the box below.

MANAGER: Hi, Mark. Rob, hi. 0It's being good to see you. 1 I'm sorry that 2 I'm being late for this meeting. I 3 have a bad day and I'm running late – 4 I'm not having much time now. 5 I'm needing to go to another meeting in the centre of town in half an hour. So, can this be a quick meeting, please? A taxi 6 is waiting to take me into town.

MARK: Well, as you know, we 7 want to make an investment in Essenzia, and we 8 need your approval for the idea. 9 You're having all the company's data in the file I sent you last week.

MANAGER: Yes, 10 I'm knowing that you want to invest in Essenzia, but 11 I'm not being sure why you want to invest in it. 12 We're needing to invest in some new companies, but we 13 want to invest in companies that make good profits.

ROB: Well, I 14 think that Essenzia is a good company to invest in. We really 15 are liking their products and 16 they're having a very modern factory. Also, the management team at Essenzia 17 seems very good and very professional. Their profits 18 are small at the moment but the company is predicting big profit increases in the next two years.

MANAGER: 19 I'm not remembering the details about the company. What products 20 do they make?

MARK: Well, they 21 sell cosmetics – perfumes, lipsticks, and so on.

MANAGER: Well, Essenzia 22 is seeming a good company. I 23 am understanding why you think it's a good company but I need to think about your plan. I need some more time. Sorry.

0 *it's*	8	17 ....
00 ✔	9	18 ....
1	10	19 ....
2	11	20 ....
3	12	21 ....
4	13	22 ....
5	14	23 ....
6	15	
7	16	

A

Read the passage below and choose the best verb from the box to put in each gap.

> 're thinking   remember   has   is publishing   are   don't remember
> explains   are becoming   runs   'm not running   thinks   has   're
> pushing   is appearing   does   is   travelling

Gordon Ramsay is a very successful chef who ⁰ *is* famous for his bad language and aggressive behaviour.

Ramsay is a very busy man. He ¹_____ marathons, ²_____ a growing restaurant empire, ³_____ a lot of charity work and motivational speaking, and he ⁴_____ a wife and four children. He ⁵_____ in a TV series called Kitchen Nightmares (which recently won a major TV award), and ⁶_____ a series of best-selling cookery books, as well as ⁷_____ all over the world.

He ⁸_____ his aggressive behaviour, saying: 'All the best chefs ⁹_____ passionate people, and the job is very hard! We ¹⁰_____ the boundaries to the extreme.   I ¹¹_____ a cheap, little bistro where there's no pressure. If you don't want pressure, go and make cheese on toast, go and make a ham salad! I'm afraid that nowadays British chefs ¹²_____ food snobs. We ¹³_____ more about exotic ingredients and we ¹⁴_____ how to cook the basic dishes.'

For Ramsay, flavour matters most; he ¹⁵_____ chefs now are too interested in the appearance of their food. He says that, after a meal, you ¹⁶_____ the flavour, and not the appearance.

B

Match the two halves of the following sentences.

0 Do you	A an abandoned dog, …
1 I really	B wants to give them a home.
2 I am	C like little puppies?
3 … who is	D have ten euros to give us?
4 Some dogs	E expecting to hear from you soon!
5 No-one	F ten euros a week to pay for our food and care.
6 It costs	G aren't as young and cute as me.
7 Do you	H write letters to everyone who helps us.
8 Luckily, good people	I you want to help us?
9 Every week, we	J are looking after us.
10 Do	K waiting to give you its love.
11 This little dog is	L hope you are a kind dog-lover.

C Read what Mark says below and use the words in brackets, and the *present simple* or *continuous*, to write Baz's questions.

BAZ HARRINGTON: (0 – what / be / an allotment) *What is an allotment* ....?

MARK LACEY: It's a piece of land in a city where people who don't have gardens can grow things.

BAZ: (1 – you / own / this allotment) ....?

MARK: No, the local council owns all the allotments here. In the past, there was an allotment for anyone who wanted one, but it's quite hard to get an allotment now.

BAZ: (2 – how much / it / cost) ....?

MARK: It costs £12 to rent an allotment here but, in some places where there is not much land available, it's a bit more.

BAZ: (3 – what / you / do) ....?

MARK: At the moment I'm picking the peas and the beans. The problem is, I eat a lot of them before they get to the kitchen! They're delicious raw!

BAZ: (4 – you / only / grow / vegetables) ....?

MARK: No, I also grow fruit and flowers.

BAZ: (5 – children / enjoy / coming here) ....?

MARK: Oh yes! Children love working with their parents in the fresh air. Not for very long, of course! They get bored after an hour or two. But it's a great education for them.

BAZ: (6 – what / they / learn / here) ....?

MARK: Well, they learn about the value of hard work, and the joy of looking after something. I think that planting a tiny little seed and watching it become a big, strong, healthy plant is a really exciting thing, at any age! And it's great spending time in the open air instead of sitting in front of a TV screen!

BAZ: (7 – why / that man / put / beer in a jar in the earth?) ....?

MARK: Oh, he's making a slug trap. The slugs climb in to drink the beer and then they can't get out!

BAZ: (8 – why / you / put / some of the green beans in that bag) ....?

MARK: These are for you! I really hope you enjoy them!

9 past simple (I listened)

The Burns family's cat, Jasper, **died** last night. He **belonged** to their youngest son, Isaac, and always **slept** on his bed. He **was** a very beautiful ginger cat, and he **had** very soft fur and a very independent character. Every night the stupid animal **ran** across a very busy road into the park, to hunt for mice and birds.

Last year Mr Burns **paid** over a thousand pounds for an operation after a car **hit** him! Last night another car **hit** him and this time he **didn't survive**. Mrs Burns **buried** him in the garden and **marked** the grave with a little stone. Isaac was very sad, and the Burns' dog, Jack, was very sad too. Now he has nothing to chase!

---

form: regular verbs

To make the past simple, we usually add **ed** to the infinitive form of the verb:

infinitive	singular	plural
follow	I / you **followed**	we / you **followed**
	he / she / it **followed**	they **followed**

- The police car **followed** the white van through the city.

If the infinitive ends with **e**, we usually add **d** in the past simple:

arrive → **arrived**   bake → **baked**   die → **died**

save → **saved**   use → **used**

If the verb ends in a *consonant* + **y**, we use **ied**:

try → **tried**   carry → **carried**   bury → **buried**   study → **studied**

With verbs that end with a *single vowel + single consonant* (e.g. **stop**), we usually double the consonant and add **ed**:

stop → **stopped**   plan → **planned**   prefer → **preferred**

Note: We don't double **w** and **y**:

snow → **snowed**   play → **played**

Exceptions: If a verb has more than one syllable and the STRESS is not on the last syllable, we *don't* double the final consonant, unless it is **l**:

LISten → **listened**   reMEMber → **remembered**

BUT   TRAvel → **travelled**

---

form: irregular verbs

A lot of frequently-used verbs are irregular – they don't have **ed** in the past simple, e.g:

be → **was / were**	buy → **bought**	come → **came**
give → **gave**	go → **went**	have → **had**
hide → **hid**	make → **made**	read (/ri...d/) → **read** (/red/)
run → **ran**	say → **said**	see → **saw**
take → **took**	think → **thought**	write → **wrote**

- We **went** to an auction yesterday and **bought** an antique clock.
- Lee Peixin **took** a brush and **wrote** some Chinese characters.

(For a complete list of irregular verbs, see page 222.)

---

use

We use the past simple to talk about *things that happened in the past and are finished*, often with a <u>time phrase</u> to say *when*:

- I **went** to the market <u>on Friday morning</u>.
- The employees **arrived** <u>before 9</u>.
- Frances **lived** in this house <u>from 2000 to 2004.</u>

We also use it to talk about *things that happened regularly or frequently in the past*, but not now:

- Darren **worked** in the warehouse on Saturdays.
- Guido **showed** his paintings each year at the Spring exhibition.

EXERCISES

A Read the text and put the verbs in brackets in the correct form below.

Charles Lutwidge Dodgson (0 – work) as a lecturer in mathematics at Oxford University from 1855 to 1881. The other tutors (1 – think) he (2 – be) a bit strange and unfriendly; he (3 – seem) more comfortable and relaxed with children. He (4 – have) a bad stammer, except when he was with children, when it completely (5 – disappear).

In 1865, he (6 – publish) *Alice's Adventures in Wonderland* and called himself Lewis Carroll. The sequel *Through the Looking Glass* (7 – appear) in 1872. He (8 – write) these two books to entertain Alice Liddell, who (9 – be) the young daughter of the Dean of Christ Church College, Oxford.

Lewis Carroll wrote many other 'nonsense' poems and books, as well as mathematical works in his real name. He (10 – live) alone and (11 – die) of bronchitis in his sisters' home in Guildford on 14th July, 1898.

0	*worked*	3	....	6	....	9	....
1	....	4	....	7	....	10	....
2	....	5	....	8	....	11	....

B Underline the errors in the past simple verbs and write the correct form at the bottom. Be careful with the irregular verbs!

Melissa Burn always <u>loveed</u> the book *Alice in Wonderland*. Her father buyed it for her fifth birthday, and he often readed it to her. She really liked the pictures, and when she getted older she enjoyd reading it herself. When her daughter Amanda was 7, she gived her a new copy of the book, with beautiful colour pictures. Amanda hate it! She sayed it was frightening, and that the animals in the story look horrible. She prefered the *Telly Tubbies*! Melissa taked the book away and hided it in the attic.

0	*loved*	3	....	6	....	9	....
1	....	4	....	7	....	10	....
2	....	5	....	8	....		

ROS: **Did** you **eat** all the apples?

TOM: No, I **didn't eat** them. I made an apple pie with them. Do you want some?

ROS: No, you know I'm on a diet! I **didn't want** apple pie, with loads of high calorie sugar and pastry. I just wanted to eat an apple!

TOM: Oh, I'm really sorry. I **didn't know** about your diet. I thought you liked apple pie!

ROS: **Did** you **finish** all the oranges as well? I can't believe it!

TOM: Oh dear! I think I gave the last one to Rob when he was here. I'm sorry. **Did** you **buy** any fruit when you went to the market this morning?

ROS: No, I **didn't go** to the market this morning. But I'll have to go now - I'm starving!

negatives

To make negatives in the past simple, we use **did + not / n't + *infinitive*:**

infinitive	singular	plural
laugh	I **did not / didn't laugh**	we **did not / didn't laugh**
	you **did not / didn't laugh**	you **did not / didn't laugh**
	he / she / it **did not / didn't laugh**	they **did not / didn't laugh**

- Kieran **did not laugh** when he fell over.
- We **didn't laugh** at Deven's stupid joke.
- Sam's really unhappy because she **didn't pass** her driving test.
- I **didn't like** that film – it was really boring.
- He **didn't buy** the picture because he **did not have** enough money.
- She **didn't go** to work yesterday because she was ill.
- Joshua **didn't seem** very pleased with his present.
- I **didn't get** home till 12 o'clock last night! (= *I finally got home at 12.*)

Note that we put *adverbs* (e.g. **really**) after **did not / didn't**:

- You **didn't get** the job because you **didn't** <u>really</u> **want** it. (= *you didn't want it very much.*)
- He **didn't** <u>really</u> **do** anything wrong. (= *He didn't do anything very wrong.*)

questions

To make questions in the past simple, we use **did + <u>*subject*</u> + *infinitive*:**

infinitive	singular	plural
stop	did <u>I</u> **stop**?	did <u>we</u> **stop**?
	did <u>you</u> **stop**?	did <u>you</u> **stop**?
	did <u>he / she / it</u> **stop**?	did <u>they</u> **stop**?

- **Did** you **stop** when the lights changed to red?
- **Did** the children **stop** talking, eventually, last night?
- **Did** you **see** Tamsin this morning?

We often use question words (e.g. **what**, **where**) with the past simple:

- **What** did you say to John last night?
- **Where** did Frank stay when he went to Rome?
- **Why** did Rob decide to leave the company?
- **How** long did you wait for a train?

We put frequency *adverbs* like **often** and **always** before the main verb:

- Did you <u>often</u> **go** to the theatre when you lived in London?

EXERCISES

A Create questions and negatives in the past simple to complete the gaps, using the words in brackets.

TANYA: Oh, that was such fun! But I spent lots and lots of money!

SIDRA: Where (0 – you / go) ..... *did you go*.....?
(1 – you / go) .... to the new Ellder's Department Store on the High Street?

TANYA: No, (2 – I / not / go) .... there because (3 – they / not / have) .... a sale on this week. I went to all the little boutiques in the Darington Mall.

SIDRA: (4 – you / buy) .... any shoes?

TANYA: No, (5 – I / not / get) .... any shoes, but I did buy a pair of boots, and a pair of furry slippers. (6 – I / show) .... you the boots?

SIDRA: No, you didn't. Let me see – oh, those are so cool! The leather is gorgeous, and I love that little heel! How much (7 – they / cost) ....?

TANYA: Oh, not very much – they were half price. But (8 – I / not / mean) .... to buy boots at all! I feel really guilty!

SIDRA: Oh, you shouldn't! You deserve something special. You work so hard. Where (9 – you / leave) .... the boys today?

TANYA: (10 – I / not / ask) .... my mother to look after them today, as she finds them very tiring. I put them in the crèche in the shopping mall.

SIDRA: (11 – I / not / know) .... they had a crèche there! That's brilliant. I'm sure they are having a great time.

TANYA: I hope so!

B Complete the questions about what happened in the underlined sentences of the story, using the past simple.

[0]Julian came to work late today because [1]he went to an evening class last night and then stayed up all night, [2]writing an essay about Pavlov's dogs for his Psychology course. He was so tired [3]he put everything in the wrong places and forgot to [4]put any milk on the shelves, so the customers were very disappointed when they came into the shop. [5]He put the tins of tomatoes with the soups, and [6]the pasta with the breakfast cereals. Then [7]he went into the store room and [8]sat down for a few minutes. [9]He slept for an hour! [10]Kofi, the manager, found him in the storeroom, fast asleep, leaning against a pile of chocolate orange biscuits!

0 Why *did Julian come to work late today*.....?

1 Did ....?

2 What ....?

3 Why ....?

4 Did ....?

5 Where ....?

6 Did ....?

7 Where ....?

8 What ....?

9 How long ....?

10 Where ....?

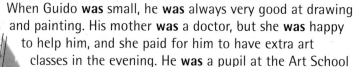

When Guido **was** small, he **was** always very good at drawing and painting. His mother **was** a doctor, but she **was** happy to help him, and she paid for him to have extra art classes in the evening. He **was** a pupil at the Art School in Palermo. The teachers there **were** young and enthusiastic, and Guido **was** their favourite. He **was** so small they had to give him a box to stand on when he was painting!

When he **was** about 15, he discovered abstract art, and **wasn't** satisfied with painting pretty pictures of flowers or people any more. He started to wear black clothes and big hats and to throw paint around. His bedroom **was** a terrible mess! His father **wasn't** very pleased! Why **was** Guido so angry?

form	The past simple of the verb **be** is irregular:

infinitive	singular	plural
be	I **was**	we **were**
	you **were**	you **were**
	he / she / it **was**	they **were**

use

We use the past simple of **be** to describe *a person or thing in the past*:
- Olga's grandmother **was** Norwegian.
- The trees in the garden **were** very tall.

or, to talk about *a situation at a particular time in the past*:
- Patrick **was** in the hall when I arrived.
- Ismah and Adnan **were** quite busy this morning.

or, to talk about *a situation which existed often or regularly in the past*:
- The dog **was** always tired after his walk.
- Giovanni **was** usually in the library in the afternoon.

negatives

We make the negative by adding **n't** or **not** after **was / were**:

singular	plural
I **was not** / **wasn't**	we **were not** / **weren't**
you **were not** / **weren't**	you **were not** / **weren't**
he / she / it **was not** / **wasn't**	they **were not** / **weren't**

- He **wasn't** in the office – he was at home.
- She said she **wasn't** angry but I didn't believe her.
- Jane and Mark **weren't** very happy about Tom's behaviour at their party last night.
- We **weren't** sure that the taxi driver knew where to go.

questions

We make questions with **was / were** + *subject*:
- **Were** <u>you</u> in the bath when I phoned?
- **Was** <u>the hotel</u> you stayed in expensive?

If we want to ask a question with a question word (**how, why, where** etc), we use *question word* + **was / were** + *subject*:
- **Where was** <u>Tom</u> this morning?
- **Why was** <u>he</u> so late?

If we want to ask about *a particular quality of something*, we use **how** + **big / long / old / hot** etc. + **was** + *subject*:
- '**How long was** <u>the meeting</u>?' 'It was three hours long!'
- '**How tall was** <u>your grandfather</u>?' 'He was more than two metres tall.'

EXERCISES

A Look at the picture and write in the missing questions or answers, using the past simple of **be** and the words in brackets.

0 'Where was Tanya at 5.30 this morning?' '(in bed) *She was in bed* .'

1 '(Tanya – asleep) ....?' 'No, she was awake.'

2 'Was she happy?' '(very unhappy) ....'

3 'Where (Freddy and Jake) ....?' 'They were in the sitting room.'

4 'Was the sitting room nice and tidy?' '(a horrible mess) ....'

5 'Where (the CDs) ....?' 'The CDs were all over the floor.'

6 'Was the plant on the table?' '(on the floor) ....'

7 '(TV – on) ....?' 'Yes, the TV was on.'

8 'Were the books in the bookcase?' '(on the floor) ....'

9 'Why (Freddy – angry) ....?' 'Freddy was angry because Jake hit him.'

10 'Were the boys dressed?' '(in their pyjamas) ....'

B

The Colossus – one of the Seven Wonders of the World

The island of Rhodes was an important economic centre in the ancient world. The Colossus of Rhodes was a huge, bronze statue near the harbour. It was one hundred and ten feet (or 33.3 metres) high. The statue stood in a traditional Greek manner: it was naked, and wore a spiked crown, with its right hand shading its eyes from the rising sun, and it held a cloak over its left arm. It was a representation of the God Helios, the Sun God, who was the patron of the island of Rhodes, and it was a symbol of the unity of the people who lived on the beautiful Mediterranean island.

The architect of this great construction was Chares of Lindos, a sculptor from Rhodes who was a great patriot and fought to defend the city.

The Colossus was there for only fifty-six years. Each morning the sun caught its polished bronze surface and made the god's figure shine. Then, in 226 B.C, there was a big earthquake and the statue collapsed.

In the seventh century A.D. the Arabs conquered Rhodes and broke the remains of the Colossus up into smaller pieces and sold the bits of metal. It was a sad end for a majestic work of art.

The Colossus was very similar to the Statue of Liberty in New York harbour.

Answer the following questions.

0 Where was the Colossus?
   It was near the harbour at Rhodes.

1 How tall was the statue?
   ....

2 Was it a traditional Greek statue?
   ....

3 Was it dressed in a long robe?
   ....

4 It was a statue of someone. Who?
   ....

5 The Colossus was a symbol of something. What?

6 Who was the architect of the Colossus? ....

7 How long was the Colossus there?
   ....

8 Was the statue made of stone?
   ....

9 When was the big earthquake that destroyed the Colossus? ....

10 When were the Arabs in Rhodes?
   ....

11 The Colossus was like a modern statue. Which statue?
   ....

past continuous (I was listening)

'I **was driving** along the High Street this morning when I heard a siren. An ambulance **was coming up** behind me. Its lights **were flashing** and its siren **was wailing**. I tried to drive my car into a layby, but I couldn't get through, and the ambulance **was trying** to get through the traffic too. All the other drivers **were** just **sitting** there, **looking** straight ahead and **not trying** to move out of the way. I was really worried that someone **was suffering** somewhere, **waiting** for the ambulance to come and help them. It's really annoying when people are so selfish!'

form

We make the past continuous by using the past of the auxiliary verb **be** (**was**, **were**) and the **ing** *form* of the main verb:

singular	plural
I **was making**	we **were making**
you **were making**	you **were making**
he / she / it **was making**	they **were making**

Note: We often use one auxiliary with more than one **ing** *form*, if the subject of the verbs remain the same:
- The people **were sitting** in their cars, just **staring** ahead.

use

We use the past continuous to talk about *something happening* at <u>a particular time in the past</u>:
- Adnan **was working** in the stockroom <u>at 8 p.m. yesterday</u>.
- The Bells **were sitting** in their garden <u>at lunchtime</u>.

We often use it to talk about *something that was in progress* <u>when an event happened</u>:
- Adnan **was driving** home <u>when Ismah phoned</u>.
- Tom **was parking** his car <u>when the traffic warden appeared</u>.

We also use it with **while** to talk about *two things happening at the same time*:
- **While** the pastry **was cooking**, Andrea prepared the tea.
- **While** Jim **was cooking**, Mary **was paying** some bills.

We also use it to talk about *repeated actions over a past period of time*:
- Last winter, Craig **was going** to Sweden every month.
- When my fridge was broken, I **was going** to the shop every day.

questions

We make questions by putting the auxiliary verb (**was** / **were**) before the <u>subject</u>:
- **Was** <u>Gaby</u> **talking** on the phone?
- **Were** <u>the customers</u> **buying** the new fashions?
- **Why** was <u>Tom</u> **shouting** at Jake?

negatives

The negative is formed by adding **not** or **n't** after **was** / **were**:
- The audience **wasn't laughing** at the comedian.
- We **weren't trying** very hard in the exam.
- Jeremy **wasn't working** for Reuters in 2004.

A Look at the chart and read the sentences below; then finish the sentences about what Melissa and Bill were doing.

Date	Melissa's week	Bill's week
Saturday 11th June	Go to the supermarket.	The plane lands in Auckland.
Sunday 12th June	Take the children to the swimming pool.	Do a tour of Auckland (the 'City of Sails').
Monday 13th June (a.m.)	Take the children to school.	Take a boat trip around 'the Bay of Islands'
Monday 13th June (p.m.)	Collect the children from school.	Cruise to Cape Brett.
Tuesday 14th June	Clean the car.	Explore Waitomo Caves and Glow-worm Grotto
Wednesday 15th June	Work in the allotment.	Visit Whakawarewa Thermal Reserve (boiling mud and geysers).
Thursday 16th June	Go shopping with my friends.	Drive to Rotorua. (redwood forests and lake Rotorua).
Friday 17th June	Change my library books.	Canoe on Lake Taupo (see the Huka Falls).
Saturday 18th June	Visit my mother-in-law in hospital.	Do the walking tour of centre of Wellington (capital city).
Sunday 19th June	Meet Bill at the airport.	Fly home to Britain.
Monday 20th June	Take the children to school, go to the supermarket etc, etc.	Sleep!

0 While Melissa was shopping at the supermarket, Bill's plane _was landing in Auckland_

1 While Melissa was swimming with the children, Bill _____

2 While Bill was taking a boat trip around the Bay of Islands, Melissa _____

3 While Melissa was collecting the children from school, Bill _____

4 While Bill was exploring the Waitomo caves, Melissa _____

5 While Melissa was working in the allotment, Bill _____

6 While Bill was driving to Rotorua, Melissa _____

7 While Melissa was changing her library books, Bill _____

8 While Bill was walking round the centre of Wellington, Melissa _____

9 While Melissa was driving to the airport, Bill _____

10 On Monday, while Melissa was doing all the usual jobs, Bill _____

B Choose a verb in the box to fit in each gap in the conversation.

| was working   was keeping   were talking   was going   was planning   was training |
| wasn't going   was studying   wasn't enjoying   ~~was waiting~~   wasn't working |

ROS: Have you heard about Julie? Well, while I [0] _was waiting_ for my dentist appointment on Thursday, she phoned me. She was on a train!

SIDRA: Oh, I thought she [1] _____ in the tax office.

ROS: So did I! But she [2] _____ . In fact, she [3] _____ to the airport, on her way to Spain!

SIDRA: Wow! We [4] _____ a week ago, and she didn't say anything about going on holiday.

ROS: Well, she [5] _____ for a holiday – she's got a job in Spain! She was really excited!

SIDRA: What kind of job has she got? I know she [6] _____ Spanish at evening classes last term…

ROS: Yes, and she [7] _____ to be a tour guide. She didn't say anything to us about that.

SIDRA: So she's got a job as a tour guide! I know she [8] _____ working in the tax office, but I didn't know she [9] _____ such a big change. Good for her!

ROS: I don't know why she didn't tell us. Maybe she [10] _____ it a secret until she got a job.

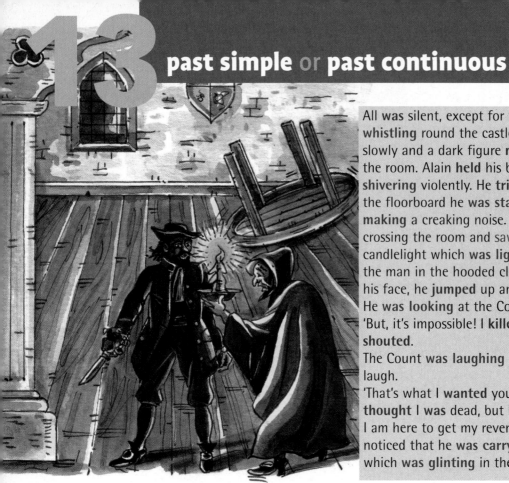

All **was** silent, except for the wind which **was whistling** round the castle. The door **opened** slowly and a dark figure **moved** silently into the room. Alain **held** his breath, but he **was shivering** violently. He **tried** to keep still, but the floorboard he **was standing** on **was making** a creaking noise. He **heard** footsteps crossing the room and **saw** the flickering candlelight which **was lighting** up the face of the man in the hooded cloak. When Alain **saw** his face, he **jumped** up and a table **fell** over. He **was looking** at the Count of Monte Bianco! 'But, it's impossible! I **killed** you a year ago!' he **shouted**.
The Count **was laughing** - a soft, sinister laugh.
'That's what I **wanted** you to believe! You **thought** I **was** dead, but I **was** still **breathing**! I am here to get my revenge!' and Alain **noticed** that he **was carrying** a large knife, which **was glinting** in the candlelight ...

past simple

We use the past simple to talk about –
events that happened <u>at a particular time in the past</u>:

- Paolo **bought** a new car <u>yesterday</u>.
- The Haywoods **went** to France <u>in 1999</u>.

situations that existed <u>for a period of time in the past</u>:

- I **lived** in Guatemala <u>for ten years</u>.
- Gary **worked** for Gargantuan <u>when he was younger</u>.

things that happened regularly or frequently in the past, but not now:

- Peter **went** to the gym twice a week.
- The milkman **delivered** two pints of milk every day.

We often use **when** or **as soon as** with the past simple:

- Sue talked to her sister **when** she **arrived**.
- We bought the new CD **as soon as** it **came out**.

past continuous

We can use the past continuous to talk about –
an activity that was happening at <u>a particular time in the past</u>:

- <u>When Helen called</u>, Jack **was working** in the garden.
- <u>At 6.30 a.m.</u> Phoebe **was making** the bread for breakfast.

repeated actions, and for something that was changing, <u>at a particular time in the past</u>:

- <u>In June</u>, Kieran **was revising** for his exams.
- The weeds **were getting** taller <u>all summer</u>.
- <u>This morning</u>, the snow **was falling** more thickly

We often use **while** with the past continuous when we are talking about *two things happening at the same time*:

- Tom fell asleep **while** the teacher **was talking**.
- The rain started falling **while** we **were walking** down the hill.

Remember – verbs which describe states or feelings are not usually used in a continuous form:

- Robin **was** ready to start the game. NOT ~~Robin was being ready to start the game.~~
- They **seemed** really excited. NOT ~~They were seeming really excited.~~

(For more on *describing* verbs, see Unit 8.)

EXERCISES

A
Put the two sentences together using **when** or **while**, and using the past continuous in one half and the past simple in the other.

0 Toni <u>be</u> in the bakery kitchen – Rosa <u>work</u> in the shop. *Toni was in the bakery kitchen while Rosa was working in the shop.*

1 A customer <u>come</u> into the shop – Rosa <u>put</u> bread rolls into a basket.

2 The supplier <u>deliver</u> the flour – Toni <u>make</u> some brown loaves.

3 The customer <u>choose</u> some pastries – Toni <u>come</u> into the shop.

4 Rosa <u>help</u> the customer – Toni <u>take</u> some money from the till.

5 The customer <u>decide</u> to buy some almond pastries – Toni <u>pay</u> for the delivery.

6 Rosa <u>put</u> the pastries in a bag – the customer <u>look</u> for her purse.

7 Rosa <u>begin</u> to think she didn't have any money – she finally <u>find</u> her purse.

8 Toni <u>ask</u> her to help him in the kitchen – she <u>give</u> the customer her change.

9 A man <u>come</u> into the shop – they <u>bake</u> the bread.

10 He <u>take</u> all the money out of the till – she <u>not watch</u>.

B
Read the text, and then answer the questions.

It was 7.15 in the evening and the choir and orchestra were changing their clothes in the dressing rooms while the audience were finding their seats. The hall looked wonderful, with great glass chandeliers and flowers everywhere. There was a big queue of people waiting to buy programmes. The conductor, in his new black suit and bow tie, was walking up and down in the corridor. He felt very nervous, as it was his first concert with a large orchestra and choir. The soprano soloist was stuck in traffic in the middle of Birmingham, but the other soloists were in their dressing rooms, practising the difficult parts of the music. She arrived at 7.25, ran into the dressing room and quickly changed into her beautiful, red silk dress, just in time to walk calmly onto the stage at 7.30. The other musicians noticed that she was breathing very heavily and her face was very red! She sang beautifully anyway, and the audience really enjoyed the concert.

0 What time was it? *It was 7.15 in the evening.*

1 What were the musicians doing?

2 What were the audience doing?

3 What was the queue of people waiting to do?

4 What was the conductor doing?

5 What was he wearing?

6 Why was he nervous?

7 Why wasn't the soprano in the concert hall?

8 What were the other soloists doing?

9 What time did the soprano arrive?

10 What did she do when she arrived?

11 What was she doing when she walked on stage?

12 What was her face like?

13 Did she sing well?

14 Did the audience enjoy the concert?

33

TEACHER: Now, class, this morning we've been to the nature reserve and we've seen some wild flowers. How many have we noticed, Harry?

HARRY: Loads, Miss!

TEACHER: You're right, we've seen lots and lots. I've listed about 20 different kinds. Have you ever been to the reserve before?

SYLVIA: No miss. But I've been to the zoo.

TEACHER: Very nice! Now, let's look at the list ... Where is it? Oh no, I've lost it!

IRVIN: I've got it, Miss. But I've made it into a paper aeroplane. Look, it flies really well!

form

We make the present perfect simple by using **have / has** with the *past participle* of the verb:

singular	plural
I **have played** (I**'ve played**)	we **have played** (we**'ve played**)
you **have played** (you**'ve played**)	you **have played** (you**'ve played**)
he / she / it **has played** (he**'s played**)	they **have played** (they**'ve played**)

We usually use the contracted form of the auxiliary (**'ve / 's**), particularly after pronouns (e.g. **I**, **he**, **they**):

- We**'ve taken** all the best sweets!   ■ He**'s had** a really bad day today.

To make a question in the present perfect, we use the *auxiliary verb* **have / has**, then the <u>subject</u>, followed by the **main verb**:

- **Have** <u>you</u> **seen** all the *Star Wars* films?   ■ **Has** <u>Toni</u> **taken** his pills?

We make the negative by adding **not** or **n't** after the *auxiliary* **have / has**:

- You **haven't forgotten** my birthday!
- Evan **hasn't contacted** the managing director yet.

use

We use the present perfect to talk about *something which happened at some time in the past but the focus of meaning is on the present*:

- Deven **has bought** a flat in Delhi. (= *He owns it now.*)
- **Have** you **used** all the shampoo? (= *Is there no shampoo now?*)

We use this form, often with **ever** or **never**, to talk about an event which happened *at some time in our lives*:

- I**'ve been** to Paris, but I**'ve never been** to Rome.
- **Has Diane ever** paid for a meal?

We also use it to talk about *a situation which began in the past and is still continuing*:

- Toni **has been** in Tasmania for three months. (*He's still there.*)
- I**'ve lived** in this village since I was a child. (*I still live in the village.*)

exceptions

The present perfect of *go* changes to **has been** when we mean *has visited*:

- Tanya **has been** to Bulawayo. (= *She has visited Bulawayo. She isn't there now.*)

but we use **has gone to (somewhere)** to mean *is there now*:

- She **has gone** to Tanzania. (= *She is in Tanzania now.*)

We often use *have got* to say we *have something now*:

- I**'ve got** a bad cold. = I **have** a bad cold.

Many common verbs have irregular *past participles*:

ending in **n / ne**: be → **been**   speak → **spoken**   drive → **driven**   give → **given**
eat → **eaten**   do → **done**   ride → **ridden**   go → **gone**
ending in **ght**: buy → **bought**   catch → **caught**   fight → **fought**
other endings: have → **had**   make → **made**   swim → **swum**
(For more irregular past participles, see page 222.)

A Put the present perfect of the appropriate verb from the box in the gaps in the questionnaire, and circle your answer.

| do | climb | ~~live~~ | be | ride | swim | speak | eat | camp | drive | make |

How brave are you?

0	*Have you lived*	in a foreign country?	(yes)/no
1	Have	in English on the phone?	yes/no
2		snails, or snake, or lizard?	yes/no
3		to a music festival?	yes/no
4		a speech in public?	yes/no
5		bungee jumping or sky diving?	yes/no
6		a sports car?	yes/no
7		in the middle of a wood?	yes/no
8		a mountain?	yes/no
9		in a deep, dark lake?	yes/no
10		on a big, fast, roller coaster?	yes/no

Now count how many *yes* answers you have given, and check what your score means in the box at the bottom of the page!

B Mr Hampton, the garage owner, has ticked (✓) all the jobs he has done. The jobs he hasn't done are crossed (✗). Now list what he has and hasn't done.

0 *He's changed the oil.*
1
2
3
4
5
6
7
8
9
10

Hampton's Garage
96 Green Avenue, Long Tilbury
LT7 4MR
Tel: 062466 282506

Customer: Mr G. Delitto   23.08
Re: green Mitsubishi, 1996

Change the oil	✓
Check the wheel balance	✓
Replace the spare tyre	✓
Measure the emissions level	✓
Mend the broken back door	✗
Repair the handle of the passenger door	✗
Clean the carburettor	✓
Wash the car	✓
Fix the wing mirrors	✓
Respray the car silver	✗
Do a test drive	✓

How brave are you?

1-3 You aren't very brave! You need to get out and live life a bit more!

3-6 You are quite adventurous, but there are still a lot more fun things to do in life. Get out and enjoy yourself!

7-10 You are crazy! Having fun is important, but don't take too many risks.

Dear Tanya,
I **arrived** here last night – the journey **was** very long and difficult, but I really **enjoyed** it. The Brazilian rainforest is wonderful! We **travelled** in a bark canoe for the last part of the journey! I **have met** several of the local Kayapo people, and they **have all been** really friendly and helpful and they **have taught** me some words in their language. I've just **eaten** monkey and bananas, and I've **made** a fire using only sticks and leaves (I'm sitting beside it now!). Oh, and a black spider **bit** me when I was collecting wood! Fortunately they **have given** me some medicine made from the bark of a tree. I **was** very frightened, but now I h**ave calmed down** a lot. In fact I'm feeling wonderful – I wonder if it is the medicine ...
Lots of love, Darren

present perfect

We use the present perfect to talk about:
something that happened in the past and that tells us something about the present:
- Karen **has passed** her driving test. Now she can drive.
- We**'ve bought** a new CD player. Listen, it's really good!
- **Have** you **missed** the bus? Are you waiting for the next one?

a situation that started in the past and continues now, or up to now:
- Andy **has lived** in Melbourne all his life. (*He's still there.*)
- We**'ve been** in the park for two hours. (*We've just left the park.*)

We often use *adverbs* (**just**, **already**, **never**) with the present perfect:
- Oh no! We**'ve** <u>just</u> **missed** the bus!
- I**'ve** <u>already</u> **seen** this film. Let's change channels.
- Martin **has** <u>never</u> **visited** the Modern Art Gallery.

When we want to ask if *someone has done something at any time in their life*, we often use **ever** with the present perfect:
- **Have** you **ever tried** surfing?
- **Has** David **ever met** Annette?

past simple

We use the past simple to talk about:
something that happened at a particular time in the past:
- Karen **took** her driving test on Monday. The examiner was really nice!
- We **bought** a new CD player last week. It broke the same day!
- **Did** you **miss** the bus? Were you late for your appointment?

a situation that existed at a particular time in the past but is finished:
- Frank **lived** in Melbourne until last year. (*He lives in Sydney now.*)
- We **were** in the park this afternoon. (*We're at home now.*)

We often use a <u>time expression</u> (**when, as soon as, at 6 o'clock** etc) with the past simple:
- <u>When</u> John **saw** the Maserati, he fell in love!
- Theo got up <u>as soon as</u> the alarm **rang**.
- <u>At half past ten</u> the children **came** out of the classroom.

When we list *things that happened in the past one after the other*, we use the *past simple*:
- Tom **changed** the tyre, then he **checked** the oil, and **cleaned** the windscreen.

EXERCISES

A

Make sentences about the picture using either the past simple or the present perfect, and the words in brackets. Some of the sentences are questions.

0 (the Marsham Ferry / already / arrive) *The Marsham ferry has already arrived.*

1 (it / arrive / at 3.00) ....

2 (the passengers / be / to Marsham) ....

3 (the ferry / be / late?) ....

4 (the two girls / miss / the boat / ?) ....

5 (the passengers / already / buy / tickets) ....

6 (when / the ferry / get here / ?) ....

7 (how many people / get off / the ferry / ?) ....

8 (the ferry / leave / Marsham on time / ?) ....

9 (the two girls / buy / sandwiches from the café) ....

10 (I / never / be / on the Bridgeport ferry) ....

B

Choose the best verb from the box to put in each gap in the text.

| have wanted | enjoyed | gave | was | has helped | hit | ~~has increased~~ | has been | helped |
| took | has worked | have been | wanted | joined | thought | were |

More and more people are doing voluntary work – that is, work that is not paid. In Britain, in the past two years the number of people that do some voluntary work 0 *has increased* by 1.6 million, to 17 million! In the year 2000, people 1 .... that society was very selfish, but there 2 .... several major disasters since then and more people 3 .... to help than ever before. When the Tsunami flood 4 .... South East Asia, people 5 .... £350 million pounds.

For two years, Tina Hannaford 6 .... two twelve-hour shifts a month at the Chiswick Lifeboat Station in London. She 7 .... the Lifeboat Association because she 8 .... sailing and 9 .... to do something useful, and exciting. She 10 .... to save lots of people when they 11 .... in trouble in boats on the River Thames. Once, a boat with sixteen people in it 12 .... stuck under a bridge and she 13 .... them all get into the lifeboat and 14 .... them to the river bank. It 15 .... very hard work sometimes, but she says it's good to feel useful!

DAVID: Hello Ian! What on earth **have you been doing**? Your clothes are all torn and dirty and there's blood on your hands!

IAN: I'm sorry I'm so late! I decided to take a short cut across the fields, instead of going by the road – but I got lost – **I've been looking** for the house for hours! I never realised how far it was from the village!

DAVID: Going across the fields is not too bad in the winter, but when the brambles **have been growing** for a couple of months, it's impossible to get through the hedges. Well, come in and rest.

IAN: Oh thank you. I suppose I've missed dinner.

DAVID: No, **I've been waiting** for you. **I've** just **been watching** the news while I waited.

form	We make the present perfect continuous with **have / has + been + ing** *form* of the main verb:

singular	plural
I **have been swimming** (I've been)	we **have been swimming** (we've been)
you **have been swimming** (you've been)	you **have been swimming** (you've been)
he / she / it **has been swimming** (he's been)	they **have been swimming** (they've been)

We usually use the contracted form (**I've**, **he's** etc), especially when we speak. (For more on the **ing** *form*, see units 5 and 8.)

To make questions in the present perfect continuous we put **has / have** before the <u>*subject*</u>:

- **Has** <u>Tim</u> **been sleeping** all morning?
- **Have** <u>your children</u> **been eating** the biscuits?

We make negatives with **not** or **n't** after **has / have**:

- Simon **hasn't been working** very hard.
- The trains **haven't been running** on time today.

use	We use the present perfect continuous to talk *about a situation or an activity which started in the past and has continued up to now*. We often use a <u>time phrase</u> to say *how long*:

- Tanya h**as been talking** on the phone <u>for half an hour</u>.
- We**'ve been revisin**g German grammar <u>all morning</u>.

We also use it for *an activity that began in the past and has very recently finished; often there is now some evidence of the activity*:

- David **has been making** dinner. (*There is a terrible mess in the kitchen!*)
- The dog **has been digging** up my roses. (*They are all broken*.)

We also use it for *repeated events up to now*:

- Halima **has been going** to yoga classes for two years.
- **I've been buying** my cheese from that shop for years.

EXERCISES

A Read these notes about the story of Amanda's favourite TV show 'Sharon Shaw'. Then complete the conversation, using the information in the notes and the present perfect continuous.

Sharon's brother, Issac: working at the beach café; stealing from the till every night.
Sharon's dad: sleeping in the garden shed;
Sharon's mum and dad: fighting for a few weeks.
Their neighbours' son, Jason: asking Sharon to go out with him every day; she refuses.
Sharon: hoping that Gareth will ask her out again.
Gareth: not going out with anyone; studying really hard for his law exams.
Linda: hiding from the police in the beach hut; the police looking for her for two weeks.
Sharon: knows where Linda is, but is lying to the police to protect Linda.

0 FRAN: Where *has Isaac been working?*

AMANDA: At the beach café. But he's in big trouble!

1 FRAN: Why? What has he been doing?

AMANDA: Well, Isaac ....

2 FRAN: No! And what about Sharon's dad? Where

....?

AMANDA: Still in the garden shed!

3 FRAN: Is there a problem between her mum and dad?

AMANDA: Yes. They ....

4 FRAN: And what about Jason? Has

....?

AMANDA: Yes, but she refused to go out with him.

5 FRAN: Why did she refuse?

AMANDA: Because ....

6 FRAN: Did Gareth ask anyone else out?

AMANDA: No, ...

7 FRAN: Why not?

AMANDA: Because ....

8 FRAN: Oh, he's such a serious boy. I don't know why she likes him so much. And where is Linda?

AMANDA: Oh, she's ....

9 FRAN: Haven't the police found her yet?

AMANDA: No, but ....

10 FRAN: Two weeks! But I thought Sharon knew where she was?

AMANDA: Oh yes, but the stupid girl

....!

B Read the phone conversation and put the correct present perfect continuous form of the verb in brackets in the gaps.

DON: Hello, is that Matt? It's Don here.

MATT: Oh, hi Don. What (⁰ you / do?) *have you been doing* today?

DON: (¹ We / walk) .... on the moors all day. (² you / enjoy?) .... the nice weather today?

MATT: Not really. (³ I / study) .... all day for my exam tomorrow morning.

DON: That's such a pity. (⁴ We / have) .... such horrible weather until today.

MATT: I know – (⁵ I / work) .... in the library mostly, but today I took my laptop and books and went to the park.

DON: So (⁶ you / revise) .... for your exam out in the sunshine! Cool!

MATT: Well, I had to come back after a couple of hours. There were too many dogs, and children, and flies! No, (⁷ I / sit) .... in my garden – in the shade!

DON: That sounds nice. Rachel and I went down to Exmoor – (⁸ we / do) .... very long hours at the hospital and we needed a day out. It was great, but we're really exhausted. She's interested in wild flowers and (⁹ she / photograph) .... plants and checking them in her book.

MATT: I didn't know you were interested in nature.

DON: Well, I wasn't, but I have to admit English plants are really interesting! And (¹⁰ I / learn) .... how to develop photographs, so I'm going to print them for her. We may put one in for a nature photography competition!

MATT: Well, you can come and take some pictures in my garden. It's full of wild flowers! (¹¹ I / not / look after) .... it at all!

17 used to

I interviewed Graham Treacher in 1998 when his band, *Treachery*, had their first successful album. Have things changed since then? He laughs and says, 'Not really! I **used to be** really scared of people changing their minds about us. And I still am! Even though we've made six albums and each one has been incredibly popular, I always think the next one's going to be a complete disaster!'

I remind him that he also **used to save** all his money, in case he never made another penny. He says he doesn't do that any more, but he is glad that he **used to be** so careful! Now he has lots of money invested and he doesn't have to worry. And now he sometimes buys things for himself, and even goes on holiday!

'I **used to be** really sad – I **didn't** really **use to enjoy** my success. But the rest of the band did! They **used to go** to parties and things after the show while I **used to go back** to the hotel and **get** a good night's sleep!'

form

singular	plural
I **used to go**	we **used to go**
you **used to go**	you **used to go**
he / she / it **used to go**	they **used to go**

We make the negative with **didn't use to**, or **used not to**, but NOT ~~didn't used to~~:

- Luigi **didn't use to be able** to speak English. OR Luigi **used not to be able** to speak English.
- We **didn't use to eat** in restaurants. OR We **used not to eat** in restaurants.

We make questions with **did** + _subject_ + **use to**:

- **Did** <u>you</u> **use to live** near the park?
- Why **did** <u>she</u> **use to be** so angry?

use

We use **used to** in the same way as the *past simple*, but only to talk about – *what we did often or regularly*:

- I **used to go** to work by by car – I travel by bus now.
- We **used to save** our data onto floppy discs but we put it onto CDs now.

or, a past situation, which has changed:

- Mr and Mrs Cavalliere **used to own** a café – now they run a bakery.
- Charlotte **used to have** a big house in the country, but she lives in a little flat in the city now.

We don't use it to talk about *a single event in the past*:

- Gary gave me a lift this morning. NOT ~~Gary used to give~~…

To describe *a past situation which has not changed*, we use the **past simple**:

- There **was** a pond in the park. It's still there.

BUT

- There **used to be** a fish and chip shop in the village. It's not there now.

with adverbs

When we use an _adverb_ like **sometimes**, **always**, **often**, **ever**, and **really**, it goes before **used to** or **use to**:

- Rita <u>often</u> **used to miss** her train.
- We <u>always</u> **used to have** coffee at eleven.
- We **didn't** <u>often</u> **use to sit** in the garden, but we do a lot now that we have a lawn.

A Read the following text and look at the past tense verbs underlined. Some of them can be changed to **used to** + *infinitive*, with the same meaning. Write the correct form in the table.

The town I ⁰<u>lived</u> in when I was a child was very small. It ¹<u>had</u> a factory which ²<u>made</u> tinned milk puddings, but then the factory ³<u>closed</u>, and there were hardly any jobs and many people ⁴<u>had to</u> leave the village. In the summer we ⁵<u>went</u> down to the bottom of the main street after school, where there ⁶<u>was</u> a bridge over the river. There isn't a bridge over the river now.

I don't think children are allowed to play outside in the country now but, at that time, parents ⁷<u>sent</u> their kids out in the morning and ⁸<u>told</u> them not to come back till tea time! Sometimes I ⁹<u>played</u> alone, and sometimes with the other children. I ¹⁰<u>organised</u> pirate games. I ¹¹<u>was always</u> the pirate captain, and my friends ¹²<u>were</u> pirates or French sailors. The pirates always ¹³<u>won</u>! We ¹⁴<u>had</u> a metal bath which we ¹⁵<u>used</u> as a boat and we always ¹⁶<u>fell</u> into the water. It wasn't very deep, and we all ¹⁷<u>learnt</u> to swim!

0 ....*used to live*....	6	12 ....
1	7	13 ....
2	8	14 ....
3	9	15 ....
4	10	16 ....
5	11	17 ....

B Read the text above and then complete the questions in this interview, using the words in brackets and **did ... use to.**

0 (the town) ' _Did the town use to_ have a factory?' 'Yes, it did.'

1 (what / the factory) '... make?' 'It used to make tinned milk puddings.'

2 (you) '... go down to the bridge?' 'Yes, I did.'

3 (parents) '... allow their children to go out and play?' 'Yes, they did.'

4 (they) '... tell them not to come back till bed time?' 'No, they didn't.'

5 (you / always) '... play alone?' 'No, I didn't.'

6 (you / often) '... play with the other children?' 'Yes, I did.'

7 (what games / you) '... organise?' 'They were pirate games.'

8 (what kind of boat / you) '... have?' 'It was a metal bath.'

9 (the French sailors / ever) '... win?' 'No, they didn't.'

10 (The pirates / always) '... win?' 'Yes they always did!'

11 (you / ever) '... fall in the water?' 'Yes, we always fell in!'

past perfect (I had listened)

Before Amelia came to Canada in 1999, she **had** never **left** Germany. She was 65. Before she retired she **had been** a nurse in her local hospital, and she **had brought** up four children. In 1994 her second son moved to Canada; her eldest son **had emigrated** there two years earlier, in 1992. They both found good jobs and decided to stay and start families there. When her youngest daughter Helga finished her education, she, too, decided to join her brothers in Ottawa. So Amelia was left alone, as her second daughter, Eva, **had** tragically **died** in a road accident when she was only 17. Amelia **had continued** to work until she was 60, and then she bought a little cottage in a pretty village called Deidesheim. After five years she decided that she didn't like retirement, and she packed a bag and left Germany forever.

form

We make the past perfect with the past of **have** (**had**, **'d**) and the *past participle* of the main verb:

singular	plural
I **had watched** (I'**d watched**)	we **had watched** (we'**d watched**)
you **had watched** (you'**d watched**)	you **had watched** (you'**d watched**)
he / she / it **had watched** (she'**d watched**)	they **had watched** (they'**d watched**)

We usually use the contracted form of the auxiliary (**'d**) after pronouns (**I**, **you**, **he** etc):

■ It was six o'clock and we'**d waited** for hours for the bus.

A lot of frequently-used verbs are irregular – they don't have **ed** in the past participle, e.g:

be → **been**	buy → **bought**	come → **come**
give → **given**	go → **gone**	have → **had**
hide → **hidden**	make → **made**	read(/riːd/) → **read** (/red/)
say → **said**	see → **seen**	write → **written**

(For a complete list of irregular verbs, see page 222.)

We make questions by putting the auxiliary **had** before the <u>subject</u>:

■ **Had** <u>Annette</u> **seen** the film before?
■ How **had** <u>Matt</u> **chosen** the car he bought?

We make the negative by adding **not** or **n't** after **had**:

■ I **had not had** a shower that morning.
■ Steve **hadn't visited** his father in hospital yet.

use

We use the past perfect to say that *something happened before something else happened*:

■ Andy **had tidied** the living room <u>before the party started</u>. (= *Andy tidied, and then they had a party.*)
■ <u>When Tina arrived</u>, Sarah **had** already **left** the house. (= *Sarah left the house and then Tina arrived.*)
■ <u>Ian waited three weeks</u> for the computer which he **had ordered**.

We use the past perfect to talk about *a situation that existed up to <u>a time we are talking about in the past</u>*, usually with a time phrase (e.g. **for ten years**):

■ <u>When she was 18</u>, Jo **had known** Sophie for ten years.
■ <u>When the phone rang</u>, Tanya **had been** in the bath for half an hour.

EXERCISES

A

Put the following pairs of sentences together, using the *past perfect*, and **before** with the *past simple*.

0 Ollie, the stage manager, closes the safety curtain. – The audience comes in: *Ollie, the stage manager, had closed the safety curtain before the audience came in.*

1 He hangs up the costumes in the dressing rooms. – The actors arrived.

2 Ollie counts the props. – The show starts.

3 The barman fills the shelves with bottles. – The first half of the play ends.

4 The actors learn their lines. – They have their first rehearsal.

5 The director reads hundreds of plays. – He chooses the play by David Thorpe.

6 The cleaner cleans up all the fake blood. – Everyone goes home.

7 The stage manager checks everything. – The play starts.

8 The lights come up. – The audience start clapping.

9 The director auditions ten different actors. – He chooses a leading man.

10 The actors have a horrible argument. – They agree about the meaning of the play.

11 They redecorate the theatre. – They put on the new play.

B

Read the story and then answer the questions about it, using the parts of the text in green. Notice that sometimes you need to use the *past simple*, and sometimes the *past perfect*.

When he was 34, Mickey Rourke quit acting to become a boxer. He had become very aggressive and self-destructive because he had had a violent step-father who had made him feel worthless. When he was a young actor, he had been very successful, and had had a very big house and a glamorous wife. He had gradually lost all his friends and his wife, and ended up in one room, lifting weights all day long. During the five and a half years he was boxing professionally, his face had been very badly damaged and he had to have plastic surgery. He realised that he had to get control of his life again, and he decided to ask for some help from a psychotherapist. It was very hard for him to do this as, in the culture he grew up in, men didn't show any weakness. He says that when he started acting again, his acting was better because of his life experience, as he had understood the problems other people can have. When he heard the director had offered him a part in a new Hollywood film, *Sin City*, he was very pleased and excited.

0 What did Mickey do when he was 34?
   He quit acting to become a boxer.

1 Why had Mickey become so self-destructive?

2 What had his step-father done to him when he was a child?

3 What had his life been like when he was a young actor?

4 What had he done before he ended up in one room?

5 What had happened to his face when he was a professional boxer?

6 What did he do to get control of his life again?

7 Why had he waited so long to ask for help?

8 Why was he a better actor when he started again?

9 How did he feel when they offered him a part in a new film?

A Read the text, and choose the best form of each underlined verb, and circle it.

Real Farm Foods
Organic produce supplier

When I was a young mother, I [0] (was)/ was being very worried about the quality of the food that I [1] was giving / have given my son. We [2] were / have been not vegetarians, and I wasn't happy to give my son the kind of meat which the supermarkets [3] sold / have sold at that time. It was full of antibiotics and artificial hormones. And there [4] had been / was being the 'mad cow' scare, as well. [5] I didn't want / was not wanting to take any risks. I [6] had studied / have studied chemistry at university and [7] understood / was understanding what those long names like 'monosodium glutamate' meant! I [8] talked / have talked to some friends and we [9] decided / were deciding to set up a business, providing good, healthy meat for our families and our customers. We then [10] discovered / had discovered there were some organic meat producers out there, and people who [11] were / 'd been happy to pay a bit more to get safe and healthy food.

Now it is ten years since we first [12] have started / started our business, and we are very proud of what we [13] 'd achieved / 've achieved. At the start, we [14] had / were having a list of priorities, and we think we've stayed true to them. We [15] 've tried / 'd tried to provide the kind of service we wanted for ourselves. We believe we can confidently say that we [16] 've brought / were bringing superb organic food and drink to our customers, we [17] offered / 've offered a friendly and efficient service, and we [18] 've tried / were trying to get all our food as locally as possible. It [19] 's always been / was always being important to us to pay our farmers well, and to take good care of the environment. We [20] 've given / were giving something back to our community, and we [21] looked after / 've looked after our staff well. It's hard work, but we love it!

B Read the story and choose the best verbs from the box to fill the gaps.

> lived   wanted   had lived   were   decided   had lived   had painted   used to go
> ordered   caught   died   ~~was preparing~~   closed   was   designed   had arrived

In 1858, the young King Pedro V of Portugal ⁰ ___was preparing___ to marry Princess Stefania of Hohenzollern-Sigmaringen. He ¹ _____ to please his young wife and so he ² _____ to decorate the future Queen's apartments in the Royal Palace, the 'Necessidades'. He ³ _____ new furniture, lamps, curtains and carpets, mainly from Paris but also from Lisbon.

He ⁴ _____ a new, ivory bedroom, overlooking a small garden, for his Queen. The King ordered their initials, P and S, to be painted on the ceiling, with the royal crown made in stucco, which

NECESSIDADES PALACE, LISBON

we can still see today. Queen Stefania was delighted when she saw her new palace, and she specially loved the doors to her dressing room, which a famous artist ⁵ _____ with pretty flowers and the date of the wedding, 1858, in the centre. The 'Necessidades' and the palace where she ⁶ _____ in Dusseldorf were similar. They ⁷ _____ both pink, quite small, built in the 18th century, and surrounded by a lovely park. She always ⁸ _____ for long walks in the park.

Tragically, the young queen ⁹ _____ diphtheria almost immediately and, on 17 July, 1859, she ¹⁰ _____ . She was only 22 years old. She ¹¹ _____ in Lisbon on 17 May 1859, and she ¹² _____ in the palace for only two months.

King Pedro V's heart ¹³ _____ broken, and he died of typhoid in 1861 at the young age of 24. After this double tragedy, the Royal family ¹⁴ _____ all the windows of the Palace out of respect for the tragic young couple. No one ¹⁵ _____ there for many years.

CLODHOPPERS HOT NEWS

Our fantastic Winter Sale **starts** on December 28th.

Our sale doors **open** at 10 a.m.

We are **reducing** ALL our prices by 20% or MORE.

We **are offering** some really fantastic savings:

50% off some women's shoes!

80% off some men's shoes!

But be quick – our sale **ends** on January 7th.

timetables

We use the ***present simple*** to talk about *events which we expect to happen*, because they are part of a *timetable* (e.g. a flight timetable, a train timetable, a school or college timetable or calendar, a cinema programme, a TV schedule, a shop timetable):

- Their flight **leaves** at 5 in the morning!
- Quick, Mike! School assembly **is** in ten minutes.
- Today is the last day of the holidays – Isaac **goes** back to school tomorrow.
- What time **does** the film **finish**?
- That TV series about doctors **ends** next week.
- Oh no, the supermarket is shut and they **don't open** tomorrow.

plans

We use the ***present continuous*** to talk about *people (or organisations) and their plans*:

- We**'re going** to the dentist tomorrow.
- Christina **is moving** into her new house next week.
- The washing machine repairman **is coming** on Tuesday.
- The company **is expanding** the sales team in Canada next year.
- The bank **is reducing** its interest rates next week.
- Marcey **isn't working** tomorrow.
- What **are** you **doing** next week? (= *What are your plans for next week?*)

We don't use **be** in the present continuous, to talk about a plan; we often use the present simple:

- Marcey is flying to Rome on Monday – she**'s** there till Thursday.

when for the future

We can use **when** to talk about *a time in the future*; we usually use the ***present simple*** after **when**:

- Will you still be here, **when** I **get** home?
- **When** I **finish** the meeting, I'll phone you on my mobile.
- **When** you **cut** your birthday cake, make a wish.

We can also use the ***present perfect*** with **when** to talk about *something that will happen first before something else will happen*:

- **When** I**'ve completed** the project, I'll send you an invoice.

EXERCISES

A Look at the travel information and insert the verbs and phrases in the box into the correct gaps in the sentences. Say if the inserted verb is talking about the future or the present.

▶ Outbound Journey	Flight No.	Depart Time	Arrival Time	Aircraft	En-Route Stops
London Heathrow – UK to Auckland Intl. – New Zealand	SL6	18:15 03-06-06	07:30 05-06-06	785	1
◀ Inbound Journey	Flight No.	Depart Time	Arrival Time	Aircraft	En-Route Stops
Auckland Intl. – New Zealand to London Heathrow – UK	SL77	19:05 20-06-06	9:00 21-06-06	796	1

gets into	lives	~~is flying~~	arrives	's coming back	's staying with	's staying in	leaves	is	is	is

0 Matt _____is flying_____ to New Zealand for a holiday. _____future_____

1 His family _____ in Auckland. _____

2 He _____ them. _____

3 His flight to New Zealand _____ at 6.15 in the evening on 3rd June. _____

4 It _____ at 7.30 in the morning on 5th June. _____

5 There _____ one stop en route. _____

6 He doesn't know where the en-route stop _____ . _____

7 He _____ Auckland for about two weeks. _____

8 He _____ on 20th June. _____

9 His flight _____ Heathrow at about 9 o'clock in the morning. _____

10 The only problem _____ that he can't find his passport! _____

B Use the words in the brackets to complete this conversation. Use the present simple or continuous.

GEORGE: Marcey, we need to plan your special report about urban foxes.

MARCEY: Oh yes, when does the report go out on the air?

GEORGE: (0 – it / go out) _____It goes out_____ on Tuesday, next week. So, can we have a meeting this week? (1 – be / you) _____ free tomorrow, Tuesday?

MARCEY: No, (2 – I / take) _____ a day off work tomorrow. (3 – I / shop) _____ in town with my sister.

GEORGE: Okay, and (4 – I / be / not) _____ here on Wednesday. (5 – I / take) _____ my kids to the seaside for the day.

MARCEY: Oh, nice. (6 – you / go) _____ by car?

GEORGE: No, (7 – we / take) _____ the train. We have to get to the station at six in the morning, because the train (8 – leave) _____ at 6.30! But (9 – it / get) _____ to Bournemouth at 9. Listen, can we have the meeting on Thursday?

MARCEY: Well, (10 – I / be) _____ here in the morning.

GEORGE: No, I can't meet in the morning. (11 – I / interview) _____ people for the new production assistant job all morning. Six candidates (12 – come) _____ for interviews. Can we meet in the afternoon?

MARCEY: No, sorry. (13 – I / go) _____ to the hairdresser's at 2, and then when (14 – I / get back) _____ to the studios, I'm doing interviews with people for the evening news.

GEORGE: Oh, no. (15 – I / be / not) _____ here on Friday.

MARCEY: What (16 – you / do) _____ on Friday?

GEORGE: Well, it's a secret but, actually, (17 – I / go) _____ for an interview for the director's job at XYC TV. Don't tell anyone.

ADNAN: That was our suppliers on the phone. They **are going to deliver** the new range of 'Rocket' boots and shoes this afternoon.

ISMAH: Good. There's plenty of space in the stockroom. The sale in the shop is going very well, isn't it?

ADNAN: Yes, it is. At this rate, we **are going to sell** all our stock before the end of the sale. The new season's shoes **are going to sell** well, too, I'm sure of it. Let's open a second shop in Swenton – let's call it 'Clodhoppers too'.

ISMAH: Yes, that's a great idea.

ADNAN : Good, I'm really glad you agree. **I'm going to start** looking for a nice location in Swenton when the sale is finished.

phone rings

ISMAH: Oh hallo, Sidra. How are things? ... Oh good. ... Yes we're fine. The sale is going very well and **we're going to try** and **open** a second shop. ... Yes, it**'s going to be** a lot of extra work for me too, but your dad **is going to share** the cooking and housework at home.

ADNAN: I didn't say that.

ISMAH: No I decided that!

ADNAN: When?

ISMAH: Just now.

form	We use **be going to** with the infinitive form of a verb:

infinitive	**be going to**	contractions
start	I **am going to** start	**I'm going to** start
	he / she / it **is going to** start	it**'s going to** start
	we / you / they **are going to** start	they**'re going to** start

In the negative we say:

	I **am not** going to start	**I'm not** going to …
	he / she / it **is not** going to start	he**'s not** / he **isn't** going to …
	we / you / they **are not** going to start	we**'re not** / we **aren't** going to …

In questions we put **am / is / are** before the <u>*subject*</u>:

- **Are** <u>you</u> **going** to buy a new car?
- **Is** <u>Stanley</u> **going** to finish his art project soon?
- When **are** <u>they</u> **going** to reply to my letter?

intentions	To talk about *intentions* (i.e. *things that people or organisations have decided to do*), we use **be going to**:

- My computer's crashed – **I'm going to phone** the help line.
- The company **is going to build** a new factory in Wales.

We use the negative to talk about *things that we have decided not to do*:

- We**'re not going to buy** a new car this year.
- Yumi **isn't going to apply** for the manager's job.
- The government **aren't going to raise** taxes before the next election.

expectations	We also use **be going to** for *things that we expect to happen*:

- Marie **is going to be** sad when her son goes to university.
- The company **is going to make** a big loss next year.

or *not to happen*:

- It **isn't going to rain** today.

EXERCISES

A Read Marcey's interview with the engineer and then complete the questions and answers, using **going to** and any other words you need.

MARCEY: So, Laura, where, exactly, ⁰ _is the new building going to be?_

LAURA: The new building is going to be in that big field, there.

MARCEY: ¹ .... that whole field?

LAURA: Yes, it's going to fill the whole area.

MARCEY: Wow! ² .... an absolutely massive building!

LAURA: Yes, it's going to be pretty big.

MARCEY: How high ³ .... , exactly?

LAURA: It's going to be 50 metres high. It's also going to have an underground railway station.

MARCEY: How deep is the station going to be?

LAURA: ⁴ .... about 30 metres deep – that's like a ten-storey building. … But can you see that river that goes through the middle of the site?

MARCEY: Oh, yes. ⁵ ....?

LAURA: Yes, it is going to be a problem.

MARCEY: Is it going to go through the middle of the building for people to paddle their feet in!?

LAURA: No, ⁶ .... through the middle of the building.

MARCEY: Are you going to send it through a tunnel under the building, then?

LAURA: No, ⁷ .... through a tunnel, because tunnels kill rivers. There are a lot of fish living in that river.

MARCEY: So, what ⁸ ....?

LAURA: Well, this is what we are going to do. We're going to build a new channel for the river.

MARCEY: Where ⁹ .... the new channel?

LAURA: We're going to build it around the edge of the field.

MARCEY: And where are you going to put the fish from the old river?

LAURA: ¹⁰ .... them in the new river.

MARCEY: Is it going to be very expensive?

LAURA: Yes, ¹¹ .... But it's ecological!

B Decide if the phrases in green are describing an _intention_ or an _expectation_.

DULCY: I've lost my camera. I think I left it on that bench ten minutes ago and it's not there now.

SAPH: ⁰ What are you going to do?

DULCY: Well, ¹ I'm not going to tell my parents that I've lost it.

SAPH: Why?

DULCY: Because it cost a lot of money and ² they're going to be really cross.

SAPH: But you must tell them. Don't worry, ³ they're not going to be cross.

DULCY: Okay, you're right but ⁴ I'm going to report the loss to the police before I tell them.

SAPH: Let's go to the police station right now.

DULCY: Okay, but first can I use your phone? ⁵ I'm going to ring Sam.

SAPH: ⁶ Why are you going to ring Sam?

DULCY: He may have my camera. We were talking on that bench ten minutes ago.

SAPH: Okay. … Oh, no. where's my phone? It was in my bag.

DULCY: Oh dear, ⁷ this is going to be a stressful day.

0	_intention_	4	....
1	....	5	....
2	....	6	....
3	....	7	....

OLAV STIGMUSSON: Well, Mr Harrison, I've done the filling. Here's some water, so you can wash your mouth. The right side of your face **will feel** numb for about three hours. The anaesthetic **will stop** working then. It's quite a deep filling and so the tooth **will** probably **be** sensitive for a few weeks. You**'ll** probably **feel** a bit of pain when you have a cold drink or eat ice-cream.

BAZ HARRINGTON: Okay, thank you. I think I**'ll go** to the mall and **have** a coffee now.

OLAV: Oh no, don't do that. **If** you have a coffee, you**'ll burn** your mouth, while it is still numb.

form	We use **will** with the infinitive form of a verb:

I / you / he / she / it **will finish**	I**'ll finish**
we / you / they **will finish**	we**'ll finish**

We prefer to use the contraction (**'ll**) in conversations, particularly after **I**, **you** etc.

We put _**adverbs**_ like **probably** or **still** before the verb:
- This **will** <u>probably</u> **hurt** a bit.

In the negative we say:

I / you / he / she / it **will not finish**	you **won't finish**
we / you / they **will not finish**	they **won't finish**

In questions we put **will** before the _**subject**_:
- **Will** <u>Silchester United</u> **beat** Swenton FC today?

expectations	

We use **will** for _things that we expect to happen_:
- Silchester **will beat** Swenton.

We use **won't** for things that we expect _not to happen_:
- They **won't sell** their house at that price. It's too high.

We often use **will** after expressions with **think**:
- I **think** it**'ll be** sunny tomorrow.
- **Do** you **think** the coach driver **will see** us?

Note: we usually avoid **think + won't**:
- I **don't think** he**'ll** wait. (NOT ~~I think he won't wait.~~)

We often use **will** with a **when** or **if** clause; we don't use **will** in the **when** or **if** clause:
- Teresa **will be** delighted <u>when she hears the news</u>.
- Productivity **will improve** <u>if the staff have new computers</u>.

plans and intentions	

We don't usually use **will** for _plans or intentions_:

We're flying to Tokyo tonight. (NOT ~~We will fly …~~)

They're going to phone the police. (NOT ~~They will phone the police …~~)

But we can use **will** for _plans_ or _intentions_ with **be** and after **I think**:
- Sanjay is flying to Berlin tomorrow. He**'ll be** there till Thursday.
- I **think** I**'ll go** to the cinema tonight.

promises and offers	

We use will in _promises_ and _offers_:
- 'Will you be ready soon?' 'I**'ll be** ready in two minutes.'
- 'I don't want to cook tonight.' 'Don't worry. I**'ll cook**.'

shall	

We don't usually use **shall** in statements, but we do use **shall I** or **shall we** (and not **will**) in _requests for advice_:
- **Shall I** ask Tom to lend us his video camera? (NOT ~~Will I ask …?~~)

EXERCISES

A

Use the words in brackets and **will** or **won't** to complete the sentences.

What will the world be like in 2050? We asked two experts – here are their opinions:

0 EXPERT A: *There won't be any oil in the world in 2050.*

(There / not / be / any oil in the world in 2050)

1 EXPERT B: ....
(We / discover / lots more oil)
There will still be lots of oil in 2050.

2 EXPERT A: ....
(No one / have / AIDS in 2050)
The disease will disappear in 2020.

3 EXPERT B: ....
(AIDS / still / be / a big problem in 2050)

4 EXPERT A: ....
(People / not / use / cars or buses in 2050)
Everyone will walk or use bicycles.

5 EXPERT B: ....
(People / have / 'skycars' / and fly through the air)

6 EXPERT A: ....
(The Amazon rain forest / not / exist / in 2050)

7 EXPERT B: ....
(The Amazon rain forest / be / bigger in 2050)

8 EXPERT A: ....
(There / be / 10 billion people in the world in 2050)

9 EXPERT B: ....
(There / not / be / 10 billion people in the world in 2050. / There / be / 8 billion)

10 EXPERT A: ....
(China / have / the biggest economy in the world in 2050)

11 EXPERT B: I don't know. ....

(China / have / the biggest economy in 2050 / ?)

B

Jim and Mary Keene are getting ready to go to a party. Complete their conversation. Use the words in brackets with **will** (or **'ll**).

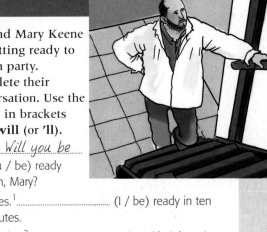

JIM: 0 ___Will you be___
(you / be) ready soon, Mary?

MARY: Yes. 1 .... (I / be) ready in ten minutes.

JIM: But the 2 .... (taxi / be) here in five minutes.

MARY: Don't worry. 3 .... (I / do) my make-up really quickly. 4 ....
(Melissa and Bill / be) at the party?

JIM: Yes, 5 .... (they / be) there.

MARY: Oh, good. Can you prepare some food for the babysitter, please? 6 .... (she / be) here in a minute.

JIM: Okay, 7 .... (I / do) that now.

MARY: Oh, and when she comes, 8 ....
(we / need) to ask her to put the children to bed at eight.

JIM: Okay, 9 .... (I / remember).

MARY: How much money do you think she 10 .... (want) for babysitting?

JIM: I don't know. 11 .... (I / ask) her when she arrives. I don't think she 12 .... (want) a lot of money.

MARY: Right here I am – all ready. Shall I wear this silver necklace or this gold necklace?

JIM: Wow! You look stunning. 13 ....
(You / look) amazing with either necklace.

MARY: Thank you! Oh, but Jim, I'm not going to a party with you in those jeans! 14 ....
(I / find) you a smart pair of trousers.

JIM: Mary, these jeans are fine for the party.

MARY: Please wear these black trousers. 15 .... (They / be) really smart.

two minutes later

MARY: 16 .... (you / be) ready soon, Jim?

JIM: I don't think these trousers 17 .... (fit) me – they look very small!

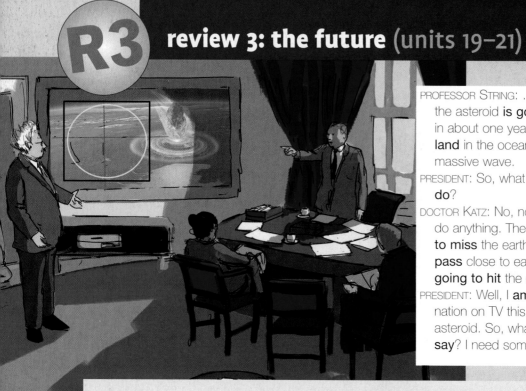

PROFESSOR STRING: … well, I predict that the asteroid **is going to hit** the earth in about one year's time. I think it **will land** in the ocean and **create** a massive wave.

PRESIDENT: So, what **are** we **going to do**?

DOCTOR KATZ: No, no, we don't need to do anything. The asteroid **is going to miss** the earth. It **will** probably **pass** close to earth but it **isn't going to hit** the earth.

PRESIDENT: Well, I **am speaking** to the nation on TV this evening about the asteroid. So, what **am** I **going to say**? I need some quick answers.

introduction

There are three main forms that we can use to talk about the future –
be going to: → I **am going to meet** her at six.
will: → I'**ll meet** her at six.
present continuous: → I **am meeting** her at six.
We use the different forms to say different things about the future.

expectations

We use **will** to say that *we expect something to happen*:
- Ismah **will** probably **come** to the wedding.
- Tanya **won't pass** her driving test.

We use **be going to** to say that *something is certain to happen*:
- The stock market **is going to go** up this year. That's what they said on the radio.
- Renzino is shooting at goal and he'**s going to score**. Yes, goal!

Note: we don't use the *present continuous* for expectations:
- It'**s going to rain** / It'**ll rain** tomorrow. (NOT ~~It's raining tomorrow.~~)

intentions

We use **be going to** to talk about *intentions* (things that we or other people have decided to do):
- Our car is very old, so we'**re going to buy** a new car soon.
- John **isn't going to go** to university.
- What **are** you **going to do** in Italy?

We use **I will** to talk about *intentions* when we *offer* or *promise* something and after **I think**:
- 'I'm thirsty.' 'I'**ll make** some tea.'
- I'**ll email** my report to you this afternoon.
- My computer's crashed. **I think I'll switch** it off for a while.

plans

We usually use the *present continuous* (and not **will**) to talk about *things that people have planned to do and have organised* (or *agreed with others*):
- I'**m meeting** Yumi tomorrow morning. We'**re going** to a gallery.
  NOT ~~I will meet Yumi tomorrow. We will go to a gallery.~~
But we do use **will** with *describing verbs* (e.g. **be**, **need**, **want**) to talk about plans:
- We **will be** in London all day. (NOT ~~We're being in London …~~)
(See unit 8 on *describing* verbs.)

A

Use the phrases in the box to complete this conversation. Use each phrase once.

| will be | ~~'ll play~~ | 'll ask | 'll ask | won't want | 's coming | 's going | 'm meeting | 's sailing |
| 's bringing | 're going to ask | am going to have | 're going to practise | 're going to organise |

RACHEL: Have you heard? Sidra's raising money for the hospital. And she wants everyone to help with ideas to make money for her appeal.

MARK: Let's do a charity concert. We can organise it for next month. I ⁰ _'ll play_ my clarinet and you can play the violin.

RACHEL: That's a great idea. But we need more people. What about Darren?

MARK: Yes, I ¹... him when we meet up this evening. He ²... for a meal at my house. He ³... his viola and we ⁴... a piece that I have written for clarinet and viola. It's called *Moon on Water*. Is there anyone else we can ask?

RACHEL: What about Christina? I ⁵... her if she wants to do a concert with us. I ⁶... her at the Café Claire for lunch today.

MARK: Oh, no, she ⁷... to do a concert with Darren. They had a big argument yesterday about something.

RACHEL: They're always arguing about stupid things, and then they forget all about it. She and Darren ⁸... friends again tomorrow.

SIDRA: Hi, Rachel, Mark, how's it going?

RACHEL: Okay, but listen, Sidra, we ⁹... a concert to raise money for your hospital appeal. We ¹⁰... Darren and Christina to do the concert with us.

SIDRA: Wonderful, but I just saw Christina and she says she ¹¹... on holiday next month. She ¹²... around the Mediterranean with some friends. She says Darren's cross because she hasn't invited him to go with her.

RACHEL: Wow! I ¹³... a lot to talk about with Christina over lunch today.

B

Choose the best form shown in green, and circle it.

SANDRA: Are you having a good time here in Tunisia?

TANYA: Oh, yes it's great. My boys love the swimming pools in the hotel and the beach.

SANDRA: ⁰ We will go / (We're going) on a coach trip tomorrow. I've just bought the tickets.

TANYA: Oh, really. ¹ Where are you going? / Where will you go?

SANDRA: ² We will go / We're going to El-Jem – it's a Roman amphitheatre.

TANYA: I read about that place in my guidebook. I'm sure ³ you'll have / you're having an amazing time there.

SANDRA: I hope so. I've got my camera and some film, because ⁴ I'll take / I'm going to take lots of photos. ⁵ I'm getting / I'll get them developed and show them to you when I get back – that's a promise.

TANYA: Oh, thanks. Actually, it sounds such a fantastic place that I think ⁶ I'm going / I'll go on that trip next week with my boys.

SANDRA: Well, ⁷ I'll show / I'm showing you my photos and then you can decide if you want to go. But the coach leaves really early. It leaves at six in the morning. So, ⁸ I'm setting / I'm going to set my alarm clock for five-thirty.

TANYA: Oh, dear, my boys ⁹ aren't wanting / won't want to get up at five-thirty. I think ¹⁰ I'll try / I'm trying to find a trip that starts later in the day.

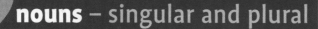

Jasmine, I want to talk to you. Come here! It's about your room.

I just tidied it, and do you know what I found on the floor? There were dirty **clothes**, of course, and **shoes**, and **books** and **magazines** – six, in fact – and three empty **bowls**, four **coffee mugs**, two **knives**, a plate, and a huge pile of empty CD **boxes**, with the **CDs** all over the place – and some of them were mine! There were empty crisp **packets** and chocolate **wrappers**, and orange **peel** – rubbish everywhere! It's not healthy to live like that!

You could get **mice**, or **cockroaches**. I wouldn't be surprised if you had **lice**!

You are not going to go on living like this. This afternoon we are going to choose some new **curtains** and a **rug**, and some **boxes** to put all your **papers** and **CDs** in – and we are going to make your room a bit more civilised...

regular plurals	Most nouns can be singular or plural. We usually add an **s** to the singular form to make it plural: a tree → two tree**s** a plane → three plane**s** a photo → some photo**s** With nouns ending in **s**, **ss**, **sh**, **ch**, or **x**, we add **es**: dress → dress**es** wish → wish**es** coach → coach**es** box → box**es** With a few nouns ending in **o**, we add **es**: potato → potato**es** tomato → tomato**es** With nouns ending in *consonant* + **y**, we use **ies**: pony → pon**ies** hobby → hobb**ies** cherry → cherr**ies** company → compan**ies** We often change **f** and **fe** to **ves** in the plural: leaf → lea**ves** shelf → shel**ves** knife → kni**ves** half → hal**ves** (For how to pronounce **s**, **es** and **ies**, see page 226.)
irregular plurals	Some nouns are the same in the singular and plural: sheep → sheep fish → fish deer → deer Some have an **en** ending in the plural: child → child**ren** man → m**en** woman → wom**en** Some change the singular **ouse** to the plural **ice**: mouse, m**ice** louse, l**ice** Some change **oo** + *consonant* to **ee** + *consonant* in the plural: tooth, t**ee**th foot, f**ee**t goose, g**ee**se (For more on irregular plurals, see page 224.)
multi-word nouns	With a *noun + noun*, we only make the second noun plural: credit card**s** ham roll**s** roller blade**s** When we talk about a *container containing something*, or a *quantity of something*, we use **of**: **a mug of** tea **three packets of** envelopes **a bar of** chocolate **2 litres of** milk
plural-only nouns	A few nouns in English are always plural, even when we are talking about one thing: jeans trousers sunglasses scissors pyjamas ■ Your new **sunglasses are** amazing! We use the word **clothes** only in the plural: ■ My **clothes are** all in the washing. **Police** and **people** are also plural; in the singular we use **police officer** and **person**: ■ The **police are** asking local **people** about the robbery. ■ A **police officer** saw a **person** running away.

EXERCISES

A You go to the *Café Blanco* with two friends.
Write sentences asking for the items in the picture using **I'd like ... please**, and a phrase from the box. You may need to make the phrase in the box plural.

> a napkin   a knife   ~~a cup of tea~~   a cappuccino
> a chair   a cheese sandwich

0 *I'd like two cups of tea, please.*
1 ....
2 ....
3 ....
4 ....
5 ....

Now you go to the newsagent, next door, and ask for some more things, using **Can I have ... please**, and a phrase from the box. You may need to make the phrase in the box plural.

> a packet of salt and vinegar crisps
> ~~a packet of tissues~~   a box of drawing pins
> a small notebook   a bar of chocolate

00 *Can I have two packets of tissues, please.*
6 ....
7 ....
8 ....
9 ....

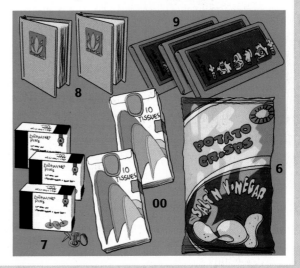

B Read the following passage and find ten errors in the noun plurals. Underline them, and write the correct plural at the bottom. Remember, not all the plurals are wrong!

The swimming pool is quite crowded, but there aren't very many <u>mans</u> here. It is four o'clock and most persons are still at work, in their officies. There are two classs of school childs, and some motheres with babys in the little pool. There are two pool attendant, sitting in tall chairies, watching the swimmers to see that everyone is safe. One of the attendants is shouting at two teenager, because they are running around the pool. You aren't allowed to run, because it is very slippery, and accidentes can easily happen.

0 *men*	2	4	6	8	10 ....
1	3	5	7	9	

TOM: We're having a **sale** at school next week to raise **money** for the Cancer Research Fund. They've asked us to bring good quality **things** we don't need, or **food**, or **plants**.

MUM: What kind of things do they need? I've got lots of nice children's **clothes**.

TOM: They said they don't want clothes. What about **CDs**, **videos**, and **books**?

MUM: Oh, yes, I'm sure we've got lots of them. Will you help me look in the **boxes** in the **attic**?

TOM: Sure. And maybe I could make some of my famous chocolate **brownies** to sell. Have you got any home-made **jam** left?

MUM: No – you've eaten it all! But I've got a lot of **fruit** in the garden this year – **apples** and **plums**. I'll ask Claire to pick some **fruit** for us.

countable nouns	We use countable nouns to talk about *one, or more, of something*. They usually have a singular and a plural form: a bird, two birds a pencil, three pencils a fan, some fans We can use **a** / **an** and **the** with singular countable nouns: ▪ We saw **an** elephant at the zoo. **The** elephant was enormous. We can use plural nouns without **the**, or with **the**: ▪ We saw **penguins** and **sea lions**. **The penguins** were sliding on the ice.
uncountable nouns	Uncountable nouns are words for *things that we see as one item and not made of separate parts*, for example: substances – milk, ice, plaster, wool, paper, glass, coffee, chicken, chocolate: ▪ Do you want some **milk** in your **coffee**? *abstract ideas* – art, law, music, hope, fear: ▪ Phil listens to **music** all day. *games and activities* – football, tennis, ice hockey; carpentry, photography: ▪ **Tennis** is my favourite game. *collections of things* – rubbish, news, luggage, traffic, money, information: ▪ The ambulance was stuck in **the traffic**. We don't use **a** / **an** with uncountables, but we can use **the**. Note: we don't use **the** with the names of games or activities. (See unit 24 on **a** / **an** and **the**.)
countable and uncountable nouns	Some nouns can be either <u>countable</u> or uncountable: ▪ 'There are four of us and I only have three **chocolates**.' 'It's okay, I don't like **chocolate**.' ▪ Does anyone want **coffee**? I only have enough **tea** for three <u>**teas**</u>. Would you like **chicken** for dinner? I have <u>a frozen **chicken**</u> in the freezer which I could defrost.
amounts	To talk about a *quantity* of something, we use **some** or **any** with a plural or uncountable noun: ▪ We need **some** *bricks* and **some** *nails*. ▪ Have you got **any** *wood* or **any** *glue*? To talk about *a container* or *a specific quantity of something*, we use **of** with a plural or uncountable noun: two boxes **of** *raisins* a lot **of** *cookies* a kilo **of** *lentils* a cup **of** *coffee* two tubes **of** *toothpaste* a bit **of** *glass*

EXERCISES

A Read the following shopping list and mark beside each <u>underlined</u> item whether it is countable (C) or uncountable (U), and then rewrite the list, buying **two** of each thing:

0 1 litre of <u>milk</u>   *U - 2 litres of milk* ....

1 1 roll of <u>toilet paper</u> ....

2 1 cleaning <u>cloth</u> ....

3 1 jar of <u>instant coffee</u> ....

4 1 packet of <u>biscuits</u> ....

5 1 kilo of <u>apples</u> ....

6 1 bottle of <u>washing-up liquid</u> ....

7 1 litre of <u>olive oil</u> ....

8 1 carton of <u>eggs</u> ....

9 1 tub of <u>black pepper</u> ....

10 1 bag of <u>potatoes</u> ....

B Read the following conversation and write the correct singular or plural form of the noun in brackets.

0 Rosie's late! I wonder if the (traffic) .... *traffic* .... was bad again today.

1 It took me two (hour) .... to get to work yesterday. It's getting crazy!

2 Shall I phone her on her mobile? I'm a bit worried – there was quite a lot of (ice) .... on the road this morning.

3 No, she can't talk on the phone while she's driving. It's against the (law) .... now.

4 I'll make some more (drink) .... Does anybody want tea, instead of coffee?

5 OK, that's three (coffee) .... and one tea.

6 Oh, Tina – I think there are some (biscuit) .... in the cupboard.

7 I bought a packet of chocolate (cookie) ...., but we may have eaten them.

8 Why don't you turn on the radio to hear the traffic (news) _____.

9 Oh, there's only (music) .... on all the local channels.

10 Well, there's no (hope) .... of rehearsing the lunchtime show now. We'll have to do it live!

An asteroid is going to pass very close to **the earth** in 2029. It will be closer than **the** telecommunications **satellites** that man has positioned in space, and only 1/10th of **the distance** to **the moon**. It will be visible without **a telescope**, and will look like **a** pale, fast-moving **star**. Professor Mark Bailey of **the** Armagh Observatory, says: 'It will be like being on **a** train station **platform** and watching **an** express **train** go by. You're close, but it's not dangerous. It is unusual, because we know about it **a** long **time** before it arrives.' **Scientists** say that asteroids of this size are expected to pass close to **the earth** every 1,300 years.

a or an	We use **a** before a consonant sound (/b, c, d,/ etc) and **an** before a vowel sound (/e, o, i, / etc):
	▪ There's **a** cat stuck in that tree.
	▪ That's **an** unusual picture.
	It's the sound that is important, and not the spelling:
	▪ Darren heard **an** SOS on his radio. (es əʊ es)
	(See page 226, for information on vowel and consonant sounds.)
a / an	We use **a** or **an** with singular countable nouns *when it is not important which particular person or thing we are talking about*:
	▪ We went to **an** Indian **restaurant** and had **a curry**.
	We also use **a / an** to talk about an *example of something*:
	▪ Neela is **a doctor** in Chicago.
	▪ Yesterday was **an amazing day**!
	We don't use **a / an** with plural or uncountable nouns.
	▪ The continental breakfast is **croissants** and **jam**.
	(See unit 23 on plural and uncountable nouns.)
the	We use **the** + **noun** when *there is no doubt about which particular person or thing we are talking about*:
	▪ **The milk** is in **the fridge**. (*There is only one fridge in the house.*)
	▪ I bought a pair of shoes and a shirt. **The shoes** were more expensive than **the shirt**.
	▪ Gary is reading **the book** that I lent him.
	▪ **The Earth** orbits **the Sun** once every year.
	▪ Yeuch! There's a fly in **the soup**! (*the soup we are eating*)
	▪ We got on a plane to Morocco, but then **the pilot** said that there was a problem with **the engines** and we had to leave **the plane**.
a, ~~the~~	To talk about *something in general*, we do not usually use **a**, **an**, or **the**:
	▪ Yumi loves **shoes** – she is always buying new pairs.
	▪ **Petrol** is getting more and more expensive.
	▪ Ellen never lost **hope**.

EXERCISES

A Write **a**, **an**, or **the** in the gaps in the following text.

I went to hear [0] _a_ new band at [1]_____ Park Street Club last night. Because it was Saturday, there was [2]_____ huge crowd of people there. When we arrived, [3]_____ dance floor was packed, and we couldn't get close to [4]_____ stage. I could hardly hear [5]_____ music, as [6]_____ speakers were broken. There was [7]_____ really bad band playing first, and some people left, but when *Spidereye* started playing, [8]_____ speakers started working again. We had [9]_____ amazing evening, as there weren't many people there and [10]_____ band was incredible!

B Match the two halves to make sentences.

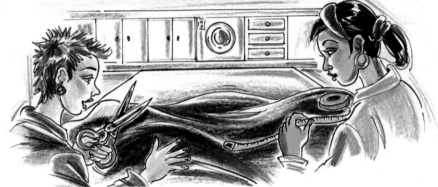

0	Where did you put the	A	pair of good scissors?
1	I think it's still in the	B	fabric that we bought yesterday?
2	Have we got a	C	kitchen table?
3	I think the	D	cups and plates in the dishwasher.
4	OK. Shall we lay out the fabric on the	E	same colour as the sofa cushions.
5	Just a minute. I'll put the	F	blue cotton. Have we got any?
6	Right. Oh, the velvet is a	G	bag in the kitchen.
7	I love it! It's almost the	H	pins?
8	Now we need some	I	long time.
9	Yes, here it is. Now, where are the	J	sharp scissors are in the workbox.
10	This is going to take a	K	really lovely colour!

C Write **a**, **an**, **the**, or *nothing* (–) in the gaps.

MELISSA: It's Dad's birthday tomorrow. Shall we make [0] _a_ special meal for him?

AMANDA: That's [1]_____ great idea. What does he like to eat?

ISAAC: The last time we ate in a restaurant, he had [2]_____ roast duck. He had [3]_____ chips with it, but he didn't eat them.

MELISSA: Ok, we'll give him duck, with [4]_____ roast potatoes, and we can have chips. Do you think we need [5]_____ starter?

AMANDA: Oh yes! It's my favourite course. I could make [6]_____ avocado salad.

ISAAC: And, of course, we need [7]_____ dessert. Dad loves puddings!

MELISSA: We all like puddings. I could make [8]_____ chocolate, orange mousse.

AMANDA: And we must have [9]_____ birthday cake.

MELISSA: Okay. I'll go to the shop and buy [10]_____ ingredients for the meal. Let's make a list!

Landscape painting in the Pyrenees

The holiday of a lifetime! Come and spend a week studying oil painting in **Paziols** in **the South of France**. Your teacher will be **Professor Lucien Mechant**, a well-known teacher from the **National Academy of Art** in **Paris**. You will stay in **the Hotel Paysan**, a small, friendly hotel which has an excellent restaurant next door, called **the Coq d'Or**. You can choose to paint the charming, ancient village, or **the** savage **Pyrenees** mountains. We will also take you down to **the Mediterranean** at **Port Vendres** to paint the beautiful coast and seascape. If you want, you can visit some of the local, historical sites: **Carcassonne** is famous for its medieval, walled town, and **Perpignan Castle** is a wonderful example of old Catalan architecture.

For more information, contact us at this address: mechant@artfest.com

You won't regret it!

people's names	We don't usually use **the** with the *names of individual people*: ■ **Martha** wants to go to the swimming pool. ■ **Mr Singh** works for a bank. ■ **Mrs Singh** is a doctor. But we do use **the** when we talk about *two or more people by their family name or by their nationality or tribe*: ■ **The Singhs** live in a big house by the river. ■ **The Kikuyu** are the largest tribe in Kenya.
names of organisations	We usually use **the** with the *names of government organisations* and *of newspapers*: **the** United Nations (**the** UN) **the** Council of Europe **the** Royal Air Force **the** New York Times **the** Daily Mail We don't use usually **the** with the *names of companies, schools*, and *colleges*: IKEA Rippon Primary School Princeton University
names of places	We usually don't use **the** before *place names*, for example: Asia Russia California Madrid Mont Blanc Lake Windermere Fifth Avenue Salisbury Cathedral Victoria Station Note these exceptions: **the** Arctic **the** Bronx **the** Matterhorn **the** White House We use **the** for *mountain ranges, deserts, seas, rivers, canals* and *waterfalls*: **the** Rockies **the** Arizona Desert **the** North Sea **the** River Seine **the** Panama Canal **the** Niagara Falls We often use **the** with the names for *hotels, museums* and *places of entertainment*: **the** Grange Hotel **the** Science Museum **the** Tate Gallery **the** Royal Opera House **the** Odeon Cinema
special cases	We usually use **the** with names that have *of* in them: **the** Duke of Edinburgh **the** Bank of Scotland **the** Isle of Wight **the** University of Essex We use **the** for places that have a *plural name* (+ **s**) or include **Kingdom** or **Republic** in the name: **the** Maldive**s** **the** United State**s** (of America) **the** United **Kingdom**

A

Write the or *nothing* (−) in each gap.

'When you are in [0] .....−..... Oxford next month, you must take a trip on the open-top tourist bus! It's great! You can see [1] .... Magdalen College, where [2] .... Oscar Wilde studied, and [3] .... Christ Church Cathedral, which is a beautiful old church. There are always lots of people in punts on [4] .... River Thames. Then there's [5] .... Broad Street, where they have a huge funfair every year ... and there's the monument where [6] .... Archbishop Thomas Cranmer was executed by burning. There is a famous, old theatre called [7] .... Oxford Playhouse. Oh, and you should take a day trip to [8] .... Blenheim Palace, which is an enormous country house with beautiful parks and gardens. I think [9] .... Winston Churchill, the former Prime Minister of Britain, was born there. It's in a small town called [10] .... Woodstock.'

B

Answer the following questions, using one of the places in the box, adding the if you need to.

| Island of Mauritius   Mediterranean Sea   Spain   ~~Rabat~~   Cape of Good Hope   Tunisia   South Africa |
| Atlas Mountains   Mount Kilimanjaro   Victoria Falls   Sahara Desert |

0 What is the capital city of Morocco? *Rabat* ....

1 What is the world's largest desert? ....

2 What is the famous waterfall on the Zambezi River called? ....

3 On which island was the last dodo seen alive?
....

4 The Canary Islands are a province of which European country?
....

5 What is the name of the highest mountain in Africa?
....

6 In ancient times, which North African country grew most of the grain for the Roman Empire?
....

7 What is the name of the Cape at the south-west tip of Africa?
....

8 Which country produces the most gold in the world? ....

9 Which sea is joined to the Red Sea by the Suez Canal? ....

10 What is the name of the mountain range that runs from Morocco to Tunisia?
....

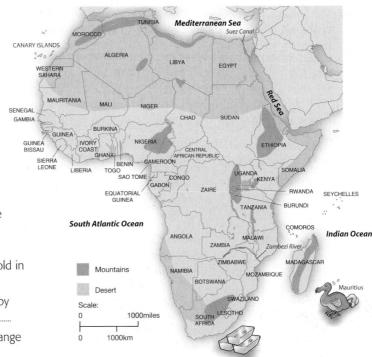

BAZ: Do you work very long hours?
KENZO: Oh yes, I leave **home** at about 7 in the morning and start **work** at about 7.30. I usually finish **work** at about 8 in the evening. I love my job. Architecture is always fascinating. But I get my best ideas at **home**, not in the office.
BAZ: Where did you get the idea for the underwater hotel?
KENZO: When I was at **home**, sitting in the bath.
BAZ: And your idea for a multi-storey airport – where did you get that thought?
KENZO: I got that idea when I was in **hospital**, when I'd hurt my leg running to catch a plane. I thought 'make the aeroplane come to you, not you to the plane'.

places with a or the	With nouns for places, we usually use **a** or **the**:

- **The bank** is in Charles Street.
- We went to **a museum** and then to **an art gallery** – it was a bit boring.
- Can you tell me where **the post office** is?
- Is there **a petrol station** near here?
- Is there **an airport** near **the city**?
- I'm late for my appointment at **the doctor's**.

places without a or the

We don't use **a** or **the** when we are talking about *being in, going to* or *coming from* a particular institution (e.g **university**, **school**, **hospital**, **church**, **prison**) when we are *using it for its intended purpose*:

- Harry is in **hospital**. He's having an operation tomorrow.
- Maya is at **school** right now, having a French class.

But if we are talking about the institution just as *a place*, we use **the** or **a**:

- They're building **a** new **school** in the park.
- Karen works in the café at **the Art College**.
- Sara is visiting her aunt in **the hospital**.

We also use **home**, **work** and **bed** without **the** to talk about *going to, being at,* or *leaving*:

- Hugo usually leaves **work** at 6.30 in the evening.
- Inti won't get out of **bed** to answer the phone.
- I'm going **home** now. I'm really tired.

activities without the

We can use some of these words to talk about an *activity*, rather than a place; again, we do not use **the**:

start / finish / like / love / hate +
work school college university

- Maria usually **starts work** at about 8 and **finishes work** around 4.
- Does Jasmine **like school**?
- Amanda **hates college**.

EXERCISES

A Where is Captain Splendid? Complete the questions, using **the** where necessary.

0 (at / zoo) '_Is he at the zoo_?' 'No he isn't.'

1 (at / work) '.....................................?' 'No he isn't.'

2 (on / bus) '.....................................?' 'No he isn't.'

3 (in / bath / at / home) '.....................................
.....................................?' 'No he isn't.'

4 (in / bed) '.....................................?' 'No he isn't.'

5 (at / dentist's) '.....................................?'
'No he isn't.'

6 (in / hospital) '.....................................?'
'Yes, he's broken his leg.'

B Insert **the**, where necessary, before the words in green in this email.

Dear Jackie,

Thanks for your email. It was great to see a message from you when I sat down at [0] _the_ computer yesterday. Finally, I've got some peace and can sit down and write some emails to friends before I start [1] .... work.

I'm really sorry that you don't like your new job at [2] .... swimming pool, but glad that you and Guido are getting on really well.

Isaac and Jasmine are at [3] .... school – Jasmine wants to leave [4] .... school when she's sixteen and work full-time in [5] .... hairdresser's where Amanda works on Saturdays. Amanda's at [6] .... college now. She should be there now but she's not feeling well so she's at [7] .... home and in [8] .... bed.

Bill has gone to [9] .... work – he was in a bit of a bad mood this morning, because he was late getting out of [10] .... bed, and he was worried about missing his train. He isn't going into [11] .... office today, he's meeting some new clients in Cambridge.

As for me, well, I'm working at [12] .... home at the moment. It's part-time work on [13] .... computer, but it's quite fun. I have to go to [14] .... hospital this afternoon to visit my aunty who is having an operation on her knee tomorrow. She'll be in [15] .... hospital for about three days and then she's staying here for a few days to recover before she goes [16] .... home. And then tonight Bill and I are going to [17] .... new restaurant in [18] .... centre of town and then to [19] .... theatre to see 'High Places'. I hope he gets [20] .... home early, so that we can eat out before we see the play.

Let's meet up soon. Perhaps we can meet for lunch?

All the best,

Melissa

A Put in **a** or **the**, where necessary, in this story about a lucky escape.

Our lucky escape in plane drama

Holidaymakers have described [0] _the_ moment that their return from [00] _a_ sunshine holiday turned to fear when their plane nearly crashed. [1]_____ doctor who was on [2]_____ holiday jet praised the quick actions of [3]_____ pilot, saying: 'I am sure that he saved all our lives.'

Shocked passengers described the screams, tears and shock when [4]_____ plane continued past [5]_____ main terminal building, towards the end of the runway at [6]_____ Leeds Airport on Wednesday.

[7]_____ Dr Jonathan Iddon, a doctor from Knaresborough, described how [8]_____ plane landed on the runway but then did not slow down.
'I realised that something was wrong when [9]_____ lights in the plane went out,' he told [10]_____ Harrogate News yesterday. 'I could hear [11]_____ brakes, but we didn't seem to slow down and then, suddenly, the plane turned round and eventually stopped.'

The plane stopped only metres away from a boundary fence of the airport and [12]_____ golf course. Its front wheel was stuck in [13]_____ muddy pond.

Emergency vehicles rushed to help [14]_____ passengers and crew.

After [15]_____ long time, the passengers got off [16]_____ jet and went to [17]_____ main terminal and then went [18]_____ home, but without their luggage.

The jet was carrying tourists back from [19]_____ Spain. [20]_____ Air Accident Investigation Branch, a government organisation, has started [21]_____ investigation into [22]_____ accident.

B Read the text and answer the questions.

Google is a company that helps people to find the information that they want on the Internet. You can type a word, a phrase, or a question into a *Google* web page and it tells you where you can find appropriate information on the Internet.

Google's founders, Larry Page and Sergey Brin, developed a new approach to online search when they were at Stanford University.

Life of a *Google* Query

The life span of a Google query normally lasts about half a second, but there are a number of different steps that happen before results are delivered to a person seeking information.

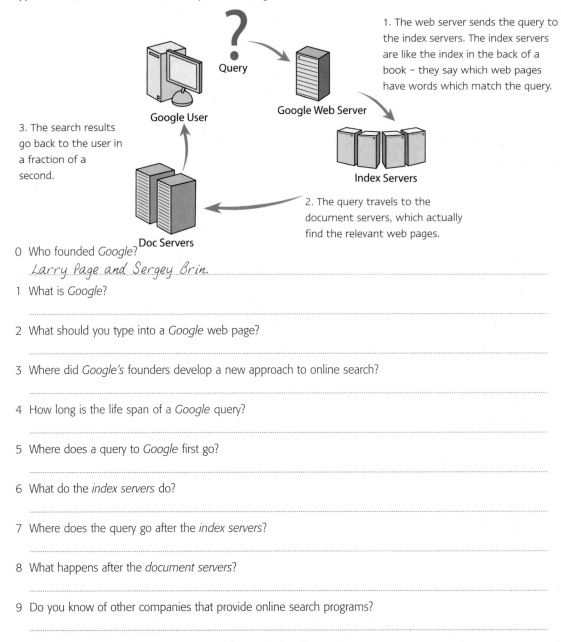

1. The web server sends the query to the index servers. The index servers are like the index in the back of a book – they say which web pages have words which match the query.

3. The search results go back to the user in a fraction of a second.

2. The query travels to the document servers, which actually find the relevant web pages.

0 Who founded *Google*?

Larry Page and Sergey Brin.

1 What is *Google*?

2 What should you type into a *Google* web page?

3 Where did *Google's* founders develop a new approach to online search?

4 How long is the life span of a *Google* query?

5 Where does a query to *Google* first go?

6 What do the *index servers* do?

7 Where does the query go after the *index servers*?

8 What happens after the *document servers*?

9 Do you know of other companies that provide online search programs?

I / me and she / her

ISMAH: Can **I** help **you**, madam?

CUSTOMER: Yes, **I**'d like to try on some of these shoes. Could **you** bring me a size 6, in blue?

ISMAH: **I**'m very sorry, madam, **we** only have that style in black or red. Would **you** like **me** to bring **you** a size 6 in black?

CUSTOMER: But my friend bought **some** the other day. **I** asked **her** where **she** bought **them** and **she** said that **she** got **them** from **you** ...

ISMAH: Well, **we** did have **some** last week, but **they**'re all sold out. **They** were very popular. **We** could order **some** for **you** ...

CUSTOMER: No. **I**'ll try the big shop on Ship Street. **I** expect **it** will have a bigger range. Thank you. Goodbye.

subject pronouns	singular	plural
	I	**we**
	you	**you**
	he / she / it	**they**

We use a subject pronoun (**I**, **you** etc) as the subject of a <u>verb</u>:

- '<u>Can</u> **I** help you?' 'Yes, **I** <u>want</u> to buy some boots.'

We use all these pronouns, except **it**, to talk about *people*:

- 'Where is Ismah?' '**She**'s in the stock room.'

We can use **it** and **they** for *things* and *animals*:

- 'Can I borrow your cellphone?' 'Yes, **it**'s in my briefcase.'
- I need to wash some plates – **they**'re all dirty.
- 'Did you ride on a camel in Tunisia?' 'Yes, but **it** was a bit grumpy.'

Note: We don't use a <u>noun</u> and a subject pronoun at the same time:

- The washing machine isn't working. OR **It** isn't working. NOT ~~The washing machine~~ **it** ~~isn't working~~.

object pronouns	singular	plural
	me	**us**
	you	**you**
	him / her / it	**them**

We use an object pronoun (**me**, **you** etc) as the object of a <u>verb</u>:

- 'Can I <u>help</u> **you**?' 'Yes, I want to buy some 'Essenzia' perfume. My wife really <u>likes</u> **it**.'

We use all these pronouns, except **it**, to talk about *people*:

- Where is Jasmine? I asked **her** to meet **me** here at six.

We use **it** and **them** for *things* and *animals*:

- Have you seen my wallet? I can't find **it**.
- I haven't fed the cats. Can you give **them** some food?

We also use **some** as an object pronoun to talk about a *quantity of something*:

- I haven't got any money. Can you lend me **some**? (= *some money*)
- We haven't got any eggs. We need to buy **some**. (= *some eggs*)

We also use object pronouns after prepositions (e.g. **for**, **from**, **to**):

- Are those flowers **for me**?! Are they **from you**?
- The man sitting next **to me** had a really bad cold.
- Ted is a fascinating person. I can talk **to him** for hours.

EXERCISES

A Read the passage and choose the best pronoun from the box to put in the gaps.

me	I	them	she	them	He	they	she	her	I	she

⁰ __I__ went to swimming practice today and Dana was there. I swam in the next lane to ¹ _____ . I can swim faster than ² _____ can, but ³ _____ talked to ⁴ _____ all the time , and I couldn't concentrate. The other girls got really annoyed too, as ⁵ _____ was talking about ⁶ _____ and ⁷ _____ wanted to hear what she was saying. The coach, Mr Ransome, was furious! ⁸ _____ said; 'If you don't stop annoying ⁹ _____ , ¹⁰ _____'ll throw you out of the team!'

B Change the <u>underlined</u> phrases or words to a pronoun.

Romeo and Juliet is one of the most famous plays in the world. ⁰ <u>The play</u> is a tragic story about two families in Verona: the Montagues and the Capulets. Juliet (a Capulet) and Romeo (a Montague) fall in love, but ¹ <u>Romeo and Juliet</u> can't tell their families, because ² <u>their families</u> would not allow ³ <u>Romeo and Juliet</u> to see each other. ⁴ <u>Juliet</u> decides to escape from their families, and ⁵ <u>Juliet</u> gets a drug from a wise man to make her seem to be dead. She sends a message to tell Romeo to go to the church where ⁶ <u>her friends</u> take her, and to run away with ⁷ <u>Juliet</u> when she wakes up. ⁸ <u>Romeo</u> does not get the message, so he thinks ⁹ <u>Juliet</u> is really dead, and he kills himself. She wakes up and finds that ¹⁰ <u>Romeo</u> is already dead, and she kills herself too.

0 _It_	3 _____	6 _____	9 _____
1 _____	4 _____	7 _____	10 _____
2 _____	5 _____	8 _____	

28 my, his etc.

JACK: **My** front garden is completely ruined! And look – **my** wife planted those roses, and all **her** flowers are broken!!

MR FRANKS: Well, I'm sorry, but it was partly **your** fault … **your** dog ran in front of **my** car and made me swerve **my** car into **your** garden. I was turning into **our** gate when he ran out in front of me…

JACK: And you hit **my** dog! I think he's broken **his** leg!

MR FRANKS: I'm very sorry about **your** dog – but he should be in **his** kennel, and not running around the street.

JACK: I'm going to call the police – and **my** lawyer!

form and use	We use **my**, **your** etc. to talk about something that someone *has*:

- That's **my** camera. **His** camera is a silver, digital camera.
- Tamara lost **her** handbag.
- **Their** hire car is a Peugeot.

singular	plural
my (= *belonging to me*)	**our** (= *belonging to us*)
your (= *belonging to you*)	**your** (= *belonging to you*)
his / her / its (= *belonging to him* etc)	**their** (= *belonging to them*)

We also use **my**, **your** etc. for:

relationships: **my** friend   **your** husband   **her** parents

parts of the body: **your** arm   **her** hand   **my** feet   **its** claws

Note: Possessive **its** does not have an apostrophe (NOT ~~it's~~). **It's** means *it is*.

singular or plural

The possessive matches the <u>person</u> who has something:

(<u>I</u> have three daughters →) **my** daughters

(<u>We</u> have a cat →) **our** cat

(<u>Maria</u> has a racing bike →) **her** racing bike

(<u>Maria</u> has black trainers →) **her** trainers

(<u>Mohammed</u> has two racing cars →) **his** racing cars

(<u>The Singhs</u> have a horse →) **their** horse

(<u>They</u> have lots of children →) **their** children

a, ~~the, this, that~~

We do not use **a**, **the**, **this**, or **that** and a possessive adjective together

- We can pick up ~~a~~ **our** hire car at six.
- That's ~~the~~ **their** house – the pink one on the hill.
- I saw ~~this~~ **your** wallet on the table in the kitchen. That is your wallet, isn't it?

But we can use a possessive immediately after **this** or **that** in questions with **be**:

- Is **this your** wallet?

EXERCISES

A

Put the words in the box in the gaps.

| my | her | his | his | our | your | their | their | their | their |

0 _My_ favourite team, Grantham, is playing at the moment. The score was 1 – 0 to Grantham, but they lost [1]............... lead just before half time, when [2]............... goalie made a mistake and let the ball into their net. [3]............... captain, Dave Enriquez, has played a wonderful match, so far. Unfortunately, [4]............... wife has been ill in hospital and [5]............... game hasn't been as good as usual for a couple of weeks, as [6]............... illness has really worried him. We all sent her [7]............... best wishes, and she's much better now. In [8]............... opinion, the team has a good chance of promotion this season, if they don't lose [9]............... confidence. Which is [10]............... favourite team, Rob?

B

Imagine that you and I are standing in a queue at a supermarket. Look at the picture and write **his**, **her**, **our**, or **their** in the gap in each sentence.

0   _Her_ loaf of bread is wholemeal.

1   .... jar of peanut butter costs £1.75.

2   .... tins of tomatoes are very heavy.

3   .... bag of apples weighs one kilo.

4   .... newspaper is the Daily News.

5   .... soap is lemon-scented.

6   .... avocado pears are not ripe.

7   .... litre of milk is skimmed.

8   .... eggs are free range.

9   .... coffee is instant.

10 .... sugar is brown.

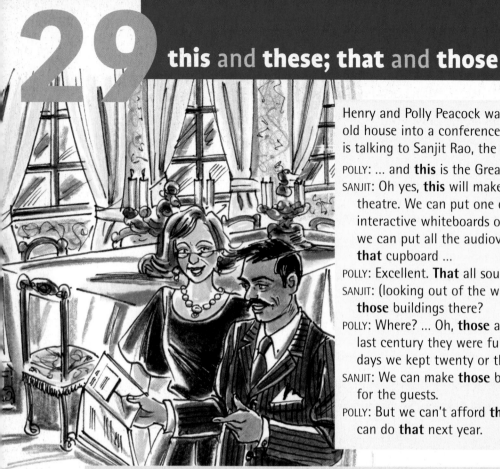

Henry and Polly Peacock want to turn their big, old house into a conference centre. Polly Peacock is talking to Sanjit Rao, the development advisor:

POLLY: ... and **this** is the Great Hall.

SANJIT: Oh yes, **this** will make a very good lecture theatre. We can put one of **these** new interactive whiteboards on **that** wall there. And we can put all the audiovisual equipment in **that** cupboard ...

POLLY: Excellent. **That** all sounds really excellent.

SANJIT: (looking out of the window) What are **those** buildings there?

POLLY: Where? ... Oh, **those** are the stables. In the last century they were full of horses. In **those** days we kept twenty or thirty horses in there.

SANJIT: We can make **those** buildings into rooms for the guests.

POLLY: But we can't afford **that** yet – maybe we can do **that** next year.

this / these		that / those	
singular	plural	singular	plural
this book	**these** book**s**	**that** book	**those** book**s**

We use **this** and **these** with nouns to talk about *things that we are holding or that are near to us*:
- **This sofa** is really comfortable. (*I am sitting on it.*)
- I need to clean **these shoes**. (*I am holding them.*)

We use **this** and **these** to talk about *a time which is now or close to now*:
- The company is expecting big sales growth **this year**. (*the current year*)
- Sophie is going to the theatre with Ahmed **this evening**. (*today*)
- **This situation** is hopeless. (*the situation now*)

We can use **this** and **these** without a noun when *it is clear <u>what</u> we are talking about*:
- **This** is a really comfortable <u>sofa</u>.
- I must buy some new <u>shoes</u>. **These** are very old. (= *these shoes*)

We use **this is** to say *who we are on the phone*:
- Hello, **this is** Guy.

We also use **this is** to *introduce someone*:
- SIDRA: Jenny, **this is** Tom.

We use **that** and **those** with nouns to talk about *things that are not near to us* (often with **there**):
- I like the wallpaper in this room, but I don't like **that wallpaper** in the hall.
- Can you give me **that box there** on the table?

We use **that** and **those** to talk about *a time in the past or in the future*:
- There was a terrible earthquake here in 1988. **That year**, many people had to live in tents in very cold weather.
- 'There's a rehearsal tomorrow.' 'Okay, I'll come to **that rehearsal**.'

We can use **that** and **those** without a noun when *it is clear <u>what</u> we are talking about*:
- 'What's **that**?' 'It's a <u>letter</u> for me.'

We often use **that** to *refer to something that someone has just said*:
- 'I've just broken my teapot.' '**That's** a pity – it was very pretty.'

We use **is that** to ask *who someone is on the phone*:
- 'Is that Angela?' 'No, it's Maria. Do you want to speak to Angela?'

EXERCISES

A Put **this**, **that**, **these**, or **those** in the gaps. Use the picture to help you.

AMANDA: Do you like ⁰ *this* blue dress, or ¹......................... red dress there on the hanger?

MIKE: They're both very nice.

AMANDA: Yes, but do you like ²......................... dress or that dress better?

MIKE: I don't really like blue, so I think I like ³......................... dress best.

AMANDA: Okay, and do you like ⁴......................... blue shoes or ⁵......................... green shoes over there in the window?

MIKE: I think I like ⁶......................... green shoes better.

TAMARA (coming into the shop): Hallo Amanda, what are you doing in ⁷......................... shop?

AMANDA: I'm buying stuff for a party. Have you met Mike?

TAMARA: No, I haven't.

AMANDA: Mike, ⁸......................... is Tamara. Tamara, ⁹......................... is Mike.

MIKE: Hallo, Tamara. (*Mike's mobile phone rings*) Hi. Hello. Is ¹⁰......................... Ahmed? Hi, Ahmed. … What, there is a football practice now ? … what, ¹¹......................... afternoon? I can't come ¹²......................... afternoon – I'm shopping with Amanda. When is the next practice? … Tomorrow? Okay. I'll come to ¹³......................... Sorry. Bye.

AMANDA: Who was ¹⁴.........................?

MIKE: It was Ahmed. There's a football practice now and I missed it.

AMANDA: Oh, ¹⁵.........................'s a pity. Anyway, I think I like ¹⁶......................... blue shoes better.

MIKE: Yes, ¹⁷......................... shoes are very nice, too.

AMANDA: Oh Mike, ¹⁸......................... is hopeless – you don't give me any real advice! Tamara, can you help me decide?

B Rob has moved into a new house and he wants to do a lot of work on his new garden. He's telling his friend his plans for the garden. Look at the garden and his plan and make sentences from the words in brackets. Use **this**, **that**, **these** or **those** in the sentences where you can.

0 (I / be going to / put a swing / in / tree) *I'm going to put a swing in that tree.*

1 (I / be going to / put / pots / around / pond) ....

2 (I / be going to / plant the clematis / beside / wall) ....

3 (I / be going to / put / small red and white flowers / in / flower bed) ....

4 (I / be going to / put / cherry tree / in / flowerbed here) ....

5 (I / be going to / make a path from / patio to / shed) ....

6 (garden / be going to / be / lovely) ....

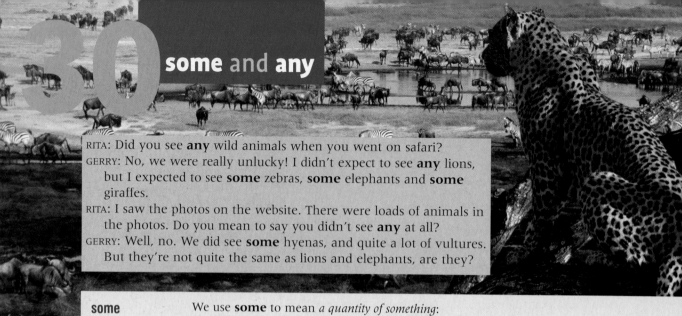

RITA: Did you see **any** wild animals when you went on safari?

GERRY: No, we were really unlucky! I didn't expect to see **any** lions, but I expected to see **some** zebras, **some** elephants and **some** giraffes.

RITA: I saw the photos on the website. There were loads of animals in the photos. Do you mean to say you didn't see **any** at all?

GERRY: Well, no. We did see **some** hyenas, and quite a lot of vultures. But they're not quite the same as lions and elephants, are they?

some	We use **some** to mean *a quantity of something*: ■ There are **some customers** in the shop. ■ Ahmed is installing **some games** onto his computer. ■ Drive carefully – there's **some ice** on the road. We use **some** in questions when we are talking about *a specific quantity*: ■ Can I have **some** chocolate **cake**, please? (*a slice*) ■ Has Sheila bought **some** new **shoes**? (*a pair*) We also use **some** idiomatically to mean *an unspecified person or thing*: ■ There was **some woman** on the TV talking about Fellini. ■ I'll come and see you **some time** tomorrow.
any	We often use **any** in questions *when we don't know if something exists or not*, or *if something is the case or not*: ■ Are there **any** living things on Mars? ■ Have you got **any** money? ■ Do you want **any** more tea? We can use **any** with a singular noun to mean *an example of something, and it doesn't matter which*: ■ He says that we can pay with **any** credit **card**. ■ **Any smoker** knows that smoking is dangerous. ■ Take **any book** that you like. We use **not … any** to mean *none of something*: ■ I can**'t** find **any** white **candles** in the cupboard. ■ There are**n't any cars** in the car park. ■ Mike does**n't** have **any money** at all.
some and any as pronouns	We can use **some** without a noun when it is clear what we are talking about: ■ 'I've never done yoga. Have you?' 'Yes, I did **some** last year.' (= *some yoga*) ■ We've made some cakes. Would you like to take **some**? (= *some cakes*) We can use **any** without a noun in negatives and questions in the same way: ■ I've looked everywhere for some candles and I can**'t** find **any**. (= *any candles*) ■ My skates are broken. Have you got **any** that I can borrow? (= *any skates*) Note: we often say **some** + *adjective* + **ones** (and not **some** + *adjective*): ■ All my brushes are useless. I need **some new ones**. (NOT ~~I need some new.~~) (See unit 37 on **something, anything** etc)
some / any of	We use **some** or **any** + **of** + **the** / **my** / **this** etc. + *noun* when we are talking about *a part of something* or *a group of things*: ■ **Some of my friends** are coming for dinner. ■ Gavin didn't drink **any of his coffee**.

EXERCISES

A Read this discussion between councillors at a Town Council meeting. Put either **some** or **any** in the gaps.

COUNCILLOR THOMPSON: Are there ⁰...*any*.... benches in the High Street?

COUNCILLOR GOPAL: No, but do we need ¹.................. benches? Do you think people will want to sit down in a busy street?

COUNCILLOR ANDREWS: Well, if we plant ².................. trees or plants in pots, it will be more restful. And there won't be ³.................. cars on the street.

CLLR. THOMPSON: That's true. We won't allow ⁴.................. traffic apart from bicycles, and delivery vans at night.

CLLR. GOPAL: OK. So we'll have ⁵.................. benches and trees at both ends of the street. What about ⁶.................. information kiosks, to provide maps and things for tourists?

CLLR. ANDREWS: That's a good idea, but we don't really need more than one.

CLLR. GOPAL: I think we need ⁷.................. safe places where people can lock up their bikes.

CLLR. THOMPSON: Aren't there ⁸.................. at the moment?

CLLR. ANDREWS: Not near the centre of town. I think it's really important to encourage people to bring their bikes into town. ⁹.................. people have told me they are afraid of thieves stealing their bikes in the centre of town.

CLLR THOMPSON: I agree. Good. And we definitely need ¹⁰.................. new public toilets! The old ones are horrible.

B Karen has bought her first home! It is a nice, little flat, near the centre of town. She is talking to her Mum on the phone. Choose one of the phrases from the box to write in the gaps in their conversation.

Is there any	there are any	any white	any new	have some	some new	need some
	some time	some old	take some	~~some of the things~~		

KAREN: … and I can move in on Saturday. It's unfurnished, but the landlady says I can use ⁰ *some of the things* that are there at the moment. The people who are living there now are going back to New Zealand, and they can only ¹................................. of their things.

MUM: ²................................. furniture in the flat? I could let you ³................................. of the things in our spare room, and from your old room. Do you need a bed?

KAREN: I could use the futon from my old room. And I'll buy ⁴................................. pillows …

MUM: We've got lots of pillows! You don't need to buy ⁵.................................ones.

KAREN: But I'd like to, Mum. New pillows are so nice! I will ⁶................................. things for the kitchen.

MUM: Well, you know I've got a cupboard full of pots and pans and bowls that I never use. Why don't you come round ⁷................................. and see if ⁸................................. that you'd like to have?

KAREN: Oh thanks, Mum! And have you got ⁹................................. paint? Some of the walls are a horrible colour!

MUM: I think we may have ¹⁰................................. tins of paint in the shed. Come and have a look.

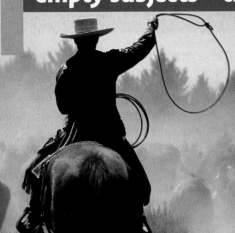

Yeah, I like living and working on the prairie. When **it's dawn** and the birds start singing, **it's wonderful** to wake up and watch the sun come up, and then have breakfast out in the open. Then I get on my horse and start work. **It's great** to spend the day riding on your horse and looking at nature. **There are** always lots of animals to see – eagles, deer, goats, and sometimes bears and wolves. **It's** often very **hot** in the middle of the day, but I have my big hat to protect me from the sun. **There are** times when I dream of working in an air-conditioned office, but **it's peaceful** here – I could never live in the city.

there + be: form		singular	plural
	present	there **is** (**'s**)	there **are**
	past	there **was**	there **were**

After **there**, the *object* makes **be** singular or plural:

- There's a bird in that tree.
- There are some birds in that tree.

We make the negative like this:

present	there **is not** (**'s not / isn't**)	there **are not** (**aren't**)
past	there **was not** (**wasn't**)	there **were not** (**weren't**)

- **There isn't** any salt in this pasta.

Note: we prefer **there isn't** before **anyone / anything**:

- **There isn't anyone** at home. (NOT ~~There's not anyone~~…)

To make questions, we put **be** before **there**:

- **Is there** a postbox on this street?
- **Was there** a letter for me in today's post?

there + be: use

We use **there is / are** + *noun* to say that *something exists*:

- **There's** some <u>shampoo</u> on the shelf in the bathroom.
- **There are** some <u>problems</u> on the roads this evening.

We use **there was / were** + *noun* to talk about *situations that existed in the past*:

- **There was** a big tree in the garden, but they cut it down.
- **There were** a lot of people in the restaurant last night.

Note: we can't use **it** or **they** in this way:

- NOT ~~It's some shampoo on the shelf in the bathroom.~~
- NOT ~~They are some problems on the roads this evening.~~

it + be: use

We usually use **it** to talk about *something that we have already mentioned*:

- 'What's that bird?' '**It's** an eagle.'
- 'Where's the phone book?' '**It's** in the sitting room.'

We can also use **it** with **be** to refer to *the rest of the sentence*, when we talk about –

distance: **It's miles** from here to the sea.

time: 'What time **is it**?' '**It's** 8.30. I'm going to go to work now.'

the nature / quality of a place: **It's freezing** in here. **It's quiet / silent / spooky / peaceful** here.

weather: 'Its raining today'.

We also use **it** + **be** + *adjective* to say *what we think or feel about something*:

- **It's** so **exciting**! The race is going to start in a few seconds.
- **It's important** to keep in contact with old friends.
- **It was great** to see Mike and Makosi last night.
- **It's** a bit **obvious** that he really likes her.

EXERCISES

A

Put it, they, or there in the gaps in this text.

We all know what elephants look like –
0 ...*they*... are big, grey animals and have large ears and long trunks. That's true, but 1 .... are two different kinds of elephant: African elephants and Asian elephants. 2 ....'s easy to tell the difference between them. African elephants have big ears, and both males and females have tusks that you can see. 3 .... have very wrinkly skin and 4 .... have hollow backs. Also, 5 .... are two 'fingers' at the end of their trunk. Asian elephants have smaller ears and only the males have tusks that you can see. 6 .... do not have very wrinkly skin; 7 .... is quite smooth. 8 .... have rounded backs and 9 .... only have one 'finger' at the end of their trunk.

In 1930, 10 .... were about 8 million African elephants. In 1989, 11 .... were about 600,000 African elephants. In 1900, 12 .... were about 200,000 Asian elephants in the world. Today 13 .... are probably about 35,000 to 40,000 Asian elephants living in the wild.

Elephants make lots of different kinds of noises for different purposes. 14 .... make sounds to show happiness, or anger, to warn of danger, or to say what 15 .... need or want.

I think 16 .... is interesting, but a bit sad, to see elephants in a zoo. 17 .... are, of course, much happier and more wonderful in the wild.

African

large ears,

tusks,

hollow back,

two 'fingers' at end of trunk

Asian

smaller ears,

rounded back,

one 'finger' at end of trunk

B

Tom is talking to Rob on the phone. Use the words in brackets, in the correct form, with it or there, to complete what they say.

TOM: Hi Rob. I'm phoning to ask how to get to your new place. (0 – be / a long way from the centre of town / ?)
Is it a long way from the centre of town?

ROB: (1 – No, / be / about twenty minutes by car / .)
....
Have you got your car?

TOM: (2 – Yes, / be / working again / .) ....
.... (3 – be / a very good garage) ....
at the end of my street. I took it there and they fixed it for me. Okay, so, I'm going to leave here in about an hour.

ROB: Great. (4 – What time / be / now / ?)
....

TOM: (5 – be / about four thirty / .)
....

ROB: So, you'll get to my place at about six. By the way, (6 – not / be / anything to eat in my fridge / .) ....
.... We'll have to eat out.

TOM: Cool. (7 – be / any good restaurants near to your place / ?)
....

ROB: Yes, (8 – be / a really good Chinese restaurant nearby / .)
....
Okay, I'll explain how to get here. Take the road south from the centre; (9 – be / a long road / .)
....

When you have passed a cinema and some shops, (10 – be / a roundabout / .) ....
....

At the roundabout, turn left. Then go along that road past two roundabouts. At the third roundabout (11 – be / a petrol station)
on the left. Oh no, wait a minute, (12 – not / be / a petrol station there now) ....
.... – they knocked it down last month. Anyway, at that roundabout, turn right, then go along that road. Near the next traffic lights, (13 – be / a supermarket) ....
.... – it's called Frisco Stores, I think.

TOM: Stop for a second, Rob. (14 – be / going to be impossible) ....
.... to remember all these directions. I need to find a pen and some paper.

ROB: Yeah, sorry, (15 – be / a bit complicated /.)
....

A Read this story about Zahra and then complete the conversation between her and Tom.

Zahra was really bored with her job and her life; she decided she needed more adventure. She saw an advertisement for lessons at a rally driving school and she phoned the school and booked a lesson. They asked her to bring her driving licence and to wear warm clothes.

Zahra was really excited and phoned her sister Sidra to tell her about it. She asked her if she wanted to do rally driving lessons with her. Sidra thought it was a crazy idea to learn to drive a rally car.

On Sunday, it was really cold and raining. Zahra got to the school at 9 a.m. The manager told her that her instructor was ill – he had flu – but he said that she could take the rally car and practise on their racing circuit. He gave her a helmet and explained to her how to drive the car, and then he said 'Okay, I hope you have a good time in the car. Come back in an hour or two.'

Zahra thought that this was a bit strange but she put on her helmet and her seatbelt and started to drive round the circuit. It was raining a lot and it was difficult to see where to go. Very soon, she was lost and then she drove off the road and the car was stuck in a ditch.

Zahra wasn't hurt but she didn't have the phone number of the driving school. She phoned her sister. 'Sidra, I'm in this rally car and I'm stuck in a ditch – can you help?' she said. 'Oh, no, you poor thing,' Sidra said, 'but what can I do to help you?' Zahra asked her to go to her flat and try to find the number of the driving school in the papers on her desk. And then Sidra said that she was staying with friends in Scotland! She was hundreds of miles away! …

TOM: Why did ⁰......*you*...... decide to do rally driving lessons?

ZAHRA: ¹...................... was really bored with ²...................... job and ³...................... life. ⁴...................... decided ⁵...................... needed more adventure. So, ⁶...................... phoned a rally school.

TOM: What did ⁷...................... say to you?

ZAHRA: ⁸...................... asked ⁹...................... to bring ¹⁰...................... driving licence and to wear warm clothes. ¹¹...................... was really excited. ¹²...................... phoned Sidra to tell her about it.

TOM: What did ¹³...................... say?

ZAHRA: ¹⁴...................... said ¹⁵...................... thought ¹⁶............... was a crazy idea to learn to drive a rally car.

TOM: Did ¹⁷...................... go to the rally school?

ZAHRA: Yes, ¹⁸...................... got there at 9 a.m, and ¹⁹............... met the manager. He looked a bit worried.

TOM: What did ²⁰...................... say to you?

ZAHRA: ²¹...................... said ²²...................... was a problem. ²³...................... told ²⁴...................... that ²⁵...................... instructor was ill. But ²⁶...................... said that ²⁷...................... could take the rally car and practise on ²⁸...................... circuit.

TOM: ²⁹...................... 's strange! So, did you do that?

ZAHRA: Yes, but ³⁰...................... was raining a lot, and I couldn't see where to go. ³¹...................... was difficult and ³²...................... drove the car into a ditch!

TOM: Oh, no, ³³...................... poor thing? Did ³⁴...................... mean to do ³⁵...................... ?

ZAHRA: No, of course not. Well, I didn't have the number of the driving school. So, I phoned Sidra. I asked ³⁶...................... to find the number of the driving school in the papers on ³⁷...................... desk.

TOM: Did ³⁸...................... help ³⁹...................... ?

ZAHRA: She couldn't help ⁴⁰...................... ! She was hundreds of miles away, in Scotland!

TOM: Oh, no! So, what did ⁴¹...................... do then?

ZAHRA: Well, two men were walking along the lane with ⁴²...................... dogs and they helped me to get the car back onto the lane. I was so grateful to ⁴³......................

B Use the words in the box to complete the conversation. Use all the words in the box.

| I | it | it | it | It | It | It | him | There | There | there | There |
| there | there | this | that | that | some | some | any | any |

MARY KEENE: Jim, where are ⁰......*you*......?

JIM KEENE: I'm in the kitchen. ¹......................'m writing a cheque.

MARY: Phew, ²......................'s very hot in here. Can I turn the heating down?

JIM: Yes, of course. I'm writing a cheque to pay for Tim's school trip to France. What's the date today?

MARY: ³......................'s the 17th of May.

JIM: Thanks. I'll write that on the cheque and then sign ⁴......................, and give it to ⁵...................... to take to school. I need to go to the supermarket in a moment. Can you look in the fridge – is there any meat in there?

MARY: Umm, no, there isn't ⁶.......................

JIM: Okay, I'll get ⁷...................... when I go to the supermarket. What's ⁸...................... piece of paper you're holding?

MARY: It's about my management training course. Did you remember that I have to go on a training course ⁹...................... weekend?

JIM: Oh, no, I'd forgotten about ¹⁰...................... Where's the course?

MARY: ¹¹......................'s in Kernall.

JIM: Wow! ¹²......................'s miles to Kernall from here.

MARY: I know. I'll have to leave at about 3 on Friday afternoon. The course starts at 8.30 and ¹³......................'s important to get to these things on time and not be late.

JIM: What do you do on the course?

MARY: Well, ¹⁴...................... are lectures in the mornings, and in the afternoons ¹⁵...................... are group workshops. ¹⁶...................... are two main topics – 'motivating people' and 'working in teams'. ¹⁷...................... are two speakers – Kim Wing from Supersizetec and Susie Barker from PersonPeople.

JIM: Hmm – it sounds fascinating! Can I see the leaflet? It says that it's a five-star hotel and ¹⁸......................'s a swimming pool and a gym! And ¹⁹...................... are tennis courts, and a sauna, and ²⁰...................... of the rooms have balconies. Can I come on the course? Are there ²¹...................... spare places?

MARY: I don't know.

JIM: Oh, and look it says here that Jim and Ted are going on the course with you, and also Melissa Summers. Is ²¹...................... that woman in the Accounts department in your company?

MELISSA: Mary, hello. So you're back from your management training weekend.

MARY: Oh, hi, Melissa. Yes, we got back last night.

MELISSA: How was it?

MARY: Well, there were **no towels** in our bathroom in the hotel. The bedroom did**n't** have **any armchairs** to sit in. The food in the restaurant was okay but there was**n't any** vegetarian **food**. Oh, and the equipment in the hotel gym was useless – **none of it** worked properly. **None of the guest speakers** came – they all said that they were ill.

MELISSA: Oh, no. That's a pity. Did you go to the training workshops?

MARY: Yes, I went to the workshops – some of them were quite interesting, actually.

no	We use a *positive* verb + **no** with a *noun*: ■ They have **no** nice **clothes** in that shop. ■ There are **no batteries** in this torch. ■ Rob has **no idea** why you phoned him.
not … any	We use a *negative* verb + **any** with a *noun*: ■ They do**n't** have **any** nice **clothes** in that shop. ■ There are**n't any batteries** in this torch. We use **not … any of** to mean *none of something specific*: ■ I haven't got **any of your CDs** – I promise. We can use **not … any** without a noun *when it is obvious what we are referring to*: ■ 'Have you got any floppy discs?' 'No, I have**n't** got **any**.' (= *any floppy discs*)
none of	We use **none of** + **my / the / these** with a *positive* verb: ■ **None of my clothes** fit me. They're all too big. ■ **None of these batteries** are the right size for my torch. ■ **None of the food** in the restaurant was organic.
use with nouns and pronouns	We can use **no**, **not … any**, and **none of the**: with plural nouns (e.g. **clothes, batteries, chairs, oranges**) with uncountable nouns (e.g. **food, fruit, information, water, chocolate**) (For more on uncountable nouns, see unit 23.) We can use a *pronoun* (e.g. **it, them, these**) after **of**: ■ There is lots of milk in the fridge. **None of it is** past its sell-by date ■ There are 52 cards in this pack. **None of them** are missing. ■ There are lots of towels in this cupboard, but **none of these** are beach towels.

A

Put any, none of, or no in the gaps.

RACHEL: Hello, is that Giles? Oh, hi, Giles. I need your help, please. I'm up in the boardroom on the top floor. I'm checking that everything is ready for the sales managers' meeting at 11, but there are lots of things missing. There are ⁰......*no*...... bottles of water and ¹.................... jugs for orange juice. And, there aren't ².................... glasses. Can you see if there are any glasses in the cupboard in your office?

GILES: There are some glasses in the cupboard, but ³.................... them are ordinary glasses – they are all wine glasses. I can get some glasses and jugs from the café.

RACHEL: Oh, great. Okay, now, there are ⁴.................... writing pads or notebooks here for the managers to write on. Are there any small pads in your cupboard?

GILES: I'll have a look. ... There are some pads, but they are all quite big – ⁵.................... them are small.

RACHEL: Oh, no, ⁶.................... the biros on the boardroom table are working. There are some pens for the whiteboard, but they are all red ones – there aren't ⁷.................... blue or black ones.

GILES: There are some blue marker pens in the cupboard here but there aren't ⁸.................... black ones. We've got a big box of yellow 'post-it's, though; they are always useful for meetings, for brainstorming activities.

RACHEL: Great. There aren't ⁹.................... up here.

GILES: Oh wait. I've just received an email from Bruce Sharpe. They've cancelled today's meeting at 11. It's now happening tomorrow. There isn't ¹⁰.................... need to panic.

B

Ros and Tom are going for a long walk in the country. They've stopped for a rest. Complete their conversation using the words in brackets. Each time add any or no in the right place.

TOM: I'm exhausted. And I'm really thirsty. And I haven't got ⁰......*any*...... water. Have you got some?

ROS: I've got a little bit of orange juice, but no, (I've got / water) I've got ¹.................... water. I told you to stop drinking all your water. You had a really big bottle. It's crazy that you haven't got ².................... now.

TOM: Okay, so we've got ³.................... water, but that isn't a problem because I've got some oranges and some grapes in my backpack.

ROS: So, you didn't need to ask me for some water!

TOM: But what I really want is some chocolate. And I didn't put ⁴.................... chocolate in my bag this morning – I forgot. Oh no, there isn't ⁵.................... fruit in my backpack. I remember – I asked you to carry the fruit.

ROS: No you didn't – I haven't got ⁶.................... fruit in my bag. What have you got in your bag? It looks very full.

TOM: Well, there isn't ⁷.................... food in here. It's full of books – books about trees, and about flowers, and about birds. Hey, look – look at those birds.

ROS: I can't see ⁸.................... birds.

TOM: Yes, you can. Look up in that tree. They're sitting on a branch.

ROS: There are ⁹.................... birds in that tree.

TOM: Yes, there are. They look like vultures!

ROS: That's impossible. There aren't ¹⁰.................... in the wild in this country.

TOM: Well, maybe they escaped from a zoo. I'm going to take a picture of them. Oh no, I can't - I've got ¹¹.................... film in my camera.

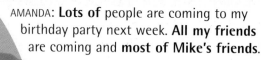

33

AMANDA: **Lots of** people are coming to my birthday party next week. **All my friends** are coming and **most of Mike's friends**.

MELISSA: That's great. But it's going to be **a lot of work** cleaning up after your party. **Every year** Dad and I have cleaned up after your parties and this year we really don't want to. We spent **all day** cleaning up after your party last year.

AMANDA: Don't worry. Mike and I will clean up the house. Oh, I need to buy some plastic glasses – can you lend me **some more money** for that?

MELISSA: But I've already lent you **a lot of money** for your party.

all, every, and **the whole**	**All of the** or **all the** mean *the complete number or amount of something*: ■ I've fed **all (of) the** animals. ■ **All (of) the energy** on the Earth comes from the Sun. In place of **the**, we can use **my / your / Jean's / these** etc: ■ **All my CDs** are in this box. **All of Jean's CDs** are in that box. **Every** + *singular countable noun* means *all the individual examples of something*: ■ **Every house** in this street has a garage. (= **All the houses** in this street have a garage.) **The whole** + *singular countable noun* means *one complete thing*: ■ We've cleaned **the whole flat**.
expressions of time	With words like **morning, evening, day, week, month, year**, we use **all** to mean *the whole of the time*: ■ It has rained **all day**, today. (= *It has rained the whole day*.) ■ Yasmin has been in the office **all morning**. (= ... *the whole morning*.) But **every morning / evening** etc. means *each time*: ■ It has rained **every day** this week. ■ Yasmin gets to her office at about 8 **every morning**.
a lot of / lots of	**Lots of** and **a lot of** mean *a large number or a large amount*: ■ There are **lots of** old **files** in this folder. ■ Mae Ling has put **a lot of time** and **effort** into this project.
more	**More** + **noun** means *a larger number* or *amount of something*: ■ **More people** came to the festival this year than last year. We often use **more** + **noun** with **than** + **noun**: ■ There are **more rats than people** in London. We use (**some**) **more** to mean *an extra amount*: ■ Would you like **some more tea**?
most (of)	**Most** (+ *plural* or *uncountable noun*) means *almost all*: ■ **Most people** would like to have a house with a garden. **Most of** (+ *singular* or *uncountable noun*) means *almost all of something*: ■ He's cleaned **most of the flat**. ■ The company makes **most of its money** from advertising.

EXERCISES

A Captain Splendid has done a lot of work this morning. Look at the pictures and choose the correct option in green.

0 He has mowed every / most of the grass on his lawn.

1 He has washed a lot / all of his suits.

2 He has hung up the whole / a lot of his laundry.

3 He has made more / most cakes than his mum.

4 He has cleaned every / all the Splendid bicycles.

5 He has painted the whole / a lot of wall.

6 He has washed a lot of the / all the bathroom floor.

7 He has put every / most of the leaves in a big bag.

8 He has done all the / most of washing-up in the sink.

9 He has done more / most of the jobs in his list of things to do.

10 He has worked very hard all / most morning.

B Look at this survey about people and their mobile phones, and then complete the summary of the results of the survey, using the phrases in the box.

	Yes	No	Don't know
Do you have a mobile phone?	70%	30%	–
Do you usually use your mobile for business?	25%	55%	20%
Do you usually use your phone to talk to friends and your family?	55%	25%	20%
Have you lost your mobile?	40%	60%	–
When you lost your mobile, did you immediately get a new one?	100%	0%	–
Do you usually use your mobile for phone conversations?	55%	35%	10%
Do you usually send text messages?	35%	55%	10%
Do you sometimes send photos or videos from your mobile?	10%	90%	–
Do you think that the mobile phones in the shops are too small?	40%	40%	20%
Do you worry that mobile phones are bad for your health?	60%	30%	10%
When you get a new mobile, are you going to buy one with a camera?	100%	0%	

A lot of people
A lot of people
A lot of people
Every person
Every person
More people
More people
~~Most people~~
Most people

The survey showed that:

0 ___*Most people*___ have a mobile phone.

1 _____ use their mobile to talk to friends and family than for business.

2 _____ have lost their mobile.

3 _____ who loses their mobile immediately gets a new one.

4 _____ use their mobile for phone conversations than for text messaging.

5 _____ don't send photos or videos from their mobile phone.

6 _____ think that the mobile phones in the shops are too small.

7 _____ worry that mobile phones are bad for their health.

8 _____ who is going to buy a new phone, is going to buy one with a camera.

many, much, a few, a bit of

GUIDO: ... Jacky, I'm tired of trying to be an artist. I don't have **many** good **ideas** these days. I don't produce **many pictures**. I spend a lot of time sitting in this studio, thinking, and I don't spend **much time** painting. And, **not many people** want to buy my pictures, so I don't make **much money**.

JACKY: But your pictures are wonderful. **Not many people** can do what you can do. You have lots and lots of talent.

GUIDO: I probably have **a bit of talent**, but not **much**.

JACKY: Don't be silly. You'll feel better tomorrow, I promise.

number quantifiers

Number quantifiers like **many** and **a few** say *how many there are of something*; we only use these with *plural nouns*:

   not many trees   **a few** people

We usually use **many** in negative sentences:
- There are**n't many people** in the pool today.
- **Not many people** have two cars.

We often use **how many** in questions:
- **How many days** are there in November?

We don't usually use **many** in positive sentences when speaking. We use **a lot of**:
- There were **a lot of** people in the pool yesterday. (NOT ~~There were many people...~~)

We can use **many** or **a lot of** in negatives and questions:
- There were**n't many customers** in the shop yesterday. Are there **a lot of people** in the shop today?

But we use many at the beginning of sentences
- Many people watch daytime TV.

A few means *some, a small number*:
- I met **a few celebrities** at the party. They were awful!

We can use **not ... many**, **how many**, and **a few** without a noun:
- 'Did you see any birds?' 'We did**n't** see **many**. We only saw **a few**.'

We can use **many of** and **a few of** to talk about *a quantity of something specific*:
- She didn't like **many of my friends**.

amount quantifiers

Amount quantifiers like **much** and **a bit of** say *how much there is of something*; we only use these with uncountable nouns:

   not much luck   **a bit of** marmalade

We usually use **much** in negative sentences:
- Tanya has**n't** got **much money** in her bank account.
- There is**n't much traffic** so I think we'll get home before nine o'clock.

We often use **how much** in questions:
- **How much coffee** have we got?

We don't use **much** in positive sentences. We usually use **a lot of**:
- Sanjay has put **a lot of** work into the project. (NOT ~~Sanjay has put much work into the project.~~)

We can use **much** or **a lot of** in negatives and questions:
- There wasn't **much** information about the accident on the radio news. Is there **a lot of** information about it in the newspaper?

A bit of means *some, a small amount*:
- We have **a bit of time** before we get on the plane – just a few minutes.

We can use **not ... much**, **how much**, and **a bit** without a noun:
- There isn't much light, but there is **a bit**.
- **How much** is that picture?

We can use **much of** and **a bit of** to talk about *a quantity of something specific*:
- **Much of the information** was wrong.

EXERCISES

A Sam and Jen are on holiday. They hired a boat and sailed out to sea. But then the mast on their boat broke … Look at the pictures and complete what Sam and Jen are saying using **many**, **much**, **a few**, or **a bit**.

SAM: We haven't had [0] _much_ luck on this holiday. We lost all our luggage and now this happens.

JEN: Look there are [1] .... boats over there. Let's shout and someone will hear us.

SAM: There's not [2] .... point. They won't hear us. Oh no, look, there are some sharks in the water.

JEN: It's okay – there aren't [3] .... sharks near us.

20 minutes later

SAM: I can only see one boat now and it's miles away from us.

JEN: It's okay. We can easily survive on this boat for [4] .... days. Someone is sure to see us in a day or two.

SAM: But we haven't got [5] .... water and we haven't got [6] .... food.

JEN: We've got [7] .... bars of chocolate. We've got [8] .... of bread. We've got [9] .... of cheese and [10] .... sweets. We haven't got [11] .... food, but we've got [12] ....

SAM: There isn't [13] .... time before it gets dark.

B Read this conversation. Notice the words highlighted in green. Then complete Alisha and Maya's report, using **many**, **much**, **a few**, or **a bit**.

ALISHA DEARLY: Oh, Maya, I have to write a report for my magazine on this fashion show. But I can't think what to say – what's your view of it?

MAYA BUKOWSKI: Well, it is divine, of course, and there are **some** new ideas in the designs. But I don't think that **a lot of** the new ideas are practical. Also, **not many** of the designers in this show have given much time or thought to quality and style. A lot of the designers in this show have created fantastic and extraordinary clothes but these clothes didn't have **a lot of** style or seem very practical. But, **some** of the clothes were beautiful – particularly Ingemar Glassman's dresses made with lots of coloured glass. Obviously **not many** people would like to try and sit down in a dress made of glass but **some** people are happy to stand up all day, especially if they are wearing a Glassman creation. Ted Murphy's designs were all very simple, black dresses, so they weren't **a lot of** fun but they did demonstrate **some** originality and they were very practical and stylish. Now, I'm thirsty darling, let's have **some** champagne. And then let's interview **some** of the designers.

ALISHA: Oh, that's brilliant, Maya. Let's write my article for the magazine together.

Alisha and Maya's report:

There were [0] _a few_ new ideas in clothes design in the *New Ideas* Fashion show this week. But a problem with the show was that not [1] .... of the new ideas were practical. [2] .... of the designers seemed to think about quality and about style, but not many of them. A lot of the designers created fantastic and extraordinary clothes but the clothes didn't have [3] .... style and didn't seem very practical. But, [4] .... of the clothes in the show were beautiful – particularly Ingemar Glassman's dresses made with lots of coloured glass. Obviously, not [5] .... people would like to try and sit down in a dress made of glass but [6] .... people are happy to stand up all day, especially if they are wearing a Glassman creation. Ted Murphy's designs were all very simple, black dresses, so they weren't [7] .... fun but they did demonstrate [8] .... of originality and they were very practical and stylish. It was thirsty work at the fashion show, so we had [9] .... of champagne, and then we interviewed [10] .... of the designers. We talked first to Ingemar Glassman …

35 each, every, both, either, and neither

MIKE: I'm trying to get ready to go to football practice and **both of my** team **shirts** are missing.

SONIA: I think I saw one or **both of them** in a pile of laundry on the kitchen table. Do you need **both shirts**?

MIKE: No, **either shirt** will be fine. I only need one. I've only got a practice session today – it's not a match. But, now, I can't find **either of my** football **boots**.

SONIA: I think I saw a boot in the dog's basket.

MIKE: Oh, no, that dog has eaten **every shoe** in this house. Hey, there's my football on the stairs.

SONIA: No, that's my football. I've put my initials, S K, on **each of my footballs**.

MIKE: Sonia, can I borrow it? Please.

SONIA: Hmmm, it's the same story **every week**.

each and every	**Each** + *singular noun* means *every individual one of two or more things or people*: ■ **Each driver** has his own van. ■ There are about 40 to 50 hurricanes in the world **each year**. **Every** + *singular noun* means *all the individual examples of something*: ■ In this exam, students must put their name at the top of **every page**. We usually use **each**, not **every**, when we talk about *a small number*: ■ I phoned three companies but **each** (NOT ~~every~~) **company** was too busy to repair my fridge this week. We can say **each of the / my / her** etc. but not **every of**; we usually use a plural noun and a singular verb after **each of**: ■ **Each of the drivers** has his own van.
both	**Both** + *plural noun* means *each of two things or people*: ■ The plane had two engines – and **both engines** were in flames! ■ It's been a very long game of tennis and **both players** are really tired. We can also say **both of the / my / her / Jane's** etc. + a plural verb: ■ It's been a hard match and **both of the** players **are** exhausted. ■ **Both of Jane's** brothers **are** really tall.
either	**Either** + *singular noun* means *one or the other of two things or people*: ■ There are two rooms free in the hotel. You can have **either room**. After **either of**, we use a plural verb: ■ Both the candidates for the job are very good. **Either of the women are** perfect for this post.
neither	We can use **neither** + *singular noun* as the subject of the verb, to mean *not one or the other of two things or people*: ■ Tina has two cars. **Neither car** is very new … After **neither of**, we use a plural verb: ■ … and **neither of her cars are** very reliable. We prefer **not … either** to **neither** as the *object of the verb*: ■ I have two books on the Pharaohs, and I ca**n't** find *either book*.
both of them etc.	We can use *pronouns* (**us, you, them, these**) after **of**: ■ I never met either of my grandfathers. **Both of them** died before I was born. ■ Sonia, Mae-ling, do **either of you** know the answer to my question?

EXERCISES

A Look at the picture and the sentences. Some of the sentences have errors of language or of fact. Write a correct version, using **both (of)**, **either (of)**, **each (of)**, or **neither (of)**; often more than one correct answer is possible. Tick the sentences that are correct.

0 Both of Bill's parents wear glasses. _X_ *Neither of Bill's parents wear glasses.*

1 Both of Melissa's daughters are wearing dresses. ....

2 Every of the children are sitting on the ground. ....

3 Both of Melissa's daughters are holding a cat. ....

4 Both of Melissa's children are holding a cat. ....

5 Both white cats has a collar. ....

6 Neither of the dogs have a collar. ....

7 Both grandfathers have a stick. ....

8 Both of the dogs are standing. ....

9 Neither of the dogs are beside Melissa. ....

10 Both grandmothers are wearing a hat. ....

11 Each adults in the picture are smiling. ....

B Put **both**, **either**, or **neither** in the gaps in this conversation.

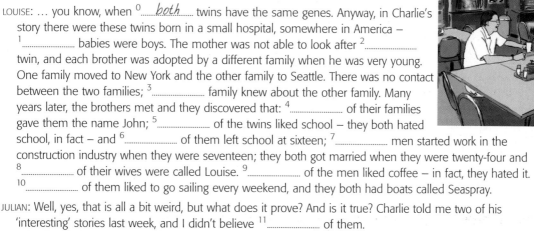

LOUISE: Charlie told me this story that he heard on TV about identical twins …

JULIAN: What's that?

LOUISE: … you know, when [0] ....._both_..... twins have the same genes. Anyway, in Charlie's story there were these twins born in a small hospital, somewhere in America – [1] .... babies were boys. The mother was not able to look after [2] .... twin, and each brother was adopted by a different family when he was very young. One family moved to New York and the other family to Seattle. There was no contact between the two families; [3] .... family knew about the other family. Many years later, the brothers met and they discovered that: [4] .... of their families gave them the name John; [5] .... of the twins liked school – they both hated school, in fact – and [6] .... of them left school at sixteen; [7] .... men started work in the construction industry when they were seventeen; they both got married when they were twenty-four and [8] .... of their wives were called Louise. [9] .... of the men liked coffee – in fact, they hated it. [10] .... of them liked to go sailing every weekend, and they both had boats called Seaspray.

JULIAN: Well, yes, that is all a bit weird, but what does it prove? And is it true? Charlie told me two of his 'interesting' stories last week, and I didn't believe [11] .... of them.

LOUISE: Oh, you and Charlie – I hate the way [12] .... of you argue all the time about everything …

JULIAN: Don't worry about that – [13] .... of us are a bit grumpy sometimes but we are very good friends really.

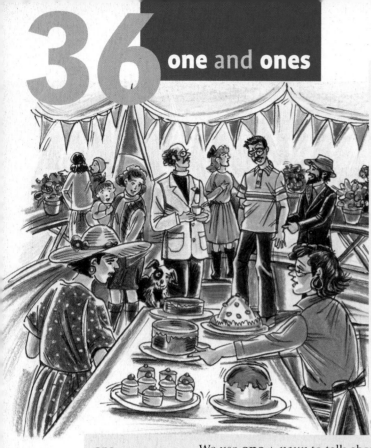

POLLY: Hello, Rosemary. I saw you arrive in your new car – it looks very smart.

ROSEMARY: Oh, yes, Jack gets me **a new one** every year. He's so silly.

POLLY: Is Jack here?

ROSEMARY: No, he's at **one of his meetings**. He's always at meetings. I say to him 'you can stop working for **one weekend**.' But he always says I'm being silly. Polly, I've never met your husband – is he here?

POLLY: Yes, Henry's over there talking to the vicar.

ROSEMARY: Oh, is he the tall man or **the handsome one** wearing a hat?

POLLY: Henry's **the one with the hat**. Is he handsome?!

ROSEMARY: Of course, he is! I'd love to meet him but first can I buy **one of your cakes**? **The ones with cherries on the top** look absolutely delicious.

one	We use **one** + *noun* to talk about *a single item or instance*: ■ We only have **one computer** in our house. We use **one day** to mean *at some time* in the past or future: ■ And then, **one day**, Roberto phoned and invited me to dinner. ■ I'll mend that gate **one day**. We can use **one** without a noun when *it is clear what we are referring to*: ■ I haven't got a black tie. I need to buy **one**. (one = *a black tie*) ■ The station was full of policemen and **one** walked towards us. (one = *a policeman*)
a / the ... one	We often use **a** + *adjective* + **one** when *it is clear what we are talking about*: ■ Your TV is so old! You should get **a new one**. (= *a new TV*) ■ I haven't got a black pen, but I've got **a red one**. We can use **the / my / her** + *adjective* + **one** to talk about *something specific*: ■ The Krugers' boat is **the orange one**. (= *the orange boat*) ■ I can't find my new hat. I'll have to wear **my old one**. We can use **the one** when <u>we explain</u> which person or thing we mean: ■ 'So, which is Rob?' 'He's **the one** <u>talking to Ros</u>.' ■ Zara's car is **the one** <u>with the massive tyres</u>.
one of the	**One of** + **the / my / his / John's** + *plural noun* means *one of a group*: ■ **One of the tyres** on the car has a puncture. ■ **One of Mark's friends** is a TV reporter. We often say **one of the** + *superlative* + *plural noun*: ■ Paris is **one of the most beautiful cities** in the world. ■ The owner of IKEA is **one of the richest men** in the world.
the ... ones	We can use **the / my / her / their** + *adjective* + **ones** to talk about *a specific group of things* when it is clear what we are talking about: ■ Shall we buy the red flowers or **the yellow ones**? (= *the yellow flowers*) We can use **the ones** when <u>we explain</u> which things or people we mean: ■ 'Are these your kids?' 'No, my kids are **the ones** <u>who are playing cricket in the garden</u>.'

EXERCISES

A Put **one** or **ones**, in the gaps to give the same meaning as the words in brackets.

Rob is thinking about leaving his job and about applying for (o – a job) ...*one*... in another company, or starting his own company (1 – sometime in the future) .... day. He's thinking about what makes a company successful, and has written this list:

❑ A good manager is (2 – a manager) .... who leads his team but also listens to his team.

❑ Successful companies are (3 – companies) .... that show all their employees that they are important and valuable.

❑ A new company needs to have a good commercial idea. If you haven't got (4 – a good idea) ...., you need to find (5 – a good idea) ....

❑ A good idea is (6 – an idea) .... that answers a need and helps to make the world a better place.

❑ Bad commercial ideas are (7 – the ideas) .... that are not new or special.

B Complete the gaps using **a / an ... one**, or **the ... one**, or **my ... one** and the adjectives in the box.

| silver | silver | ~~new~~ | old | electric | electric | red | blue |

☐	VIRTUALLY NEW SPEEDY ELECTRIC BICYCLE	£392.00	6
☐	Boys 6-speed universal silver mountain bike ********Pre-assembled and ready to ride********	£46.00	10
☐	PRO GENTS ALLOY MOUNTAIN BIKE	£31.00	7
☐	BRAND NEW TRAILER BIKE CONVERTOR Have safe fun with the kids!!!!!	£36.00	6
☐	FANTASTIC IMMACULATE CLASSIC MEN'S RACING BIKE	£460.00	8

AMANDA: What are you doing Mike?

MIKE: I'm looking for a new bike on Ebay on the Net. I need to get [0] ...*a new one*... because the pedals on [1] .... are broken. [2] .... looks very good but it's very expensive. It's £460.

AMANDA: [3] .... looks quite cheap – it's only £46. It says [4] .... is almost new. I'd love an electric bike!

MIKE: But it says [5] .... is a boy's bike. Which is [6] ....?

AMANDA: [7] .... at the top of the list. But it's quite expensive; it's £392 – maybe you can get cheaper electric bikes.

MIKE: I don't know, but I don't want [8] .... I need to get lots of exercise in order to keep fit.

A nothing day

I thought **someone** knocked at the door; I opened it and
    nobody was there.
I expected **something** in the post; and **nothing** came.
I wanted to go **somewhere** today; I went **nowhere**.
Is **anything** better than **nothing**?
Anywhere better than **nowhere**?
Anyone better than **no one**?

someone

Someone means *a person*:
- **Someone** has taken my pen.

Anyone means *any person*; we usually use it after negatives and in questions:
- I did**n't** meet **anyone** that I knew at the school reunion.
- Has **anyone** seen Sheila today?

Everyone means *all (the) people*:
- **Everyone** likes getting presents. (*All people …*)
- **Everyone** in the room started clapping. (*All the people …*)

No one means *no person*; we use it as the *subject* of a *positive* verb:
- I phoned home but **no one answered**. Everyone must be out.

If we want to talk about *no one* as the <u>*object*</u> of the verb, we usually use a
negative verb + **anyone**:
- Petra does**n't** know <u>**anyone**</u> in the class.

Note: **somebody**, **anybody**, **everybody** and **nobody** are used in the same ways.

something

Something means *an unspecific thing*:
- Please eat **something** – we've got lots and lots of food.

We usually use **anything** after negatives and in questions:
- Tom has**n't got anything** to do.
- Is there **anything** in the box?

Everything means *all (the) things*, or *all of something*:
- We sold **everything** on the stall.
- 'Did you see the accident?' 'Yes, I saw **everything**.'

We usually use **nothing** before a *positive* verb:
- **Nothing is** nicer than strawberries and cream!

If we want to talk about *nothing* as the <u>*object*</u> of the verb, we usually use a
negative verb + **anything**:
- We did**n't** say **anything**.

somewhere

Somewhere means *an unspecified place*:
- It's impossible to find **somewhere** to park the car.

We usually use **anywhere** in questions and negatives:
- Is there **anywhere** to eat near here?

Everywhere means *all the places*:
- I've looked **everywhere** in the house and I can't find my purse.

Nowhere means *no place*:
- Ismah really wants to buy a big piano but she has **nowhere** to put it.

Note: we usually say **go / has been** etc. + **somewhere / anywhere** etc,
without **to**:
- Tom's been **everywhere**. (NOT … ~~been to everywhere~~.)

adjectives

We use *adjectives* after **something**, **anything** etc:
- There's **something strange** and **weird** about this place.
- Did you get **anything nice** on your birthday?

EXERCISES

A

Put the words in the box in the right place in this story, to match the meaning in brackets. You will need to use some of the words more than once.

| someone | anyone | no one | something | anything | somewhere |
| anywhere | everywhere | | | | |

Many years ago, I rented a villa – it was (0 – in a place) _____somewhere_____ in Tuscany, in Italy. Every evening I sat (1 – in a place) .... in the garden – sometimes under the trees, and sometimes on the grass. It was always very quiet. And then one evening, I heard (2 – a noise) ....; it was like the noise of (3 – a person) .... opening a door or a window. And then I heard some music; (4 – a person) .... was playing the piano; it seemed to be (5 – a piece of music) .... by Chopin or by Tchaikovsky. It was a beautiful piece of music, and also quite sad. I didn't do (6 – a thing) ....; I didn't move a muscle – I just sat and listened.

I listened and I thought, 'How can (7 – any person) .... play so beautifully?' I turned to look at the villa and I noticed that one of the windows was open and I thought 'the music is coming from (8 – a place) .... inside the villa.' This seemed strange because I didn't think there was a piano (9 – in any place) .... in the villa. The music suddenly stopped. I got out of my chair and looked through the open window. There was no piano, and (10 – no person) .... was in the room.

I searched (11 – in every place) .... in the villa but I didn't find (12 – any person) .... in the house and I didn't find (13 – any type of thing) .... that looked like a piano. It was (14 – an experience) .... I shall never forget.

B

Use the words in brackets and the words in the box to complete these sentences.

| someone | someone | someone | nobody | something | anything | anything | somewhere | everywhere |

HENRY: Hallo, Roberto. How are you?

ROBERTO: I'm fine. How are you?

HENRY: I'm okay, but (strange / happened / last night) 0 _____something strange happened last night_____

ROBERTO: Oh, yes? – (Is there / I can do to help) 1 ....?

HENRY: Well, I don't know. I was sitting in the garden and (I heard / – / playing the piano / inside the villa) 2 ....

ROBERTO: Yes?

HENRY: Well, there isn't any piano in the villa and the house was empty (– / was / inside the house) 3 ....

ROBERTO: Oh, no, (there / isn't / – / strange about that) 4 .... It's very simple. Many years ago, a young man lived in the villa. One year, he went on a very long holiday. (He / went / – / in Europe) 5 ....; he went to Germany, France, Spain, Sweden – lots of countries. And he went to Finland (where / he / met / –) 6 .... She was very beautiful. (They / got married / – / in Germany) 7 .... Then they came to live in the villa. But then one year, (the lady / died of / –) 8 .... Before she died, every evening she played the piano for her husband. And for (– / special) 9 ...., like you, she still plays the piano.

HENRY: Roberto, you're making fun of me! You are, aren't you?!

SOPHIE: Hi, Mum. Sorry I'm late back home. I went to **Jemima's** house today. It was great.

JUNE: That's okay. Who's Jemima?

SOPHIE : You know, Jemima Proudly from school. The **Proudlys'** house is amazing – it's massive. The front **of the house** is like a palace. **Jemima's** mum looks really young and slim. At the end **of their garden** they have a swimming pool and **Jemima's** mum swims for two hours everyday! You should do that, mum. **Jemima's** dad's got a Porsche. Jemima's coming here in an **hour's** time and we're going to **Jemima's mum's** gym in her **dad's** car to play tennis.

JUNE: Great.

's	We usually use **'s** with a *person*, to mean *belonging to*: ■ Which is **Anne's** room? ■ **Mr Singh's** office is on the fifth floor. ■ Can you sign **Mark's** card? We can use **'s** without a noun after it *when it is clear what we are talking about*: ■ 'Is this your camera?' 'No, that's **Layla's**.' (= *Layla's camera*) ■ I saw this ring in a **jeweller's**. (= *a jeweller's shop*) ■ I've got an appointment at the **doctor's** in five minutes. (= *the doctor's surgery*)
s'	We usually use **s'** with *people*, to mean *belonging to them*: ■ I have marked all the **students'** essays. ■ Our **neighbours'** dog barks a lot.
of	We usually use **of** with *things*: ■ The real star **of the film** was Jenny Lindon. ■ What is the name **of this road**? We often use expressions like **the back of**, **the middle of**, **the centre of** etc: ■ Let's sit at **the back of the minibus**. ■ We climbed to **the top of a** big **hill**.
two possessives	We can use two possessives together: ■ **Sidra's father's** shop sells boots and shoes. (= *The shop belonging to the father of Sidra* …) ■ What was the name **of Columbus's ship**? ■ The noise **of the builder's drill** woke me up.
exceptions	We sometimes use **of** when we are talking about *a person and their role or job*: ■ He's the **President's** husband / husband **of the President**. ■ It's the **director's** job / job **of the director** to make difficult decisions. We can use **'s** with *companies and organisations*: ■ The **committee's** decision / decision **of the committee** is final. ■ The **company's** problems / problems **of the company** are worse. We can use *place + 's + superlative*: ■ Every year a new building is the **world's tallest** building. ■ She is **India's most popular** film star. We use **'s** in expressions about *the future* with **time**: ■ Guido will finish the picture in **a month's time**. (= *in one month from now*) ■ Where will you be in **five years' time**?

EXERCISES

A

Look at the picture and complete the sentences, using a word or phrase from box **a** with one from box **b**. Each time, decide if you need to add **'s** or **of**, or *nothing*.

a

Freddy	the roof	~~the handle~~	the top
granny	the lid	the world	a leaf

b

the cherry tree	the fence	the box	hand
the shed	most beautiful	hat	~~the teapot~~

TANYA: Look, at that beautiful butterfly. It's on
0 *the handle of the teapot.*

JAKE: Where is it now? Oh look, it's on ¹ ....

MUM: Does it tickle, Freddy? Now it has landed on ² .... !

JAKE: I think it's going to land on ³ ....
Be careful, Granny!

TANYA: It's on ⁴ .... I hope it doesn't eat the cherries.

JAKE: Now it's gone inside the sandwich box!

TANYA: Don't shut ⁵ .... Let it fly free.

GRANNY: It's on ⁶ .... Now it's flown away. Wasn't it lovely? Butterflies are one of ⁷ .... creatures.

B

Baz is developing an idea for a new TV show called *The Hart Sisters*. He is selling the idea for the show to a producer. Complete the gaps using the words in brackets, and **of** or **'s** where necessary.

BAZ: So, the (0 – name / this show) ..... *name of this show* ..... is 'The Hart Sisters'. The main characters in the show are Jenny Hart and (1 – Jenny / sister) .... Trudy. The (2 – sisters / company) .... is called 'Hart Design'. (3 – The office / Hart Design) .... is in a houseboat on the river. Two other characters in the show are Eric Neilson and Mark Trent; Eric is (4 – Jenny / boyfriend) .... and Mark is (5 – Trudy / husband) .... Jenny and Eric want to sell the (6 – sisters / houseboat) .... to Jimmy Bond, but Trudy and Mark don't want to sell it.

Okay, one day, Trudy is in the town and she is putting some shopping in (7 – the boot / Mark / taxi) ...., in the (8 – car park / a supermarket) .... She looks up and she notices (9 – Eric / black BMW) .... drive past. She thinks she sees (10 – Eric / face) .... through the (11 – window / the car) .... She notices the car stop and park near (12 – an estate agent / office) .... Now she is suspicious – she thinks that Eric is enquiring about selling the houseboat.

PRODUCER: Wait a minute, wait a minute – I'm confused. Who is in the black car?

BAZ: Eric is in the black car. Trudy thinks that the black car is (13 – Eric) ....

PRODUCER: And Eric is (14 – Trudy / boyfriend) ....?

BAZ: No, Mark is (15 – Trudy / husband) .... Eric is (16 – Jenny / boyfriend) ....

PRODUCER: So the black car is (17 – Jenny / boyfriend / car) ....?

BAZ: Yes, yes, that's right.

39 mine, myself etc.

CAPTAIN SPLENDID: Hello, Amazing Woman – did you fly here?

AMAZING WOMAN: No, Captain Splendid, I came here in my new machine. I built it **myself**. It's got six gears.

CAPTAIN SPLENDID: Oh, I've got a new machine too. I built **mine** too. It's got 21 gears.

AMAZING WOMAN: Oh, really? I put two steering wheels on **mine**.

CAPTAIN SPLENDID: **Mine** just has handle bars.

AMAZING WOMAN: Wait a minute, Captain Splendid. My new machine is a tank. What is **yours**?

CAPTAIN SPLENDID: **Mine** is a bicycle.

mine, hers etc.	We can use **my**, **her** etc. before nouns (e.g. **that's my book**, **it isn't her pen**), but when it is clear what we are referring to, we can also say **that's mine**, **it isn't hers**:

- 'Have you seen my 'Radiohead' CD?' 'It's not your CD; it's mine.' (= *it's my CD*)

singular	plural
mine (= *my thing(s)*)	**ours** (= *our thing(s)*)
yours (= *your thing(s)*)	**yours** (= *your thing(s)*)
his / hers (= *his / her thing(s)*)	**theirs** (= *their thing(s)*)

Note that **yours** is the same in the singular and plural.

use	**Mine**, **hers**, **ours** etc. refer to <u>*the person*</u> and not *the thing possessed*:

- Ann: <u>Sheila</u> can't find **her** notes.
  Ben: Are these **hers**?
  Ann: And she's lost **her** pen.
  Ben: Is this **hers**?

We can use **mine**, **hers** etc. as the ***subject*** of the verb:

- 'Is this your pen?' 'No, **mine is** a blue one.'

myself, herself etc.	singular	plural
	myself	**ourselves**
	yourself	**yourselves**
	himself / herself / itself	**themselves**

use	We often use **myself** etc. to emphasise the ***subject*** of the verb:

- <u>Kate</u> is building the boat **herself**.
- Did <u>you</u> pack these bags **yourself**?

We also use **myself** etc. as an object to say that the ***subject*** and the object *refer to the same person or thing*:

- At the end of the play, <u>Juliet</u> kills **herself**.
- Be careful or <u>you</u>'ll hurt **yourself**.

We often use **myself** etc. after a *verb + preposition*:

- To be successful <u>you</u> have to **believe in yourself**. (= ... *you have to believe that you are clever / skilled*.)
- <u>He</u> was really **angry with himself**.

To talk about *things that people do for themselves*, we can say:

- <u>Melissa</u> is buying lots of expensive things **for herself**. OR Melissa is buying **herself** lots of expensive things.
- <u>I</u>'ll make a cup of coffee **for myself**. OR I'll make **myself** a cup of coffee.

EXERCISES

A Put **mine, yours, hers, ours,** or **theirs** in the correct gaps. Use the table to help you.

DVD	belongs to			
	Youssef	Jacky	Teresa	Frank and Linda
Amélie		✓		
Star Wars	✓			
Chocolat		✓		
Lord of the Rings			✓	
The War of the Worlds				✓
Batman Begins			✓	
Equation	✓		✓	
Planet X	✓			

YOUSSEF: Hi, Teresa. What are you doing?

TERESA: Well, I'm moving to my new flat tomorrow, and I'm trying to sort out our DVDs. I want to take ⁰ *mine* but I'm not sure which ones are mine, which are ¹............... , and which ones are Jacky's.

YOUSSEF: Okay, maybe I can help.

TERESA: Is *Amélie* Jacky's DVD?

YOUSSEF: Yes, that's ²............... . All the *Star Wars* DVDs are ³............... .

TERESA: Okay, and I know that *Chocolat* isn't ⁴............... or ⁵............... . So, it must be Jacky's.

YOUSSEF: Yes, it's definitely ⁶............... . *Lord of the Rings* is ⁷............... .

TERESA: Yes, that's ⁸............... , I'm sure. Whose is *The War of the Worlds*?

YOUSSEF: Oh, Jacky borrowed it from Frank and Linda.

TERESA: Yes, you're right, it's ⁹............... . And *Batman Begins* is ¹⁰............... , isn't it?

YOUSSEF: Yes, that's ¹¹............... .

TERESA: Is *Equation* your DVD?

YOUSSEF: No, it isn't ¹²............... . Do you remember that we bought it together one day – so, actually, it's ¹³............... . But you can take it if you like.

TERESA: That's kind of you, Youssef, thanks.

YOUSSEF: Right, I'll put all of your DVDs in this bag and ¹⁴............... and Jacky's can stay in that box. So, whose DVD is *Planet X*?

TERESA: That's ¹⁵...............

B Put the words in the box in the correct places in this conversation.

| ~~myself~~ myself myself myself myself |
| yourself himself himself ourselves I |
| I you you you my |

BILL: Would you like a cup of tea?

AMANDA: No, it's okay, thanks. I'll make ⁰ *myself* a cup of coffee in a minute.

BILL: Okay. So, Amanda, what are ¹............... doing today?

AMANDA: Well, I'm going to the theatre and then to a posh restaurant with Mike. He organised it all ²............... .

BILL: That sounds great.

AMANDA: Dad, can ³............... borrow the car this morning? I want to go into town and buy ⁴............... a new dress. I need something smart for this evening.

BILL: Sorry, I need the car ⁵............... today. I'm going into town with your mum.

AMANDA: Well, can I come with ⁶............... ? Then both Mum and I can get ⁷............... new dresses at the same time.

BILL: Yes of course. And then we can have lunch in town.

MELISSA: Mike's on the phone – apparently he injured ⁸............... playing football yesterday. He's hurt his leg quite badly.

AMANDA: Oh, no, Mum. ⁹............... hope this doesn't mean that we can't go out tonight.

MELISSA: By the way, Amanda, have you looked at ¹⁰............... in the mirror this morning?

AMANDA: No, why? ... Oh, no, I've got an enormous spot on ¹¹............... chin. I'll have to buy ¹²............... some cream in town today. Dad, why didn't ¹³............... tell me?

BILL: Sorry, I didn't notice it ¹⁴............... .

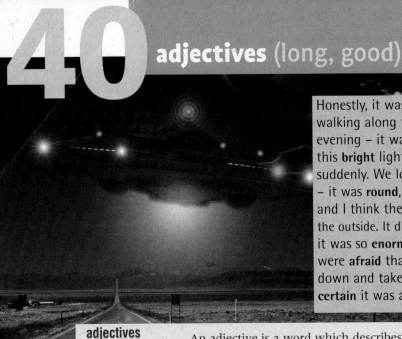

Honestly, it was amazing – my wife and I were just walking along this **narrow** lane and it was **early** evening – it was almost **dark** – and then we noticed this **bright** light in the sky. It appeared really suddenly. We looked up and saw a **huge, silver** shape – it was **round**, with a **flashing** light in the middle, and I think there were lots of **small, blue** lights around the outside. It didn't make any noise, which is **strange**, as it was so **enormous**. We were really **scared**! I think we were **afraid** that **little, green** Martians would come down and take us away in their **shiny** space ship! I'm **certain** it was a flying saucer.

adjectives before nouns	An adjective is a word which describes *things* or *people*. It can go before a **_noun_**: ■ My **black** <u>gloves</u> are in the car. ■ There was an **amazing** <u>sunset</u> last night. Adjectives can describe the *size*, *age*, *colour* etc. of things or people. We usually put a *size* adjective before another adjective: ■ Can I have a **small, strong** coffee, please? ■ There are hundreds of **big, red** ants in the tent! Some adjectives give *our opinion* of something, for example **lovely, pretty, horrible, nice, ugly** etc. These usually go before other adjectives: ■ Look at that **pretty, little, pink** house! ■ Jurgen needs a **nice, clean** suit. Note: we use commas between adjectives, but not immediately before the noun. (See unit 37 on adjectives AFTER **someone, anyone, nothing** etc)
adjectives after verbs	We use adjectives after a **_describing_ verb** (**be, seem, feel, look** etc): ■ John <u>seems</u> **tired**. ■ The house <u>was</u> **empty**. If we use two adjectives after a verb we put *and* after the first adjective: ■ Heather was **tired and hungry**. ■ Gareth felt **bored and frustrated**. (For more on describing verbs, see unit 8.)
colours	Some colour adjectives are made from two words together (**pale, dark, bright** etc. + *colour*), without a comma: ■ Where is my **pale green** scarf? ■ Look at that **bright yellow** butterfly!
ing and ed adjectives	We can use the **ed** *form* of feeling verbs as adjectives to describe *how someone feels*: ■ I showed Dan my essay, and he was really **interested**. ■ Keith seems **depressed** at the moment. We can use the **ing** *form* of feeling verbs to describe *how something makes us feel*: ■ I saw a very **frightening** film last night. (= *it made me feel frightened*) We also use the **ing** *form* of other verbs to describe *what something is for*: ■ There's a new **swimming** pool in the town. (= *a pool for swimming*) and we use the **ed** *form* of other verbs to say *what something is like*: ■ I'm afraid the CD player is **broken**. (For more on **ing** and **ed** *forms*, see units 74 and 63).

EXERCISES

A

Read the brochure and answer the questions.

Are you completely happy with the design of your home? Do you feel calm and relaxed in your flat or house? If your answer is, 'No, not really!', you need our expert help!

Our talented designers can work with your family to create the perfect environment for you. Every family is different and we want to create a world that is right for each family's needs.

Saleem and Sidra Ashraf wanted a cool, sophisticated home, that always looked tidy and clean. We designed a beautiful home for them, using pale colours and low, modern furniture, with natural fabrics and pale brown, wood floors. We gave them lots of cupboards and shelves, so they could keep everything tidy.

Another customer, the Duval family, preferred lots of bright colours and rich patterns. They already owned a lot of valuable, antique furniture, so we created a warm and original decor that they loved!

So come and talk to our friendly team and we guarantee to change your life – for the better!

0 What kind of help are we offering? ..*expert help*..

1 What kind of designers do we have?
....

2 What kind of environment can they create for you?
....

3 What kind of home did Mr and Mrs Ashraf want?
....

4 How did they want their house to look?
....

5 What kind of colours did we choose for them?
....

6 What kind of furniture? ....

7 What kind of fabrics and floors? ....

8 What kind of colours did Mr and Mrs Duval prefer?
....

9 What kind of furniture did they have? ....
....

10 What kind of decor did we create for them? ....
....

11 What is our team like? ....

B

Look at the pictures of the flowers and put the correct adjectives from the box in each description.

| tall yellow ~~light pink~~ small pale green black poisonous common tiny famous thick blue |

0 Herb Robert

Herb Robert has small flowers with five [0] ..*light pink*.. petals.

1 Love-in-a-mist

The flower of *Love-in-a-mist* has five
[1] ....,
[2] .... petals. The leaves below the flowers are [3] .... and feathery.

2 Great Mullein

Great Mullein is a very
[4] ....
plant, with a
[5] ....,
stem and
[6] ....
[7] ....
flowers.

3 Deadly Nightshade

The *Deadly Nightshade* has a shiny [8] .... berry. Don't eat it! It is extremely
[9] ....!

4 Wild Daffodil

This medium-sized, yellow flower is very
[10] .... in the spring. It is [11] .... partly because of the Wordsworth poem, 'The Daffodils'.

Illustrations from Wild Flowers by Colour ©Marjorie Blamey, used with kind permission of Domino Books.

The Tempest

Last night I went to Shakespeare's Globe Theatre and had an **amazing** evening! I saw *The Tempest* in a **fascinating**, new production directed by Tim Carroll. He only used three male actors (who were all extremely **talented**), three funky female dancers, six **highly-trained** singers and a long piece of rope! It is quite a difficult play, with the usual, **complicated**, Shakespearean story. In some productions I have seen, the long speeches can be **boring** and **confusing**, but everything seemed quite clear in this production. The comedy scenes were very **amusing** indeed, and the tragedy was extremely **moving**.

It was really **interesting** to see how a short-haired man can successfully act the part of a beautiful, young woman without the help of a long wig and make-up. The actor has to believe in himself, and *feel* female, and then he can appear as a **convincing** woman. The audience feels it too, and is **convinced**.

If Shakespeare's ghost is here somewhere, I think he must be very **pleased** and **excited** that his work is still alive, and giving so much pleasure.

ed *form* adjectives

We use the **ed *form*** of feeling verbs as adjectives to describe *how someone feels*:
- Dan was really **interested** in my story.
- Helen looks **scared** when she goes to the dentist.

We use **ed *forms*** to say *what has happened to something*:
- The sewing machine is **broken**.
- There is a tent for **lost** children.

We also use **ed *forms*** to describe *the pattern of something*:
- I like your **striped** duvet cover.
- Where did you find that **spotted** wallpaper?
- Lennie has a nice, **checked** shirt.

ing *form* adjectives

We use the **ing *form*** of feeling verbs to describe *how something makes us feel*:
- That's an **interesting** story.
- I saw a really **frightening** film last night.

We use **ing *form*** adjectives when we want to say *what something does*:
- There was a **ticking** clock on the wall.
- Maria was the **dancing** champion this year.

We also use the **ing *form*** of other verbs to describe *what something is used for*:
- There's a new **swimming** pool in the town. (= *a pool for swimming*)
- Karen needs some **walking** boots. (= *boots for walking*)

We often use these kinds of adjectives with another adjective or adverb. We use a hyphen when they are before the noun:
- John was very **hard hearted**.
- The clematis is a very **fast-growing** plant.
- Tanya's son is **good looking**.
- Radiohead is a **well-known**, local band in Oxford.

A Choose and circle the right form of the adjective.

DON: Have you ever been to Africa? It's a very
⁰ varying / varied continent, but a lot of people
think it's all the same.

MATT: No, I haven't been there, but I know that the
African desert is getting bigger all the time, and it's
a very ¹ worried / worrying situation.

DON: That's true, but lots of Africa is fertile, green and
full of wildlife. Where I come from in Botswana,
there are ² amazed / amazing safari parks and the
well-³ known / knowing Savuti marshes. You really
should come and see them.

MATT: Is that a serious invitation? I would be ⁴ delighted
/ delighting to come with you any time – if you're
paying!

DON: Well, of course I can't pay your airfare – I can't
afford to go home to Botswana very often myself –
the cost is ⁵ frightening / frightened! But I'm sure
my family would be ⁶ pleased / pleasing if you
came to stay at any time.

MATT: Where do you live exactly?

DON: In Gaborone – which is Botswana's fastest- ⁷ growing /
grown city. It's right next to the border with South Africa.

MATT: Well, let's go! I haven't planned my next holiday yet.
Wow, that's really ⁸ exciting / excited! My computer is
⁹ broken / breaking, or I'd go online to get some
information.

DON: My computer is fine. Let's go to my flat now and look at
the Botswana government website. It's really
¹⁰ interested / interesting.

B Read the following sentences, and write the correct adjective in the gap.

0 The magician amazed the audience. He was an ....*amazing*........ magician.

1 Everyone knows him. He is very well-..

2 His tricks confused everyone. His tricks were ....

3 But his act was not boring at all. We weren't .... at all.

4 Some of the people at the front were frightened. His performance was quite ....

5 He was wearing a suit with purple spots on it. He was wearing a purple-.. suit.

6 He pretended to break the man's watch. The man thought his watch was ....

7 He asked a girl with dark hair to go and help him. He asked a .... girl to help him.

8 He hypnotised her and told her she was a famous singer. He told her she was a .... star.

9 When she sang, it sounded like someone was strangling her! She had a .... voice.

10 When she sat down again, she was really embarrassed. It was an .... occasion for her!

The snow was falling on the silent hills. Harriet walked along the lane; her boots were getting **heavier and heavier** with packed ice. It was odd, she thought, that snow flakes looked **blacker than** the sky as they fell in the dark. It was **more difficult** to recognise the familiar landscape, as the valley was gradually filling with snow. She felt thankful that her sister had lent her a **warmer** coat. An owl suddenly flew past her in the darkness; it was **as white and silent as** a huge snowflake. It must be **easier** to hunt for mice when everything is covered with white, she thought. She heard the sound of a car engine behind her. It sounded **softer** and **more muffled than** usual, and it sounded far away. Distances seemed **greater** in the snow, probably because it took a **longer** time to move through it.

adjective + er	If an adjective has one syllable, to make a comparative we add **er**:
	    old → old**er** long → long**er**
	When the adjective ends in one <u>*consonant*</u>, we double it and add **er**:
	    hot → hot**ter** mad → mad**der**
	We don't double **w**:
	    few → fewer low → lower
	With adjectives ending in **e**, we add **r**:
	    nice → nice**r** pale → pale**r**
	Some common adjectives have an irregular comparative:
	    good → **better** bad → **worse**

more + adjective	If an adjective has more than one syllable, we usually add **more** before it:
	    intelligent → **more** intelligent expensive → **more** expensive
	But if a two-syllable adjective ends in a **y**, we use **ier**:
	    pretty → prett**ier** happy → happ**ier** easy → eas**ier**

use	We use a comparative adjective when we want to say that *something has more of a particular quality*. We often use it with **than**: ■ Ian is **older than** Francis. ■ My bedroom is **more untidy than** yours. (= *than your bedroom*) ■ This box is **bigger than** that. (= *than that box*) But we can also use a comparative without **than**: ■ She lent me a **warmer** coat. (= *It was warmer than **my** coat.*) ■ Jacky is a fast runner but Tina is **faster**. (= *Tina is faster **than** Jacky.*) We can use **a bit** and **much** before comparatives: ■ Mike is 18, Bill is 36 and Sanjit is 34. Bill is **much older** than Mike and **a bit older** than Sanjit.
as … as	If we want to say that *two things are equal* in some way, we use **as + *adjective* + as**: ■ The cottage is **as cold as** ice. ■ Robyn looked **as angry as** Tamsin. To say things are *not equal* we use **not as … as**: ■ Tea is **not as** expensive **as** coffee. We use **less**, to say the opposite of **more**, often with **than**: ■ Diane's **less enthusiastic than** Grace. ■ She's feeling **less energetic** today.

A

Read the text and put in the comparative form of the adjectives in brackets.

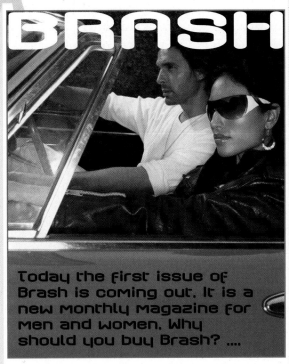

BRASH

Today the first issue of Brash is coming out. It is a new monthly magazine for men and women. Why should you buy Brash? ....

Because:

0 – the first issue is (cheap) ....*cheaper*........ than a bottle of cola!

1 – it's (modern) .... than all the other magazines.

2 – it's (big) .... than other magazines at the same price.

3 – it is for men and women, and it's (daring) ....

4 – it's got (funny) .... stories.

5 – it's full of (exciting) .... articles.

6 – the real-life stories are (shocking) .... than any you've read!

7 – it's (cool) .... than all the competition.

8 – the regular features are (interesting) .... than other magazines'.

9 – it has (original) .... features.

10 – it's actually (brash) .... than any magazine – ever!

B

Read the conversation and fill in the form that's missing. Some are + (more or er forms), and some are – (not as ... less ... forms).

TANYA: I really need to earn some money, Sidra! I'm just (– independent) 0 ...*not as* ...*independent*......... as I used to be. I can't even afford a holiday!

SIDRA: Your Mum is happy to look after the boys sometimes. Maybe you could get a part-time job. It's (– difficult) 1 .... to find part-time work than full-time.

TANYA: What kind of jobs are there in the paper? I used to work as an accounts clerk – but there are (+ stimulating) 2 .... jobs than that. I don't want to be stuck behind a desk all the time.

SIDRA: Well, here's a job working in a shop. You'd meet lots of people. It's a bit (+ sociable) 3 ....

TANYA: But people are (– polite) 4 .... as they used to be. I think I'd prefer to work alone.

SIDRA: What about dress-making? Can you use a sewing machine? It's a bit (+ easy) 5 .... if you can work at home, as you have the boys to look after.

TANYA: Me! Sewing! You're joking! Don't you remember? I was even (+ bad) 6 .... than you at sewing when we were at school! I can cook ... but I don't really enjoy it.

SIDRA: Well, what about cleaning? There are always lots of people who need cleaners. Some cleaning jobs are (+ interesting) 7 .... than others.

TANYA: That's a possibility. Let's see ... oh, here's something ... Artist ... happy to pay someone (+ sensitive) 8 .... and intelligent a (+ good) 9 .... wage to help me organise my studio ... .

SIDRA: Hey, that sounds cool! Why don't you give him a call? It'll be much (+ rewarding) 10 .... than cleaning someone's dirty kitchen!

I have always loved Scotland, as it has **the most beautiful** mountains and lakes in Britain. It is also **the coldest** part of the UK and has **the longest** winters, but winter there is beautiful, as well. I think **the loveliest** city in Scotland is Edinburgh. You must visit the castle, which is on the top of an extinct volcano!

In 1767, architects started planning a new area of the city, and this was, at that time, **the** world's **largest** planned city development. It was completed in 1810. By then, Edinburgh was Britain's **most important** financial centre outside London and, because of the neo–classical architecture, it was called 'the Athens of the North'. Edinburgh has produced many famous writers. **The most famous** are Robert Burns, Sir Walter Scott and Robert Louis Stevenson.

adjective +est	If an adjective has one syllable, to make a superlative we add **est**: old → the old**est** long → the long**est**
	With adjectives ending in one *consonant* (except w), we double the consonant and add **est**: hot → the hott**est** mad → the madd**est**
	With adjectives ending in **e**, we add **st**: nice → nice**st** pale → pale**st**
	Some common adjectives have an irregular superlative: good → **best** bad → **worst**
	If the adjective ends with *consonant* + **y**, we change the **y** to **i** and add **est**: dry → dr**iest**
most + adjective	If an adjective has more than one syllable, we usually add **most** before it: stupid → the **most** stupid elegant → the **most** elegant
	But if a two-syllable adjective ends in a **y**, we often use the **est** form: pretty → the prett**iest** silly → the sill**iest**
comparing things	We use a superlative adjective when we want to say that someone or something *has the most of a particular quality*: ■ Ivan is **the oldest** boy in the class. ■ This tomato is **the ripest** of them all.
	The opposite of **the most / the ...est** is **the least**: ■ Harriet is the **least busy** of us all. ■ Which shoes are **the least** expensive?
with and without the	We sometimes use the superlative form without **the** when it is at the end of a sentence: ■ All these watches cost a lot, but that one is **most expensive**. ■ Sarah's hat looks **prettiest**.
	We can use a possessive (e.g. **his**, **her**, **Britain's**) in place of **the**: ■ That was **her fastest** shot of the match. ■ The tower is on **the island's highest** hill. (= *the highest hill of the island*)

A Read the conversation and answer the questions.

MIA: When can I see the doctor, please? I've been waiting for 3 hours!

THOMAS: I've been here for 3 hours and 15 minutes, and I'm feeling really bad, but I can see that all the doctors are very busy.

MIA: I think my wrist is broken. I really think I'm the most urgent case, so I should go first.

THOMAS: I have a really bad headache and I'm seeing spots in front of my eyes. I might faint at any moment.

SIDRA: My son Adnan is very ill and he's only 2. The doctor should see him first, because he's the youngest.

MIA: But you've only just arrived! You'll have to wait.

THOMAS: There are so many sick people. We have to be patient. At least it's warm in here and we can sit down.

SIDRA: Don't tell me to sit down. Adnan is screaming and shouting and disturbing everyone. Can't we go first?

THOMAS: Why don't you get him something to eat from the cafe? It sells delicious cake. Your little boy may be hungry.

SIDRA: He doesn't want food! He's just eaten at home with me. He's ill, you stupid man!

MIA: There's no need to be so rude. He's only trying to help. Oh, I'm absolutely starving!

THOMAS: So am I. Would you like me to get something for us from the cafe? Coffee – sandwiches – crisps?

MIA: Thank you, you're very kind. A sandwich would be great – and a coffee. I'm sorry I was impatient, it's just that my wrist hurts so much. Look, it's really swollen.

THOMAS: Well, you sit still and I'll buy you a coffee and sandwich.

0 Who has been waiting for the longest time?
   Thomas

1 Who is the most talkative? ....

2 Who is the youngest patient? ....

3 Which patient is the least impatient? ....

4 Who are the most recent to arrive? ....

5 Who is the noisiest? ....

6 Who sounds like the rudest person? ....

7 Who is the least hungry? ....

8 Which patient is the most generous? ....

9 Which part of Mia's body is the most swollen?

   ....

B Look at the houses in the picture and complete the sentences about them, using the adjective in brackets and a superlative, either **the most / ...est (+)** or **the least (–)**.

0 (+ big) Number ....._30 is the biggest house._....

1 (+ small) Numbers ....

2 (– tidy) Number ....

3 (+ colourful) Number ....

4 (+ dirty) Number ....

5 (+ fast) The car at number ....

6 (+ large) The garden of number ....

7 (– well-kept) Number ....

8 (+ frightening) The dogs at number ....

   ....

9 (+ pretty) Number ....

10 (+ modern) Number ....

... and this is going to be the new office – it's really nice. The old one didn't get **enough light**. It was **too dark** to work in without artificial light. With these lovely, big windows this office will be **light enough**. And it's going to be **roomy enough** to keep the filing cabinets here, too, for easy access. The old office was **too small**, and we had to put all the files in another room. The new classrooms will be smaller, but there are more of them. That means they wo**n't be big enough** for the classes we used to have, so we're going to have to divide the students up into smaller groups. The classes in the old school were **too big** and impersonal. It means we won't have **enough teachers**, but I don't think it will be **too difficult** to find some good, new ones.

adjective + enough	We use **enough** after an adjective to mean *sufficiently*: ■ I hope this suitcase is **big enough**. (= ... is sufficiently big) ■ The soup is **hot enough** now. We often use **not** + *adjective* + **enough** when something is *not sufficient*: ■ These shoes are**n't big enough**. They really hurt. ■ I can't make ice cream, because my freezer is**n't cold enough**. We use *adjective* + **enough** + **for** + *noun* to say *sufficient for a purpose*: ■ The string isn't **long enough for** the parcel. (= to tie round the parcel) ■ William is **intelligent enough for** the job. (= to do the job) We also use *adjective* + **enough** + **to** + *verb* to say *sufficient, or insufficient, for a purpose*: ■ The lamp is **bright enough to** light the picture. ■ The cloth was**n't wide enough to** cover the table.
enough + noun	When we use **enough** with a noun, it goes before the noun: ■ Do you think we've got **enough plates**? ■ There are **enough eggs** in the fridge. We can also use **enough** without a noun *when it is clear what we are talking about*: ■ There aren't many sandwiches. Have you had **enough**? ■ I've got £10. Is that **enough**? or **enough** + *noun* + **for** + *noun*: ■ We've got **enough chairs for** the guests. ■ There is **enough rice** for everyone. or **enough** + *noun* + **to** + *verb*: ■ Deven bought **enough flour to** make chapattis for the family. ■ I have **enough paint to** finish the picture.
not + verb + enough	To make the negative, we use a *negative* verb + **enough**: ■ We **didn't buy enough** milk. NOT ~~We bought not enough milk~~.
too + adjective	We use **too** before an adjective to mean *excessively*: ■ I can't sleep, because it's just **too hot**! ■ Gary is **too lazy** to work for the exam. We often use **not too** to mean *not very*, especially with **sure**, **bad** and **good**: ■ Kerry was**n't too sure** where Marcia lived. ■ That play was**n't too good**. I was really bored.
too + many / much	We also use **too** with **many** (*for a number of things*), and **much** (*for a quantity of something*) meaning *an excess of something*: ■ There are **too many** cars on the road. (*a number*) ■ I can't carry the shopping. There's **too much**! (*a quantity*)

A Read the text and put **enough** or **too** with the word in brackets in the gaps. Each time **enough** or **too** needs to go either before or after the word in brackets.

ZOE: Didn't you have your audition for drama school today? How was it?

PAULETTE: Well, it wasn't (0 bad) ....*too bad*....... I was stuck in traffic and I was nearly (1 late) .... for the audition, but I got there just in time. In fact, I had (2 time) .... to have a cup of coffee and calm down before the audition.

ZOE: What did you have to do?

PAULETTE: I had an interview first. That wasn't (3 terrifying) .... The interviewers were quite friendly, but I don't think I was really (4 positive) .... to impress them. I was so nervous! There were (5 many) .... girls there and, as usual, not (6 men) .... I did my Shakespeare speech, which was OK, but I'm not (7 sure) .... that they liked it. And I found it hard to concentrate as there was (8 much) .... noise in the room. I don't think I acted with (9 passion) .... I don't think they'll offer me a place.

ZOE: Never mind. I believe you are (10 talented) .... to get a place eventually. You mustn't give up!

B Choose and circle the best of the underlined words or phrases.

MELISSA: I'm making a quiche for the picnic tomorrow. I just hope the weather is going to be 0 (warm enough) / too warm to sit out in the park. Six eggs are enough 1 for / to six people, aren't they? And I need flour and butter. I think there is 2 enough flour / flour enough in this bag. Oh dear! I think I've put in 3 not enough / too much! This tin looks 4 too / enough small. I'll make two small quiches. Now, I need enough pastry 5 to / for cover the bottom of the tins. I like lots of cheese – but some people don't like it 6 too / enough cheesy. I'll put some onion in it – enough 7 for / to make it nice and tasty, but not 8 too / too much. I hope the oven is 9 enough hot / hot enough. Amanda, have we got 10 too many / enough salad? Amanda?

A

Underline and list all the adjectives in the following passage.

It is a ⁰beautiful, clear day here at Willstree. There is a gentle breeze, and the ground is quite dry. It is a perfect day for racing! The race track is in very good condition, and the horses are all ready at the starting gate. Oh dear, one of the horses is obviously feeling a bit nervous – and the jockey is not happy! He's managed to get the horse back into the right position. This large, enthusiastic crowd is excited and impatient to see the start of first race of the day. No – the black horse is still not standing still. And now the big, grey mare has turned around. Behind me is Titania Harcourt in the Royal box, the special guest of young Prince Stephen, wearing an amazing, pink hat in the shape of a flamingo! Her mother, Lady Julia Harcourt, is beside her, dressed in a long, flower-patterned, silk dress, with a huge hat with red roses and white feathers. They both look gorgeous!

Now, I think – yes – the horses are all ready – and they're off! The crowd gives a loud cheer and everyone is on their feet. … This is going to be a great day for everyone!

0	*beautiful*	12		24	
1		13		25	
2		14		26	
3		15		27	
4		16		28	
5		17		29	
6		18		30	
7		19		31	
8		20		32	
9		21		33	
10		22			
11		23			

B

Now read the interview with Titania Harcourt and choose the best adjective for each of the gaps.

> smoked   proud   younger   ~~lovely~~   original   Spanish   first   brave   favourite   wonderful   well

JIMMY: Excuse me, Miss … Can I say how [0] _____lovely_____ you are looking today?

TITANIA: Oh thank you so much! I'm having a [1] _____ time!

JIMMY: Is this the [2] _____ time you have been to Willstree?

TITANIA: Oh no! I used to come when I was [3] _____.

JIMMY: And I must say your hat is very [4] _____ I've never seen one like it!

TITANIA: It was designed for me by my [5] _____ hat designer, Juan Mendez. He's [6] _____.

JIMMY: Well, I think you are very [7] _____ to wear it! And how is the Prince today?

TITANIA: Oh, he isn't feeling very [8] _____ at the moment. I think he ate too much
  [9] _____ salmon at breakfast. But I feel very [10] _____ to be here with the Prince.

C

Choose the best adjectives in the box to put in the gaps in the text.

> young,   athletic   smaller   little,   white   comfortable   depressing   difficult   tired   old
> ~~great~~   unfit   favourite   public

Tennis is such a [0] _____great_____ game! Every summer, when the tennis tournament at Wimbledon starts, thousands of British people get out their [1] _____ tennis rackets and try to squeeze into their [2] _____ shorts (why do those shorts seem to be a bit [3] _____ each year?). Then they go out onto the tennis court to share again in the excitement of their [4] _____ tournament of the year. But it's a [5] _____ game, if you're not an expert, so it can be a [6] _____ experience. The next day they always feel [7] _____, so they probably leave their rackets in the cupboard for another year. The problem is that when you play on [8] _____ courts, there are always some [9] _____ players on the next court who make you feel really [10] _____ . In the end, it's just as much fun to watch the Wimbledon tennis tournament on television, sitting on your [11] _____ sofa at home!

BRAVE COUPLE SAVES KNIFE VICTIM

This brave couple **probably** saved the life of a teenager yesterday. They say it was very lucky that they were in the right place at the right time to help save the teenager, who was **brutally** stabbed three times with a knife. Mr and Mrs Khazir had just come out of a shop near their home, when they saw a young man **desperately** defending himself from five boys who were punching him. Mr Khazir and his wife shouted **loudly** at them to stop, but the boys started shouting 'stab him, stab him'. He managed to escape, and ran right past his own house and into the next street. Mr Khazir said: 'If he had gone inside his own house the youths **almost certainly** would have killed him, because they were **definitely** not going to stop until he was dead.'

probability and manner	Two common types of adverb are: *probability adverbs* – these tell us how *likely* or *unlikely* something is (e.g. **probably**, **certainly**, **possibly**) *manner adverbs* – these tell us *how* something happens (e.g. **quickly**, **loudly**, **beautifully**)
form	These kinds of adverbs are usually formed by adding **ly** to an adjective:

adjective		adverb	adjective		adverb
bad	→	**badly**	soft	→	**softly**
quick	→	**quickly**	certain	→	**certainly**

If the adjective ends with **le**, we take off the **e** and add **ly**:

probable → probab**ly**   horrible → horrib**ly**

If the adjective ends in *consonant* + **y** we change the **y** to **-ily**:

happy → happ**ily**   pretty → prett**ily**

We can modify probability adverbs with another adverb, e.g. **almost**, **absolutely**, **really**.

■ Delia has **almost certainly** failed her Chemistry exam.

exceptions	Some adverbs are irregular:

good → **well**   fast → **fast**   hard → **hard**   late → **late**

Some words change their meaning when we add **ly** to make an adverb:

real (= *true*) → **really** (= *very*)   hard (= *solid, difficult*) → **hardly** (= *almost not*)
fair (= *just*, or *pale hair/skin*) → **fairly** (= *quite, not very*)
late (= *not on time*) → **lately** (= *recently*)

probability adverbs	Probability adverbs usually go before the *main verb*: ■ We'll **probably** *miss* the train. ■ Olaf has **definitely** *brought* back his book. If the main verb is **be** we put the adverb after it: ■ John **is certainly** the best student in the class.
manner adverbs	Manner adverbs often go after the <u>verb</u>, or after the <u>verb phrase</u>: ■ The students <u>worked</u> **silently** in the library. ■ Mrs Braithwaite <u>cooked the food</u> **well**. We often use, **really**, **very** etc. before a manner adverb to make it stronger: ■ The children were listening **really carefully**! We often use a manner adverb, before an **ed** adjective: ■ That picture is very **badly painted**. ■ Tim is **heavily built**.

EXERCISES

A

Read each line of this conversation. Tick it if it is correct, or underline any errors and write the correct form.

0 Did you see that man? He was running really <u>fastly</u>!
.....*fast*.....

1 He was trying probably to catch a bus. ....

2 I don't think so. He kept looking behind him nervously.
....

3 Oh, look at that other man – he's walking quick and looking very angry. ....

4 He's following definitely someone. ....

5 Shall we follow them? If we go carefully they won't notice. ....

6 What do you mean, carefully? We should behave natural. ....

7 You're right! Let's just walk normally. ....

8 Oh my goodness – there he is! He's following definitely him! ....

9 Don't watch them obviously so. Let's hide.
....

10 He's really tightly holding his arm. ....

11 He's arresting him. Look, he's a policeman and the other man is definitely a dangerous criminal!
....

B

Put the adverb in brackets into one of the two gaps in the following sentences.

0 (probably) Narcissus was .....*probably*..... the .... most beautiful young man in mythology.

1 (cruelly) But he also .... behaved .... to other people.

2 (desperately) People .... fell .... in love with him all the time.

3 (insanely) A nymph called Echo .... was .... angry with him, and called to the Goddess Diana to punish him.

4 (definitely) Diana heard her, and said that she would .... make him suffer ....

5 (deeply) Narcissus saw his reflection in a pool one day, and .... fell .... in love with himself!

6 (elegantly) He thought that what he saw was .... a beautiful water spirit, floating .... in the clear water.

7 (lovingly) He sat by the pond day and night, and stared .... at his .... reflection.

8 (immediately) Every time he tried to touch the reflection, ... it .... disappeared in the ripples.

9 (sadly) He sat there for so long that he became .... a flower, bending its head down .... beside a pool.

10 (certainly) It was .... a .... poetic punishment.

When Tanya needs a holiday her mother **usually** looks after her grandsons so Tanya can go **away** for the weekend. She has **just** phoned Tanya to tell her she can't have them **this weekend**. Tanya has **already** arranged to stay with her friend Julie, who lives **down in Dorset**, but fortunately she hasn't bought her train ticket **yet**. **This time**, she will have to take them with her. They have **never** been **there before**, and they're very excited.

how often **adverbs**	*Time adverbs* tell us *when* or *how often* something happens. *How often* adverbs (**never, not ever, sometimes, often, frequently, usually, always**) go before the main verb: ■ Tomas **never** shops at Frisco stores. ■ My aunt **often** visits me at the weekend.
when **adverbs**	*When* adverbs (e.g. **now, then, soon, later, today**) and adverbial phrases (e.g. **in June, last week, at once, at 6 o'clock, by now**) tell us about *the time when something happens*. They often go at the end of a clause: ■ I'm flying to Reykjavik **next month**. ■ Come here **now**! *When* adverbs can also go *at the beginning of a clause*, followed by a comma (,): ■ **The next morning**, the ice melted. ■ **Later**, she regretted it all.
just	**Just** is a *when* adverb, and we use it to say that something has happened very recently. We usually use it with the *present* or *past perfect*, and it goes before the main verb: ■ Liv has **just** passed her driving test! ■ When Dana arrived, Paul had **just** left.
soon	We use **soon** to say something will happen *in a short time from now*; it goes at the end of the clause: ■ I hope you will feel better **soon**. ■ Gary is leaving **soon**.
(not) yet	We use **not yet** to say that something *hasn't happened, but will happen*. We use **yet** with *perfect verbs*, and it goes at the end of the clause: ■ The letter has**n't** arrived **yet**. ■ Are**n't** you ready **yet**?
since	We use **since** with perfect verbs, to say *when* something *began*. It goes after the verb phrase: ■ Ken has lived in Leeds **since** 1997. ■ I've been working **since** 8 o'clock.
where **adverbs**	*Place adverbs* tell use *where* or *in what direction* something happens. *Where* adverbs (**here, there, out, in, at home, away, everywhere**) usually go after the main verb phrase: ■ I really like living **here**. ■ Gavin is **away** at the moment.
direction **adverbs**	*Direction adverbs* (**down, up, home, forwards, backwards, in, out, away, off**) also go after the verb: ■ The lift went **up** to the fourth floor. ■ Shall we take the bus **home**? ■ The train started moving **backwards**.
two adverbs together	If we use a *place* and a *time adverb* together we put the *place adverb* first: ■ Steve and Gary are going **out this evening**. ■ Shall I bring the washing **in now**?

EXERCISES

A Choose and circle the best adverb in the following text.

Sue has [0] since / (just) arrived in London, and she is [1] today / sometimes confused. It is a very big city and everyone [2] always / here hurries [3] sometimes / everywhere. They speak differently from how she speaks, and she [4] often / there has to ask them to repeat things. She has [5] since / already found a nice room in a shared house, and she is busy taking her things [6] up / now to her room. She will finish unpacking [7] yet / soon and [8] then / always she will be able to relax. She is very happy to be living [9] up / always in London, but she is looking forward to going back [10] tomorrow / home to Devon to tell her family all about it.

B The adverbs in **green** are in the wrong places in this conversation. Put an arrow where the adverb should be.

GARETH: Hello, Toni! What are you **there** doing ?

TONI: I'm cleaning the kitchen. **Here** I have to work all morning.

GARETH: But, it's Sunday, Toni! Why don't you come with us **out**? We're going to play golf!

TONI: But I really have to **today** clean the kitchen.

GARETH: Can't you **later** do that?

TONI: The inspectors **tomorrow morning** are coming. I have to **now** do it.

GARETH: If you **this morning** come and play golf, we'll help you clean up this evening!

TONI: That's a good idea! I'd love to **now** come and play golf.

GARETH: **Here** shall we meet? Come to my house and we can go together.

TONI: Great! I'll be in half an hour **there**!

Dana, our dream expert says:

Dreaming is **really** important! Apparently, we need to dream. Scientists have found that if someone wakes us up every time we start to dream, we go crazy **very** quickly. It is possible to learn how to remember all our dreams. We can **even** choose what we dream about! We **just** have to say 'I will dream about getting my exam results' or something, just before we go to sleep, and it will **really** happen. We can **even** agree to meet other dreamers at a certain place and time.

It takes **quite** a long time to learn to understand what our dreams are telling us, but it can be **very** useful. Dreams always tell us the truth, but **only** if we know how to 'read' them.

focus adverbs	Focus adverbs (**just**, **only**) go before the word or phrase we want to stress, usually after **be** or before the **main verb**. They tell us that *something is unexpected or significant in some way*: ■ There were **just** three people in the audience. (*Three is an unexpectedly small number for an audience*.) ■ Kerry can swim although he is **only** five years old. (*Five is very young*.) ■ I **only** got one birthday card. (*I usually get more*.)
even	**Even** is a focus adverb, but is only used with a *comparative* (**bigger**, **better**): ■ The plane was **even** bigger than a jumbo. (*Jumbos are very big, so this plane must be huge!*)
modifying adverbs	There are two types of *modifying adverbs*; they usually go before an *adjective* or an *adverb*. *Diminishers* (**not very**, **not really**, **fairly**) make the meaning *less strong*: ■ The new film by Guido Minelli is **fairly** dull. ■ We're **not really** ready to start the meeting. *Intensifiers* (**very**, **really**, **so**) make the meaning *stronger*: ■ This music is **really** wonderful! ■ I'm **so** sorry. It was a **very** stupid thing to say. ■ Alma was walking **very** slowly. **Really** can be used as an *intensifier*, before a <u>*describing verb*</u>: ■ I **really** <u>love</u> that song! (= *I love it very much*.) (See unit 8 on describing verbs.)
quite	**Quite** can be used in four ways: before most *adjectives*, it usually makes the meaning *less strong*: ■ Tanya's new boots are **quite** nice (but not really my style). ■ It's **quite** hot in Barcelona, but I like it. but when we use it with some *absolute adjectives* (e.g. **perfect**, **right**, **wrong**), it means *completely*: ■ I think Venice is **quite** perfect! (= *totally perfect*) ■ His theory is **quite** wrong! (= *completely incorrect*) we often use **quite** with **a / an** + *adjective* + *noun*, or with **a lot of**: ■ There's **quite a big scar** on my leg. NOT … ~~a quite big scar~~… ■ Julia had **quite a lot of letters** this morning. NOT … ~~quite lots of letters~~… we use **not quite as** … **as** to mean *a bit less than*: ■ Tsien is **not quite as** clever as Liao. (= *Liao is a bit cleverer than Tsien*.)

EXERCISES

A

Circle the right explanation for the underlined phrase in the following sentences.

0 Did you know that <u>Tamsin's only fifteen</u>? = (She's very old. / (She's very young.))

1 No! <u>That's quite surprising</u> … = (That's very surprising. / That's a bit surprising.)

2 … but I knew <u>she wasn't quite as old as us.</u> = (She was a lot younger. / She was a little bit younger.)

3 If they put her in our class <u>she must be really clever.</u> = (She must be very clever. / She must be quite clever.)

4 Yes, there are <u>only two other people</u> who are less than 17 in our class. = (That's a small number of people. / That's a big number of people.)

5 Yes. I think <u>it's fairly unusual.</u> = (It's very unusual. / It's a bit unusual.)

6 She seems <u>quite mature</u> for her age. = (completely mature / a bit mature)

7 And <u>she's even better at French</u> than you! = (It's surprising that she's better at French. / She isn't better at French.)

8 <u>That's only because</u> she used to live in Lyons! = (The reason is … / It's surprising that …)

9 Oh! <u>I really thought</u> she was American. = (That is a surprise to me. / I wasn't sure about that.)

10 No, she said she was Scottish, but <u>she has only been here for a few weeks.</u> = (She arrived recently. / She hasn't been anywhere else.)

B

Put the adverb in brackets in the right place in the following sentences.

0 (really) The price of oil is rising fast.
   The price of oil is rising really fast.

1 (quite) There are a lot of reasons for this.

2 (only) An increase in oil prices doesn't change the price of petrol.

3 (even) It can make food more expensive.

4 (quite) It may mean a big increase in the cost of travel.

5 (fairly) Since 1999, the increase in oil prices has been steady.

6 (very) Because of world events, the price has increased suddenly.

7 (really) Before now, the price of oil in European countries was not affected.

8 (even) The USA, which used to be safe, may run out of oil soon.

9 (really) We have to change the way we live.

10 (even) It is more important, now, to develop other ways of producing power.

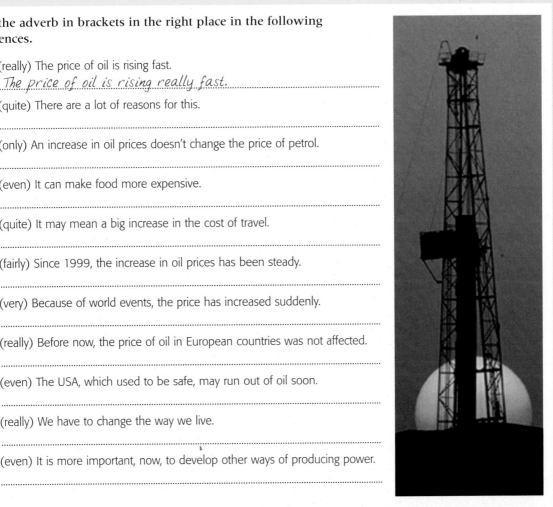

review 7: adverbs (units 45–47)

A Read the following biography and put an arrow where the adverbs in brackets should go in each sentence. Sometimes more than one position is possible.

0 Josephine Baker was ↓ the most famous black singer and dancer in Paris in the 1920s. (probably)

1 She was born in St Louis in the USA and she began dancing on stage when she was 13. (only)

2 When she went to Paris in 1925 she became successful. (immediately)

3 Her style of dance was daring and original. (extremely)

4 She was well known in Europe. (everywhere)

5 She used the traditions from her American black culture in her acts. (always)

6 During the war she worked for the French Intelligence Service. (secretly)

7 She entertained the troops in Africa and the Middle East. (often)

8 She fought for racial equality. (hard)

9 She refused to work in any club which did not have a policy of racial equality. (always)

10 She was accused of being a communist and couldn't get work. (unfairly)

11 In 1963 she made a speech in Washington, supporting Martin Luther King. (bravely)

12 After this, she lost all her money. (gradually)

13 She had to leave her villa. (eventually)

14 She started another successful career on the stage. (then)

15 She died of a stroke in 1975, as she was becoming successful again. (just)

B Choose the best adverbs from the box to go in each gap in the text. The first letter is given.

> a lot really only often recently Even still probably continuously totally
> carefully Usually clearly ~~really~~ quite even always without

Smoking cigarettes used to be ⁰r......*really*...... cool. Hollywood films used to show glamorous and

attractive people, smoking ¹c .... ²E .... women film stars used to smoke

³a .... Think of Marlene Dietrich, who ⁴a .... seemed to be in a cloud of

smoke, ⁵e .... when she was singing! And of course, Humphrey Bogart, who couldn't get out of bed in the morning [6] w .... a cigarette in his mouth. A survey has [7] r .... been done of smoking in Hollywood films. Things have [8] r .... changed! In the 1980s, tobacco companies paid millions of dollars to make sure their product was [9] c .... seen in movies. Now advertising cigarettes in films is [10] t .... illegal.

Doctors were [11] s .... afraid that the cinema was encouraging people to smoke, by showing positive examples of actors smoking, but the survey has proved [12] q .... the opposite. In the majority of films from the past year, the survey found that [13] o .... the bad people smoke. [14] U ...., the people who smoke in films are poorer, and less successful than the non-smokers. Next time you go to the cinema, watch [15] c ....! Count the number of times you see someone smoking a cigarette, and think about what kind of characters they are. They will [16] p .... be baddies, or losers.

The problem is, young people [17] o .... think it's good to be bad!

C Read the conversation and choose and circle the best adverb from the two in green.

ISMAH: Good morning, Madam. Can I help you?

DANA: Yes, I'm looking for some sandals – I [0] quite / (really) need some comfortable sandals that look good.

ISMAH: I'm sorry, but you look [1] very / probably familiar … have you been in the shop [2] before / still?

DANA: No – well, maybe [3] once / only, years ago – but I've been [4] off / away for several years.

ISMAH: We've only had the shop for two years, [5] now / soon. But I've [6] fairly / definitely seen you somewhere …

DANA: Well, [7] actually / certainly, I'm a tennis player. You've [8] probably / badly seen me on TV.

ISMAH: How exciting! Have you won any championships? I [9] absolutely / well love tennis!

DANA: I [10] usually / recently played in the finals in the OCCTA – that's in the US. [11] Unfortunately / Badly I lost! And I won at Eastbourne the year before, but I've [12] even / never played at Wimbledon – not yet!

ISMAH: Oh yes – of course! I've seen a picture of you in the paper. But you looked [13] completely / always different. I [14] just / always thought you had blonde hair.

DANA: Yes, my hair is [15] only / really blonde, but I [16] often / here wear a brown wig when I go shopping.

ISMAH: Well, I am [17] so / just pleased to meet you. [18] Before / So we bought the shop I [19] quite / usually played tennis at the weekends, but we are [20] certainly / so busy with the shop, I haven't played for months.

DANA: Well you [21] certainly / even should try to find time. It keeps you [22] definitely / really fit, and it's fun.

ISMAH: I know. You're [23] just / quite right. I must start playing [24] once / again, but I'm sure I won't be able to play very [25] well / so. Anyway … what about those sandals?

DANA: Well, these white ones look as if they would [26] here / probably be comfortable. Can I try [27] up / on a size 6, please?

TANYA: Jake, where is your *Captain Splendid* lunchbox? I put it **on** the table, but it's not there now.

JAKE: I don't want to go to nursery. Freddy doesn't have to go to nursery.

TANYA: Freddy's a baby, and you're a big boy. I don't understand it. I just took the lunchbox **out of** the cupboard to put your lunch **in**. Have you hidden it?

JAKE: It's lost.

TANYA: Well, you can take your lunch **in** a bag.

JAKE: Maybe it's **in** the bathroom.

TANYA: Oh Jake, you are so naughty! Go **into** the bathroom and get it immediately!

position prepositions: in	Position prepositions (e.g. **in**, **on**) tell us *where something is*. They usually go before a ***noun phrase***. We use **in** to say that something is in a *defined space or context*: ■ I left my bag **in** the Post Office. ■ Harriet still lives **in** the Netherlands. ■ I read about Tom Cruise **in** an article **in** the paper. ■ The island is **in** the middle of the lake. Note: we can use **in** without **the/a** with **hospital**, **bed** and **prison**: ■ Is it true that Mr Franks is seriously ill **in hospital**? ■ The children are all **in bed**. ■ John wrote a book when he was **in prison**.
position prepositions: on	We use **on** to say that something is: *supported by something*: ■ The cat was sleeping **on** the chair. or *attached to something*: ■ Your coat is hanging **on** the hook. or *covering* or *in contact with something*: ■ Jake's shoes were **on** the wrong feet. Note: we use **on the train / boat / plane** to talk about *where we are when we are travelling*: ■ I hope I don't feel sick **on the boat**.
movement prepositions	Movement prepositions (**out of**, **onto**, **into**) tell us *something is moving to or from a defined space*, and also go before a ***noun phrase***: ■ The train came **into** the station. ■ Jake threw his lunch box **onto** the floor. ■ A big, black bird flew **out of** the forest.
at the end of a clause	We can use space prepositions at the end of a sentence without a ***noun***, when we have already said <u>what thing or place</u> we are talking about: ■ Have you got <u>a purse</u> to keep the money **in**? ■ I visited <u>the island</u> Salvator was born **on**. ■ It was dark in <u>the room</u> we went **into**.

A Choose the best prepositions from the alternatives in these instructions for making a model boat.

Take all the pieces ⁰ to / (out of) the box and lay them out ¹ on / in the table, as shown ² onto / in the diagram.

Carefully press the main sections (A,B,C, and D) ³ on / out of the frame.

Put a small amount of glue ⁴ on / out of all the parts marked G.

Put the glued edge of section A ⁵ into / on the hole ⁶ on / in section B.

Take the sail ⁷ out of / into the plastic bag, and lay it flat ⁸ out of / on the table. Put the strings through the holes ⁹ in / into the sail and tie them. When the glue is dry, attach the sail to the mast. Do not put the boat ¹⁰ into / out of water until you have painted it.

B Read the text and put either **in, on, into, onto** or **out of** in the gaps. Then read the questions and answer them.

Tanya walked ⁰ ....*into*........ into Guido's studio and stood ¹ .... the middle of the room, staring around. Guido had phoned her when she was ² .... the bus and warned her about the mess. He must have had a party ³ .... the studio the night before, because there were empty glasses and plates ⁴ .... the floor and all the paintings were piled up ⁵ .... the corner. Someone had put a hat ⁶ .... the statue. She took all the dirty dishes ⁷ .... the kitchen and piled them ⁸ .... the sink. There was a lot of food ⁹ .... the table, so she put it all ¹⁰ .... the fridge and took the vacuum cleaner ¹¹ .... the cupboard. This was going to take her a long time.

0 Where did Tanya go? *She went into Guido's studio.*

1 Where did she stand? ....

2 Where was Tanya when Guido phoned? ....

3 Where had Guido had his party? ....

4 Where were the glasses and plates? ....

5 Where were the paintings? ....

6 Where was the hat? ....

7 What did she do with the dishes? ....

8 Where was the food? ....

9 What did she do with the food? ....

10 Where was the vacuum cleaner kept? ....

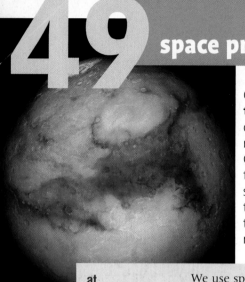

On Thursday, NASA changed the date of the launch of a spacecraft **to** Mars because of a problem with the software in the rocket. They decided to launch the rocket three days after the shuttle Discovery returned **to** earth. The two-ton space vehicle will travel **from** Cape Canaveral **to** Mars to collect data on the weather on Mars, and on the geology of Mars. The spacecraft carries the biggest telescope ever sent **to** another planet. It will circle Mars for four years, looking **at** the surface. Scientists hope to learn something about the history of the ice on the planet. The journey **from** earth will take about seven months, so it should arrive **at** its destination in March next year.

at

We use space prepositions to talk about *where something is*, or *where it is going to*. We use **at** when we want to talk about *someone or something arriving, or staying at a particular place*:

- I've just arrived **at** the cinema.   ▪ The train didn't stop **at** this station.

We do not use **at** for larger areas, like towns, cities, and countries:

- The plane landed **in** Germany NOT ~~The plane landed at Germany~~

We also use **at** to talk about *places we go to for particular purposes*:

at the bus stop (*waiting for a bus*)   **at** school (*studying*)
at the office (*working*)   **at** the theatre/cinema etc. (*watching a play, film etc*)
(For more on this, see unit 52)

We also use phrases with **at** to talk about the *position of someone or something* (**at** the back of, **at** the side of):

- The policeman was standing **at the back of** the room.
- **At the front of** the queue, my friend was waiting.

We use **at** when we want to say that someone is *behind or in front of* a table, counter, door etc:

- Miss Franks is **at** the reception desk.
- Harry isn't sitting **at** the table.

Note: we say **in the middle**, NOT ~~at the middle~~:

- There's an island **in the middle** of the lake.

We also use **at** after certain verbs (e.g. **look**, **point**, **shout**, **throw**) when we want to talk about *doing something in the direction of something*:

- **Look at** the sunset! It's lovely.   ▪ Maria **threw a stone at** the rat.
- Please don't **shout at** the children.

to

We use **to** to talk about *movement towards something*:

- Paul has never been **to** Holland before.
- Renée swam **to** the middle of the river.

We also use **to** after certain verbs (e.g. **talk**, **give**, **throw**) when we want to say that *two people are involved in the action*:

- Harry was **talking to** Tom when I saw him. (= *and Tom was talking, or listening, to Harry.*)
- **Give** the bag **to** me! (= *I will take the bag.*)
- Mitsue **threw** the ball **to** Chen. (= *Chen caught the ball.*)

from

We use **from** to talk about *where a journey starts*:

- Jane has just arrived **from** Ireland.
- How long does it take to get here **from** your village?

We also use **from** after some *adverbs* (**away**, **down**, **up** etc):

- Jenny is working **away from** the office at the moment.
- Karl came **up from** the cellar with a bag of coal.

A

Choose **to**, **from** or **at** to fill the gaps in the following text.

Dear Simon,

I am so excited that you are coming to stay [0] ...*at*... my house next week! What time are you arriving [1] .... Heathrow? I can come [2] .... the airport to meet you, if it isn't too early in the morning. It takes about two hours to get there [3] .... Weymouth. If you are arriving in the middle of the night, you can stay in the hotel [4] .... the airport. My dad says he will pay for it. Then we can come and pick you up the next morning. At the moment, my sister is away [5] .... home, so you can have her room. We live very close to the sea, so we can spend every day [6] .... the seaside, if the weather is good. We are also going [7] .... London on Friday, as my dad has tickets for The Lion King, which is on [8] .... the Regent's Theatre.

Is this the first time you have been [9] .... England? When I was [10] .... college in France I wanted to come and visit you, but it was too far to go [11] .... Avignon [12] .... your house in Percy.

Text me to say what time you're arriving.

Looking forward to seeing you,

Damien

B

Look at the picture and then answer the questions, making sentences using the words in brackets with either **at**, **to** or **from**. Now write the names on each of the characters in the picture.

0 Where is Yumi? (sit / her desk) ...*She's sitting at her desk.*..

1 Where is Paul going? (go / water cooler) ....

2 What is Mr Tranter doing? (look / a map) ....

3 What is Emma doing? (talk / Paul) ....

4 What is Rachel doing? (give / a cup of tea / Yumi) ....

5 Where is Liam coming back from? (come back / the photocopier) ....

6 What is Jurgen looking at? (look / some papers) ....

7 Where is Rachel standing? (stand / Yumi's desk) ....

8 What is Keith doing? (throw / a paper aeroplane / Kamila ....

ADNAN: The new winter shoes and boots have arrived. We need to re-organise the shop. I think we need the really funky boots **in the middle** of the shelf **opposite** the entrance, so that people see them first when they walk into the shop.

ISMAH: But, at this time of year, we sell lots of school shoes – maybe we could put them **above** the boots on this shelf?

ADNAN: Yes, that's a good idea. And what about the new range of trainers? They're very popular, so I think they should be **in front of** the counter. Or what about here, **under** the socks and tights, **next to** these slippers?

ISMAH: OK, and the party shoes and men's casuals can go at the back, **beside** the stock room door ...

under

- My wallet is **under** the car.

above

- The price is on the sign **above** the car.

behind

- Be careful **behind** the car, Sam!

in front of

- The gate **in front of** the car is closed.

in the middle / front / back (of)

- David is **in the front** of the car, and the dog is **in the back**.
- The car is parked **in the middle** of the car park.

in the way (= *blocking*)

- David can't drive out of the car park because a bicycle is **in the way**.

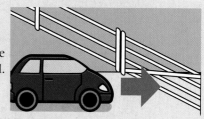

opposite

- My car is parked **opposite** Gary's car.

beside / next to / by

- Is that your car, **next to** the blue Jaguar?
- No, my car is **beside** the black Honda.
- His car is parked **by** the exit.

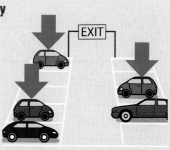

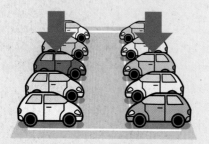

A Answer the questions using the word in brackets.

0   Where is Tanya? (under)
    She's under the table.

1   Is the TV beside the sofa? (opposite)
    ....

2   Where is Jake? (beside)
    ....

3   Where is the cat? (behind)
    ....

4   Where are the toys? (under)
    ....

5   Where is the mirror? (above)
    ....

6   Where is Jake's shoe? (in front of)
    ....

7   Where is Harry? (behind)
    ....

8   Is the door opposite the window? (opposite)
    ....

9   Where is Harry's breakfast? (under)
    ....

10 Is Harry under the sofa? (in front of)
    ....

B Look at the picture and choose the best phrase from the box to finish the sentences.

> under the vegetables   ~~beside the sugar~~   under the ham   opposite the fruit   above the cakes
> beside the butter   above the biscuits   beside the fish   below the sugar   opposite the ham   above the vegetables

0   The rice is *beside the sugar* ....
1   The fruit is ....
2   The cakes are ....
3   The ham is ....
4   The herbs are ....
5   The honey is ....
6   The bread is ....
7   The biscuits are ....
8   The cream is ....
9   The salad is ....
10 The bacon is ....

The hurricane hit the city **at** 8.30 **on** Monday morning. **By** 10.30 it had moved down the coast, but **during** those two hours it almost completely destroyed the city. The city was flooded with water **after** the storm passed. It is three days **since** the disaster, and people are still waiting to be rescued, some of them on the roofs of their houses. The experts thought the hurricane might change direction **before** it hit the city, but, in fact, it got stronger as it moved over the city, and **in** two hours it was all finished. **For** several days before the hurricane, people were preparing for the storm, but they were not prepared for this.

in	We use **in** to talk about something happening *at some time during a longer period of time*: ■ We went to Ireland **in** June. We also use **in** to talk about *how long* something *takes to complete*: ■ The guests finished their meal **in** half an hour. We also use **in** to say *how long before something is going to happen*: ■ Let's meet **in** an hour (from now). We use **in the end** to say something *takes longer than we expect*, or *the result is unexpected*: ■ The essay took me three days, but I finished it **in the end**. ■ Delia thought she had failed the exam but, **in the end**, she did really well. We use **in time** (for) to say that something *is early enough*: ■ I hope the Bells arrive **in time** for dinner.
at	We use **at** to talk about *the time (usually by the clock)* when something happens: ■ The train left **at** 4.45 p.m. ■ Jane woke **at** dawn. We say **at the end/beginning** to say *what happens when something starts or finishes*: ■ Lennie was excited **at the beginning** of the show, and she was tired **at the end**. Note: we also say 'at the weekend' and use **at** for festivals like Diwali, Easter, Eid etc.
on	We use **on** to talk about *the day or date* when something happens: ■ I think the party is **on** June 8th. Yes, it's **on** her birthday. We use **on time** to say that something happens *at the right time*: ■ I hope we get to the station **on time**! I don't want to miss the train.
during	We use **during** before a noun to talk about something that happens *at the same time as something else, or in a longer period of time*: ■ **During** the night Kevin filled the supermarket shelves.
before	We use **before** to talk about something that happens *at an earlier time than something else*: ■ Tom talked to Yvonne **before** the exam.
after	We use **after** to talk about something that happens *later than something else*: ■ They went and had a pizza **after** the play.
for	We use **for** to talk about *how long something lasts*: ■ Jane talked on the phone **for** twenty minutes.
from – till / until	We use **from** to say *when* something *starts happening*. We use **until** or **till** to talk about something *continuing up to a moment in time*: ■ Pietro played chess **from** three **until** ten last night!
since	We use **since** to talk about *when something, that is still continuing, started*: ■ Yuko has worked at the library **since** August.
by	We use **by** to talk about *something that happens or finishes before a particular time*: ■ Jack will be here **by** this evening. ■ **By** the time we got there, the meal was over.

A Choose the best preposition from the box to put in the gaps in the conversation.

on ~~from~~ in before by at for since for during before

TANYA: Oh no! The landlord is increasing my rent ⁰ *from* the beginning of March. I can't afford it. I'll have to find a cheaper place ¹ .... the spring. I'll buy a paper ² .... I go to work and we can look at the flats available.

MUM: I'm afraid I've got an appointment at the doctor's ³ .... 3.00 this afternoon so I can't help you today. But I'm free ⁴ .... the day ⁵ .... Wednesday.

TANYA: OK. I'll phone and try to make appointments to visit some flats then, so you can come with me. Actually, I'm quite excited! I've been living here ⁶ .... a long time. A change will be good.

MUM: Yes, it might be fun to live somewhere new. Listen, I have to meet Sarah ⁷ .... twenty minutes, but tell me how much the increase in your rent is ⁸ .... I go.

TANYA: It's going up by 25%. I suppose it's not so bad. I have been living here ⁹ .... almost five years and the rent hasn't changed.

MUM: 25%! I think that's terrible! Well, I'm sorry, but I must go now. I haven't seen Sarah ¹⁰ .... she went to live in Austria – almost ten years!

TANYA: OK, Mum. Say Hi to Sarah from me. Bye!

B The underlined prepositions are wrong in the following phone conversation. Write the correct word at the bottom.

MATT: Hello? Is that you, Don? I've been waiting here ⁰ <u>at</u> half an hour!

DON: Hi Matt. I'm sorry. I've been stuck in the traffic ¹ <u>in</u> ages.

MATT: Where are you now? I can't stay here ² <u>by</u> much longer, as I've got a parking space ³ <u>to</u> another ten minutes, but, ⁴ <u>for</u> that, I'll have to move my car.

DON: I'm still on the Harrow Road, but the traffic is moving a bit faster now. I should be there ⁵ <u>for</u> about ten minutes.

MATT: Maybe I should move my car now. We'll still need some time to discuss my contract ⁶ <u>from</u> you get here. I'll wait ⁷ <u>on</u> 4.30 and then move the car, so, if I've gone ⁸ <u>at</u> you get here, just wait here. I'll be back ⁹ <u>at</u> a few minutes, when I find a new parking place.

DON: We shouldn't have planned to meet ¹⁰ <u>in</u> a Saturday, and ¹¹ <u>until</u> the busiest time of day! Honestly, I sometimes think public transport would be easier.

0 *for*	3	6	8	10 ....
1	4	7	9	11 ....
2	5			

52 preposition + noun (on holiday, in love, by mistake etc)

ELLEN: Yes, Mr Dawson, Carl is still **on holiday**. He didn't go **by himself**, this time. He took his new wife. It's sweet, they're really **in love**!

MR DAWSON: Good, but I need to talk to him before the meeting, so maybe I could talk to him **on the phone**. **By the way**, have you chosen a new picture for the reception area?

ELLEN: Yes, I chose that painting **by** Guido Delitto. It's very **up to date**.

MR DAWSON: Fine. Did you pay him **in cash**, or by cheque?

ELLEN: I paid him by cheque. But he left the cheque in the office **by mistake**. He's very – artistic!

MR DAWSON: I know! When we went to his studio it was **in a** terrible **mess**. Well, just send the cheque by post.

on + (the) + noun	**on holiday** (= *away from work/school*) ■ Tom went **on holiday** last week. **on fire** (= *burning, usually accidentally*) ■ Oh no! The Town Hall is **on fire**! **on the phone** (= *talking to someone using a telephone*) ■ Don't interrupt your sister when she's **on the phone**. **on the TV/video/radio** (= *by means of the TV etc*) ■ Declan heard his mother interviewed **on the radio**.	**on purpose** (= *deliberately*) ■ Harry hit Jake **on purpose**!
in + (a) + noun	**in cash** (= *with paper money or coins*) ■ I prefer to pay for things **in cash**. **in a mess** (= *very untidy*) ■ Dad's really angry because the house is **in a mess**. **in case** (= *because this may happen …*) ■ I'll take my coat **in case** it rains.	**in love** (= *loving someone*) ■ The song was about being **in love**.
by + (the) + noun	**by + person's name** (= *a work of art created by …*) ■ My favourite painting is **by** Monet. **by myself, himself** etc. (= *without another person,* or *without help from anyone*) ■ Saima was sitting **by herself** in the park. ■ The children had to do the test **by themselves**. **by mistake/accident** (= *not deliberately*) ■ Ellen wrote the wrong name **by mistake**. **by the way** (= *now I'm talking about something different …*) ■ Here is your ticket, and, **by the way**, the flight leaves at 5.	
at + (the) + noun	**at home / work / school** (= *using the place in its usual way*) ■ No, Eric isn't here. He's **at work** at the moment. (= *he's working*) **at the school/office** etc. (= *at a place*) ■ The bus arrived **at the school**.	
other prepositions + noun	**for example** (= *as an example, e.g.*) ■ I love Italian food; I love pizza, **for example**. **out of date** (= *old fashioned,* or *not correct now*) ■ The information he gave was **out of date**. **up to date** (= *modern,* or *correct now*) ■ The décor in the office is really **up to date**.	

EXERCISES

A

Circle the best explanation of the underlined part of the following sentences.

0 When Ellen arrived at the meeting, Mr Dawson was waiting <u>by himself</u>. = (*alone*) OR *with other people*

1 When the others arrived, they watched a new advertisement for their company <u>on the video</u>. = *played using the video machine* OR *on top of the video machine*

2 Ellen played the wrong video <u>by mistake</u>. = *she didn't mean to* OR *she wanted to play the wrong video*

3 Mr Dawson's wife <u>called him on the phone</u>. = *she asked him to answer the telephone* OR *she phoned him*

4 He said, 'please, <u>don't call me at work</u>.' = *don't phone me when I am in the office* OR *don't phone me when you are in the office*

5 Ben said, '<u>the advert is out of date</u>.' = *the advert is old-fashioned* OR *the date on the advert is wrong*

6 Ellen said, 'the advertising company <u>made the advertisement in the style of the 1960s on purpose</u>.' = *didn't want the advertisement to have a 1960s style* OR *wanted the advertisement to have a 1960s style*

7 Ben said, 'our company needs to seem <u>more up to date</u>.' = *more modern* OR *to have the date on the screen*

8 Su Yen suggested, 'the advert <u>could use Doggydog Dog's music, for example</u>.' = *it could use music like Doggydog Dog's* OR *it will definitely use Doggydog Dog's music*

9 Ben said he didn't use that kind of music <u>on purpose</u>. He hated it! = *as a deliberate choice* OR *without thinking*

10 He preferred <u>music by</u> bands like The Cuties. = *music different from* OR *music they have written and performed*

B

Choose the best phrase from the box to put in the gaps in the dialogue.

| on fire | in a mess | ~~at work~~ | By the way | by accident | at home | up to date | in case | by myself | on holiday |

MELISSA: Oh Bill – I'm sorry to phone you ⁰ ....*at work*........, but I really need to talk to you.

BILL: That's OK. I'm ¹ .... in the office at the moment, everyone else has left. What's wrong?

MELISSA: Well, I think the Grants' house next door is ² ....! There's smoke coming out of the window.

BILL: Are you sure? Is anyone ³ .... there?

MELISSA: I don't think so. I knocked on the door, and then looked through the window. The sitting room was ⁴ ...., there was rubbish everywhere, but I couldn't see anyone. Maybe they left the oven on ⁵ ....

BILL: I think the Grants may still be ⁶ .... They went to Spain last week. Have you phoned the fire service?

MELISSA: Yes, of course, but I wanted to tell you, ⁷ .... there was something else I should do. I'm afraid it might spread to our house.

BILL: Well, the fire service should be there soon. Don't worry. ⁸ ...., did you pay our house insurance this month?

MELISSA: I always do. The payments are ⁹ ....

BILL: That's good. Well, I'll be home in half an hour. Bye!

SIMON: I think I'll go down to Newquay **by** coach this time. It's cheaper.

KASHI: But the coach is so slow! The train goes **at** 100m.p.h. The coach takes hours, and you might get delayed **by** traffic jams.

SIMON: Yes, I know, but I've got to write a talk **about** surfboard technology, so I can start that on the journey.

KASHI: Have you been to Newquay before?

SIMON: Oh yes, I was really keen on surfing **at** the age of 20, and I spent a summer near there. It's a beautiful place.

KASHI: I once went surfing in Cornwall – **without** a wetsuit. It was freezing!

by

We use **by**:

after <u>passive verbs</u>, to say *who* or *what* did the action:

■ The shoe factory <u>was hit</u> **by** a bomb.

to say *how*, or *what we use*, to do something, when it is followed by a noun without **the / a**:

■ I'll send the letter **by post**.
■ Emile paid the bill **by cheque**.
■ I prefer to travel **by train**.

at

We use **at**:

for a person's **age**:

■ **At the age of 18**, Kasia went to university.
■ Sam had a mid-life crisis **at 45**.

for the *speed or temperature* that something is done:

■ The bullet train travels **at** 300km an hour.
■ The pie must be cooked **at** 250°.

about

We use **about**:

for *the topic* of a book / story / talk etc:

■ Ms Foster gave a talk **about** Argentina.

for *the topic* after certain verbs (e.g. **talk**, **think**, **read**, **write**):

■ Saleem talked **about** life in Beirut.

with and without

We use **with**:

to say that *two or more things are together*:

■ Lucy went for dinner **with** Juanita and Pedro.

to say *what we use* to do something:

■ You must cut the meat **with** a sharp knife.

to describe the *features* someone has:

■ A tall man **with** a beard opened the door.

to describe *what someone is carrying or holding*:

■ Lorraine was the woman **with** the green bag.

to describe *what someone is wearing*, sometimes with **on** at the end of the clause:

■ Lucia is the woman **with** the blue dress (on).

We use **without**:

to say what someone *is not wearing or carrying*:

■ Martin went out **without** his coat and bag.

and to say what features a person *does not have*:

■ Graham is the man **without** a moustache.

EXERCISES

A

Put either by, at, about, or with in the gaps in the following text.

Last night, I went to a talk in the Technology Institute; the talk was given
0 ....*by*........ Anthony Parsons. It was 1 .... his new book, *Triumph and
Tears*. The book is 2 .... the history of British motorcycles. He is a small,
plump man 3 .... very bright eyes; his wife was sitting 4 .... him
on the stage, 5 .... a motorcycle helmet on her knee.

He said that, although he doesn't like travelling 6 .... high speed any more, he still enjoys riding his
collection of old bikes. He said he started riding a motorbike on his father's farm 7 .... the age of 12! He
said he doesn't normally travel 8 .... bike now because he has a family and, in the winter, 9 .... low
temperatures, biking can be very uncomfortable!

The book is published 10 .... Jardines, and has lots of lovely photos which were taken 11 .... the
author.

B

Look at the picture and answer the questions. Use the words in brackets and add by, at, about, with, or without.

0 How are they travelling? (plane) *by plane* ....

1 Which is the pilot? (man / the blue cap) ....

2 How did the passengers get their drinks? (were served / the air steward) ....

   ....

3 Which is the air steward? (the young man / the drinks trolley) ....

4 What is the woman reading? (a magazine / yoga) ....

5 How is the child eating her yogurt? (her finger) ....

6 What is she thinking? (being a pilot) ....

7 Who is sitting next to the woman? (young man / glasses) ....

8 How is the man opening his orange juice? (his teeth) ....

9 Which man is a passenger? (man / uniform) ....

10 How fast is the plane flying? (530 mph) ....

54 for, from, of

Recently, Ismah got back **from** a business trip to Milan. The reason **for** her visit was to buy shoes **from** a factory there. Milan is famous **for** its fashion industry, and Ismah's customers love shoes **from** Italy. The factory was not in the centre **of** the city; it was in San Donato, so Ismah tried to find the bus **for** San Donato. She was not sure **of** the way to the bus stop, so she asked a woman. The woman took her to the bus station. Fortunately, some **of** the bus drivers spoke English, so Ismah bought a ticket **for** San Donato and got on the bus. It took her an hour!

for after nouns	**cheque** ■ Matt wrote **a cheque for** £55. **train, ferry, platform ticket** etc: ■ Have you got a **ticket for** the **bus for** York? **reason, excuse:** ■ What is **the reason for** all the excitement?
for before example, ever and **always**	**example** ■ Oliver loves rock music from the 1970s – the band, Queen, **for example**. **ever** (often written as one word: **forever**): ■ I would like to stay here **for ever** ■ The universe may not exist **forever**.
for after adjectives	**famous** ■ Torun is **famous for** its beautiful old buildings. **good/bad:** ■ Fresh vegetables are very **good for** you. **sorry** (= *to feel pity*): ■ Paul felt **sorry for** the beggar and gave him a cup of tea. (For **for** after verbs, see unit 80.)
from after nouns	a **person's name** (= *where they live or were born*) ■ Do you know **Antonella, from** Bologna? a **product** (= *where, or when, it was made*) ■ I bought a **violin from** Germany. ■ The furniture was **all from** the 1930s. (For **from** after verbs, see unit 80.)
of after nouns	a **cup, glass, tin, box** etc. (= *what it contains*) ■ I'd like a **glass of** water, please. **centre, middle, edge, bottom, top** (= *position*): ■ The house is **in the middle of** the village. **taste, smell, feel** etc. ■ Do you like the **smell of** fresh coffee? **danger, risk, hope, fear** ■ There is a **danger of** deep snow tonight.
of after adjectives	**full** ■ Jane's room is **full of** toys. **afraid** ■ The dog is **afraid of** fireworks. **sure** (we also use **about**) ■ Are you **sure of/about** the time the concert begins? **tired** (= *bored by something*) ■ The class is really **tired of** studying.
of after quantifiers and superlatives	**a lot, a bit, some, most** etc: ■ Can we have **some of** that pie? **the best, the last, the first** etc: ■ The **first of** the contestants was Cheung.

A Choose whether to use **of, for** or **from** in the gaps in the following text.

Porcelain is the finest [0] ...._of_.... all the different types of china. It is called china because, originally, this kind of fine pottery came [1] .... China. As well as being the whitest, it is also famous [2] .... being the hardest and strongest [3] .... all types of china. It is very expensive, because people love the look and feel [4] .... it. It is used for vases, ornaments and tableware, [5] .... example, teacups. If you are not sure [6] .... the type of china you have, try tapping it! If it rings like a little bell, then it is porcelain. In England, they say that if you drink a cup [7] .... tea from a porcelain cup, it tastes better. In the 17th century, English people loved things that came [8] .... the Far East, and we have many words in English which are [9] .... that time, such as _tea caddy_. If you are careful with your porcelain, it will last [10] .... ever, and it will become more and more valuable. If you look in an antique shop in Britain, you will find it is full [11] .... lovely, old porcelain.

B Read the dialogue and put the right word from the box in the gap.

~~ticket~~ middle come ever some good cup cheque reason sure away

JACKY: What's this, Guido? It looks like a [0] ...._ticket_.... for Sicily! Are you leaving?

GUIDO: Oh Jacky! I didn't want you to suffer any more! I am always in the [1] .... of a crisis, and I can't make any money.

JACKY: So you are running [2] .... from me without telling me? What is the real [3] .... for this decision?

GUIDO: I told you – I am not [4] .... for you.

JACKY: Look, let's sit down and have a [5] .... of coffee and talk about this. What's happened?

GUIDO: No. It's too late. I have never been so [6] .... of anything in my life. So I'm going back to where I [7] .... from.

JACKY: Look, there's a letter you haven't opened, from the gallery. Oh, Guido! It's a [8] .... for £3,000! It's for that portrait you did.

GUIDO: What? Let me see!

JACKY: Look – and the gallery owners want you to show them some more of your work. Let's take [9] .... of your best drawings round this afternoon.

GUIDO: Yes, you're right. They liked it! I'm sorry, I will stay - I'll stay here for [10] ....!

A

Read the text and choose the best preposition from the box to go in each gap.

> for ~~on~~ on on about about about with from of of in in at

A new species of giant squid was found ⁰ ....*on*............ a Tasmanian beach ¹ .... the weekend. The squid weighs 250 kilograms and is 18 metres (60 feet) long, the Australian Broadcasting Corporation reported ² .... Monday. Scientists came ³ .... the Tasmanian Museum and Art Gallery to study the squid; they are trying to decide if it is a new species.

Only two other giant squid have been found ⁴ .... Tasmanian shores, ⁵ .... 1986 and 1991. People have told stories ⁶ .... giant squid ⁷ .... more than two thousand years, but no-one knows much ⁸ .... the animal, because very few ⁹ .... these creatures have been seen ¹⁰ .... the last century. The giant squid is a meat-eating mollusc, ¹¹ .... a beak which is strong enough to cut through metal, and it has the biggest eyes ¹² .... any animal in the world. These eyes can grow up to 45 centimetres (18 inches) wide. There have been several stories ¹³ .... fishermen seeing giant squid fighting with whales!

B Read the travel itinerary and answer the questions.

11.30	Arrive Okecie Airport
2.00	The Hotel Polska, central Warsaw, lunch
3.00	Visit the Palace of Culture and Science (by high-speed lift to the top of the tower)
4.00	Visit the Old Town (on the left bank of the Vistula River)
5.00	Tea (café, in the centre of the Old Town)
6.00	Free to explore Old Town
7.30	All meet: Lobby of Hotel Polska
8.00	Dinner: the hotel restaurant (2nd floor)
10.30	Bed time

0 What time do we arrive in Poland? ..... *at 11.30*

1 Where is the Hotel Polska? ....

2 Where are we having lunch? ....

3 Where are we going after lunch? ....

....

4 How do we get to the top of the tower of the Palace? ....

....

5 Where is the Old Town? ....

....

6 Where are we having tea? ....

....

7 What do we do after tea? ....

8 Where do we have dinner? ....

9 What time is dinner? ....

10 Where is the restaurant? ....

11 What do we do at 10.30? ....

C Choose and circle the best preposition of the two.

MATT: Don! Will you help me make this bookcase? I bought the kit last month, but I have been too busy to make it ⁰(since)/ from I bought it.

DON: OK. There are a lot ¹ in / of pieces! Where do we begin?

MATT: ² In / At the instructions it says 'put piece 1 ³ on / under the floor and put the large screw ⁴ from / into the hole marked A'.

DON: Do you attach all the pieces ⁵ with / of screws, or do you have to glue them, as well?

MATT: Only screws. ⁶ At / By the way – how many screws are there?

DON: Wait a minute – six, seven, eight – and here's one ⁷ under / without the box. Nine.

MATT: Oh dear! There should be 12! Are there any more ⁸ to / in the packet?

DON: Oh yes – sorry. I put the packet in the bin ⁹ by / on mistake.

MATT: Now, where is the screwdriver? Pass it to me, please. It's ¹⁰ behind / into the box.

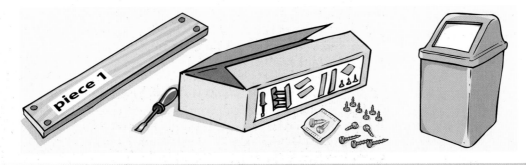

Build up your muscles with the *Miracle Muscle Machine*. **Exercise** with the *Miracle Muscle Machine* for twenty minutes a day and **see** your muscles develop – in days!

Buy the *Miracle Muscle Machine*, **assemble** it in minutes, and **start** the creation of a new 'you'. Captain Splendid bought the *Miracle Muscle Machine* and **look** at him now!

And, at a special discount price, **get** the *Miracle Exercise Steps* and **get** really fit too. **Hurry** – this special offer ends in two weeks.

form	The imperative has the same form as the *infinitive*:

- **Hurry** up! The coach is about to leave.
- **Switch** the light on, please – this room's too dark.

We use **do not / don't** + *infinitive* in a negative imperative:

- **Do not open** your exam paper before the examination starts.
- **Don't answer** the phone.

common uses

We use the imperative to say *you must*, and the negative imperative to say *you mustn't*:

in *commands*:

- **Put** that vase back on the shelf – it's very valuable.
- **Don't laugh** at Isaac – he's getting upset.

Note: we can 'soften' the command with **please** (**Please** put that vase back …).

in *instructions about how to make or do something*:

- **Mix** the flour and sugar in a bowl.
- **Do not take** this medicine without food.

in *advice*:

- **Remember** to take an umbrella – I think it's going to rain later.
- **Phone** the help line – they may be able to tell you what to do.
- **Don't feel** nervous – it's a nice, friendly dog.

when we *encourage*, or *ask someone to do something*:

- **Go on**, keep trying, **don't give up** now. You can still win the competition.
- **Help** me, I'm drowning!

on *notices and signs*:

- **Stop**   ■ **Keep out**   ■ **Don't walk** on the grass.

Note: In the UK, we don't usually use the negative imperative in *signs*. We usually use **No + ing** form:

- **No parking** NOT ~~Don't park~~   ■ **No smoking**

in a *mix of command, advice, and encouragement*:

- **Lose** weight fast with *Miracle Diet Pills*

Note: advertisers often use the imperative.

let's

We use **let's** (= *let us*) to make a *suggestion about what we can do*:

- '**Let's have** a party this weekend to celebrate your new job.'
- '**Let's wait** a bit. I don't know if I have got the job yet.'

EXERCISES

A Use the words in the box to complete the gaps in this recipe.

Pour   Take   Do not cook   check   Fry   Fry   Heat   Serve   Press   do not boil   mix   Use   ~~Put~~

Recipe for 'Steak with Black Pepper and Cream sauce'

Ingredients (serves 4 people)
15 grams of crushed black peppers
4 large beef steaks
50 grams of butter
1 tablespoon of olive oil
1 small, chopped onion
150 millilitres of double cream
a small amount of salt

Method

0   ....*Put*........ the butter and oil in a frying pan.

1   .... the crushed black pepper into each steak.

2   .... steaks in the butter and oil.

3   .... the steaks for more than five minutes on each side.

4   .... the steaks out of the pan and put them in a hot dish.

5   .... the chopped onion in the steak pan for 2 minutes.

6   .... the cream into the steak pan and .... it with the chopped onion and oil.

7   .... cream but .... it. It should not bubble.

8   Add salt, and .... the taste.

9   Put the steaks on plates. .... a wooden spoon to put the sauce over each steak.

10 .... the steaks immediately.

B Leanne is having a driving lesson in London with Mr Bolan, her instructor. Use the information in brackets to write what they say, using an imperative.

0   (He wants Leanne to look in her rear-view mirror and her side mirror.)
    MR BOLAN: *Look in your rear-view mirror and your side mirror.*

1   (He wants Leanne to slow down and park the car behind the white van.)
    MR BOLAN: Please ....

2   (He wants Leanne to take her foot off the accelerator.)
    MR BOLAN: ....

3   (He tells Leanne not to forget to check her mirrors again.)
    MR BOLAN: ....

4   (He tells Leanne to move the indicator switch up.)
    MR BOLAN: ....

5   (He tells Leanne to push the clutch pedal down with her left foot.)
    MR BOLAN: ....

6   (He wants Leanne to change down into second gear.)
    MR BOLAN: ....

7   (He tells Leanne to notice the edge of the pavement.)
    MR BOLAN: ....

8   (He doesn't want Leanne to hit the pavement.)
    MR BOLAN: ....

9   (She suggests that they try parking again.)
    LEANNE: I did some driving when I was in America but they drive on the right side of the road there. It's difficult for me to drive on the left, now.

10 (He encourages Leanne to keep practising and not to give up.)
    MR BOLAN: ...., ... and you'll soon have no problems with driving on the left.

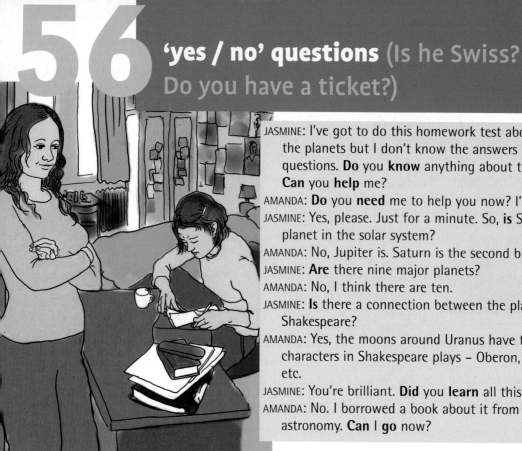

JASMINE: I've got to do this homework test about the sun and the planets but I don't know the answers to some of the questions. **Do** you **know** anything about the solar system? **Can** you **help** me?

AMANDA: **Do** you **need** me to help you now? I'm about to go out.

JASMINE: Yes, please. Just for a minute. So, **is** Saturn the biggest planet in the solar system?

AMANDA: No, Jupiter is. Saturn is the second biggest planet.

JASMINE: **Are** there nine major planets?

AMANDA: No, I think there are ten.

JASMINE: **Is** there a connection between the planet Uranus and Shakespeare?

AMANDA: Yes, the moons around Uranus have the names of characters in Shakespeare plays – Oberon, Titania, Ophelia etc.

JASMINE: You're brilliant. **Did** you **learn** all this stuff at school?

AMANDA: No. I borrowed a book about it from Mike. He loves astronomy. **Can** I **go** now?

be + subject	When we make a question with **be** in the present or past simple (**am**, **is**, **are**, **was**, **were**), we put the *subject* after the verb: ■ Harry is in Sri Lanka. → **Is** <u>Harry</u> in Sri Lanka? ■ This camera is Zahrah's. → **Is** <u>this camera</u> Zahrah's? ■ Sachiko was in Tokyo last week. → **Was** <u>Sachiko</u> in Tokyo last week? ■ They were hungry. → **Were** <u>they</u> hungry? We often use the empty subjects <u>**it**</u> and <u>**there**</u> in questions with **be**: ■ **Is** <u>it</u> exciting living in Paris? ■ **Is** <u>there</u> space in the cupboard for this big bag? ■ **Are** <u>there</u> any good films on television tonight? (See unit 31 for more on empty subjects.)

do / did + subject	To make a question in the present simple with all verbs (except **be**, **have** and *modals*), we use **do / does** + *subject* + *infinitive*:

singular	plural
do I / you **know**?	**do** we / you **know**?
does he / she / it **know**?	**do** they **know**?

■ You know the truth. → **Do** <u>you</u> **know** the truth?
■ Adnan drives a Lexus. → **Does** <u>Adnan</u> **drive** a Lexus?

To make a question in the past simple with all verbs (except **be**), we use **did** + *subject* + *infinitive*:

(Note – with **have** we often use **have got** in British English (see unit 67.)
■ **Has** Juan **got** a beard?
■ She complained. → **Did** <u>she</u> **complain**?
■ Tim bought a new suit. → **Did** <u>Tim</u> **buy** a new suit?

other verb forms	With a *verb + verb*, we put the *subject* after the first verb in questions: ■ **Is** <u>Ben</u> **working** today? ■ **Are** <u>they</u> **running** to catch the bus? ■ **Will** <u>you</u> **be** late tonight? ■ **Have** <u>they</u> **spent** all their money? ■ **Would** <u>you</u> **like** a sandwich? ■ **Can** <u>you</u> **see** the sea?

A

Ros has received this email from Julie. Sidra phones Ros. Read the email and complete Sidra's questions.

> Hi Ros,
>
> Well, here I am in Alicante. I'm working as a holiday rep for a travel company. I've been here for two months. It's really hard work, but I'm enjoying it.
>
> I went to Granada last week and saw the Alhambra Palace – it's amazing.
>
> Here's the big news. I've got a boyfriend – he's called Enrique. He's quite good-looking and he's really funny.
>
> I'm coming back to England for a short holiday in two weeks. Enrique's coming with me. Can we stay with you?
>
> Lots of love,
>
> Julie

ROS: Hallo, Sidra. Listen, I've just received an email from Julie.

SIDRA: 0 _Is she_ all right?

ROS: Yes, she's fine.

SIDRA: 1 .... in Spain, like we thought?

ROS: Yes, she's in Alicante.

SIDRA: 2 .... as a holiday rep?

ROS: Yes, she is. She says it's really hard work.

SIDRA: I can imagine, but 3 .... fun?

ROS: Yes, she says it's fun. And she says she went to Granada last week.

SIDRA: 4 .... the Alhambra when she went there?

ROS: Yes, she saw it. She says it was wonderful. And she has some big news!

SIDRA: 5 .... new boyfriend?

ROS: Yes. She's got one already!

SIDRA: 6 .... Spanish?

ROS: I think he is. His name is Enrique.

SIDRA: 7 .... what he's like?

ROS: Yes, she says he's good looking and really funny. And they're coming to England in two weeks.

SIDRA: 8 .... to stay with you?

ROS: Yes, you're right. They want to stay with me.

SIDRA: 9 .... enough space in your flat for two more people?

ROS: Yes, there's enough space for two more for a short time.

B

Change the statements in brackets into questions to complete this conversation. Add do or did, where necessary.

POLICE OFFICER: (0 you saw the accident)
Did you see the accident, madam?

MRS BURN: Yes, I saw the whole thing.

POLICE OFFICER: (1 you can tell) ....
.... me what happened, please?

MRS BURN: Well, this man was driving along Rectory Road.

POLICE OFFICER: (2 he was driving) ....
.... fast?

MRS BURN: No, he was going quite slowly. Then suddenly a girl on a bicycle came out onto the road in front of him.

POLICE OFFICER: (3 he saw) .... the cyclist?

MRS BURN: No, he was talking on his mobile phone. (4 it is) .... against the law to talk on your mobile phone when driving?

POLICE OFFICER: Yes, it is. (5 he knock) ....
.... the girl off her bike?

MRS BURN: Yes, he did, and she hit her head on the road.

POLICE OFFICER: (6 she was wearing) ....
.... a helmet?

MRS BURN: Yes, she was, luckily.

POLICE OFFICER: (7 the man in the car stopped) ....
......................................?

POLICE OFFICER: Yes, he did, and he parked there.

POLICE OFFICER: (8 he talked) ....
to the girl?

MRS BURN: Yes, but he was very angry.

POLICE OFFICER: (9 he helped) ....
the girl?

MRS BURN: No, he went back to his car and drove away. I helped the girl.

POLICE OFFICER: (10 you have phoned) ....
.... for an ambulance?

MRS BURN: Yes, it seemed like a good idea. (11 you think) .... I was silly?

POLICE OFFICER: No, madam, I think you did the right thing. (12 you remember) ....
the number on the man's car?

MRS BURN: Well, actually, yes, I do. (13 you would like) ....
.... me to give you the number?

POLICE OFFICER: Yes, please, madam.

JEAN: Hi, Rob. It's Jean.

ROB: Hi, Jean. **How**'s life? **What** are you doing these days?

JEAN: It's good. I'm a reporter on the business section of the paper.

ROB: That sounds great. **What** can I do to help?

JEAN: Well, I have heard that your company is making a big investment in a media company in India. **What** can you tell me about it?

ROB: **What** sort of information do you want to know?

JEAN: Well, **what** is the company's name? **Where** exactly is it based? **How much** are you investing? **Why** are you making the investment? That kind of thing.

ROB: Jean, I can't talk about it now. **When** can I phone you back?

who, what, which, whose	We use **who** to ask about *people*: ■ '**Who** was that on the phone?' 'It was Uncle Fred.' ■ **Who** did they arrest for the robbery? We use **what** to ask about *things*. We can use it with or without a **_noun_**: ■ **What** <u>time</u> is your flight? ■ **What** did you say to Serena? We use **which** when there is more than one *thing* or *person* to choose from: ■ **Which** shirt shall I wear for the party? ■ **Which** player scored that goal? We use **whose** to ask *who something belongs to*: ■ '**Whose** dog is that in my pond?' 'Oh, sorry, it's mine.' ■ '**Whose** is that beautiful sports car?' 'That's Tina's. She's really rich.'
why, when, where	We use **why** to ask about *the reason for something*: ■ '**Why** do you like Ellen?' 'Because she's always happy.' We use **when** to ask about *times* and **where** about *places*: ■ '**When** does your plane arrive in Mumbai?' 'At 05.35.' ■ '**Where** did I put my glasses?' 'They're on the table.'
how	We usually use **how** to mean *in what way*: ■ **How** do you make an omelette? We also use **how** + *adjective / adverb* to ask for *specific information*: ■ **How old** is your house? ■ **How fast** does your new car go? We use **how many** with *countables* and **how much** with *uncountables*: ■ **How many** (people) came to the party? ■ **How much** (milk) do you want in your coffee? (See unit 23 for more on **countable** and **uncountable nouns**.)
common idioms	We use **what + be ... like?** to ask for a *description of something*: ■ '**What's** your new flat **like**?' 'It's very big and comfortable.' ■ '**What was** Janet's boyfriend **like**?' 'He wasn't very friendly.' We use **how + be** to ask someone *whether something is good or bad*: ■ '**How are** the sandwiches?' 'They're lovely, thanks.' ■ '**How was** the film?' 'Really boring.' We use questions with **how** to ask someone *about their life*: ■ **How** are you? ■ **How** are you doing? ■ **How** are things? ■ **How**'s it going? ■ **How**'s life?

EXERCISES

A Use the correct question words to complete the questions in this conversation.

TAMARA: So, Amanda, 0 ...*what*... are you doing these days?

AMANDA: Well, I'm still at college, but I'm working at the hairdressers at the weekend, and that's a lot of fun.

TAMARA: And 1 .... are the other girls there like?

AMANDA: They're really friendly. We laugh and chat a lot.

TAMARA: And 2 .... 's life?

AMANDA: It's OK, but I'm not getting on well with my boyfriend, Mike, at the moment.

TAMARA: 3 .... 's the problem? 4 .... are you two having problems?

AMANDA: Well, it's because he likes football and astrophysics, and I like music and shopping. Mike hates shopping.

TAMARA: 5 .... 's astrophysics?

AMANDA: I don't know really – it's something to do with the stars.

TAMARA: 6 .... does Mike hate shopping?

AMANDA: He says it's boring and he's not interested in clothes.

TAMARA: 7 .... have you and he been boyfriend and girlfriend?

AMANDA: I think we first met at Ellen's 17th birthday party.

TAMARA: 8 .... was that?

AMANDA: It was about two years ago.

TAMARA: Well, maybe you need to tell Mike how you feel.

AMANDA: Maybe. But, anyway, 9 .... are things in your life?

TAMARA: Well, 10 .... do you think happened to me yesterday?!

B Use the words in brackets and the words in the box to complete the questions.

will	is	is	's	are	are	does	do	do	did
				did					

ROB: Hi, Jean. It's Rob. I'm sorry that I couldn't talk about the investment deal this morning. But I can talk about it now.

JEAN: Great. Thanks for phoning me back. By the way, (0 what / the name) _what's the name_ of your company now? Has it got a new name?

ROB: Yes, we're called *Investness* now.

JEAN: (1 Why / they / change) .... the name?

ROB: I think they changed it because they wanted a more modern name. (2 What / you / want) .... to know about the deal?

JEAN: Well, I want to know a few things. (3 how big / the investment) ....?

ROB: It's £28 million. It's the biggest investment we have made in the Indian entertainment industry.

JEAN: And, (4 who / you / investing) .... the money in?

ROB: We're investing in a company called *Realspace Communications*.

JEAN: (5 Why / you / choose) .... to invest in *Realspace*?

ROB: We decided to invest in it because we like companies like *Realspace*, that don't take a lot of financial risks.

JEAN: (6 What / *Realspace* / do) ....?

ROB: It makes films and TV programmes in Indian languages and in English.

JEAN: (7 What / *Realspace* / use) .... your money for?

ROB: It will use it for new films and programmes. By the way, (8 which / your favourite restaurant) .... in town, Jean?

JEAN: (9 Why / you / asking) ....?

ROB: Because the directors of *Realspace* are coming here next week and I want to take them to a really good restaurant.

JEAN: (10 What / you / think) .... of Greek food?

RADIO DJ: That was a bit of *Dreaming my life away* by *The Z-Sisters*. And now, we have Mr Doggydog Dog in the Studio. **How's it going**, Doggydog?

DOGGYDOG: Everything's cool.

DJ: Great. This year has been good for you and your band. **How many hit singles have you had this year?** Is it three?

DOGGYDOG: Yeah, that's right. It's been a cool year, so far. And we have a new single coming out next month.

DJ: **What's the name of the single?**

DOGGYDOG: It's called *Give me all of your love*. But I didn't write it.

DJ: **Who wrote** it?

DOGGYDOG: My good friend Mr Smiles wrote the music and the words.

DJ: **What**, in your opinion, **makes** a hit single?

DOGGYDOG: Truth and love and a cool beat.

object questions

We can use a question word as the object of the sentence:

- **What** do you eat for breakfast?
  You eat something.
- **Who** are you phoning?
  You are phoning someone.
- **Where** did Petra go to school?
  Petra went to school somewhere.

When the question word is the object, we need an *auxiliary verb* after it:

- **Whose** (scarf) **did** you borrow?
- **Which** (magazine) **do** you want to buy?
- **When are** you arriving from Paris?
- **How shall** we find each other?
- **Why is** the door open?
- **Where do** you go for your holidays?
- **What was** the name of the hotel?

subject questions

We can use **who**, **whose**, **what**, or **which** as the **subject** of the sentence:

- **Who** likes apple pie?
  Someone likes apple pie.
- **Whose** essay is the best?
  Someone's essay is the best.
- **What** was making all that noise?
  Something was making a noise.

When we use a question word as the subject of a sentence we don't need to add **do**, **does**, or **did** for the present and past simple.

- **Who** wants an orange? I've got loads.
- **Whose** car is parked outside?
- **What** made you so angry?
- **Which** is my box?

EXERCISES

A

Complete each quiz question to make a subject or object question. Use the quiz answers to help you. Sometimes you will need to use **do**, **does**, or **did**.

questions

0 Who ....._invented_..... the sewing machine?

1 Who .... at 55B Baker Street? .

2 Who .... the character, Sherlock Holmes.

3 What .... Mahatma Gandhi .... for in his life?

4 Which city in the world .... the largest population?

5 What .... the two main political parties in America?

6 What .... Marilyn Monroe's real name?

7 What .... colds?

8 What .... the speed of light?

9 What .... 'nanotechnology'?

10 What .... _The Titanic_?

11 What .... bees .... honey from?

12 What mammals .... in the sea?

13 What .... the extinction of the dinosaurs?

14 Who .... the music for the film 'Cinema Paradiso'?

15 What .... a thermometer .... ?

16 What .... we .... plastic from?

17 Who .... the Eiffel Tower?

answers

0 Elias Howe invented it in 1846.

1 The fictional detective, Sherlock Holmes, lived there.

2 Sir Arthur Conan Doyle created him.

3 He worked for Indian independence from Britain

4 Tokyo has the largest population; about 35 million people live in Tokyo.

5 They are the Democrats and the Republicans.

6 Her real name was Norma Jean Mortensen.

7 Viruses cause colds.

8 The speed of light is kms per second.

9 It's the manufacture of very small machines.

10 It was a big ship that sank in the Atlantic Ocean in 1912.

11 They make it from the nectar of flowers.

12 Whales, dolphins and porpoises are mammals that live in the sea.

13 A big meteorite hitting the earth caused their extinction.

14 Ennio Morricone wrote the music for 'Cinema Paradiso'.

15 It measures temperature.

16 We make it from oil.

17 Gustave Eiffel designed it.

B

Use the words in brackets to complete this conversation. Use **do**, **does**, or **did**, where necessary.

MARK: Rachel tells me that you have a new job. (0 What / be / it / ?) ....._What is it?_.....

DARREN: I've got a job as an editor for a publisher.

MARK: So, how do we make books? (1 What / a publisher / do / ?) ....

DARREN: A publisher asks an author to write a book or agrees to publish a book that an author has already written.

MARK: (2 What / an editor / do / ?) ....

DARREN: An editor reads what the author has written and suggests to the author changes and improvements.

MARK: So (3 what / the author / do) .... then?

DARREN: She, or he, makes changes to the book and sends it back to the editor.

MARK: But (4 what / happen) .... if an author thinks his book is perfect and does not want to make any changes?

DARREN: Well, then the author and editor try and agree to some changes, but perhaps not all of them. Then an editor checks the spelling, and punctuation in the book.

MARK: (5 Who / decides) .... what is correct punctuation and what is incorrect?

DARREN: Well, there are books about correct punctuation. Anyway, then the author's text goes to a designer.

MARK: (6 What / a designer / do?) ....

DARREN: A designer makes the book look smart, and clear, and easy to understand.

137

PHOTOGRAPHER: Hallo there. You have a very pretty face. You should be a fashion model, you know.

TAMARA: Oh yes, I've heard that before. No thanks.

PHOTOGRAPHER: Listen, I'm a professional fashion photographer. I know what I'm talking about. Why **don't you want** to become a model?

TAMARA: **Don't you have** to work very hard as a model?

PHOTOGRAPHER: Yes, but **wouldn't you like** to make lots of money?

TAMARA: Not really. I'm a student.

RACHEL: Tamara, it's five o'clock. **Isn't it** time we got the bus to go home?

TAMARA: Yes, you're right. Let's go. Bye.

PHOTOGRAPHER: Bye.

RACHEL: Why **didn't he ask** <u>me</u> to be a model?

form

We make negative questions in the same way as ordinary questions (see unit 56) but we add **n't** after the first verb:

present:
- Is it time to leave? → **Isn't** it time to leave?
- Have you got a Russian car? → **Haven't** you got a Russian car?
- Are there any eggs in the fridge? → **Aren't** there any eggs in the fridge?
- Is Jack playing golf? → **Isn't** Jack playing golf?
- Does Ismah work in a shop? → **Doesn't** Ismah work in a shop?
- Do you think she's pretty? → **Don't** you think she's pretty?

past:
- Was Tom on that flight? → **Wasn't** Tom on that flight?
- Were you angry? → **Weren't** you angry?
- Did they like the meal? → **Didn't** they like the meal?
- Has Ros phoned yet? → **Hasn't** Ros phoned yet?
- Had you met Sanjay before? → **Hadn't** you met Sanjay before?

future and modals:
- Will you see Mike today? → **Won't** you see Mike today?
- Is it going to rain tomorrow? → **Isn't** it going to rain tomorrow?
- Can I come to the party? → **Can't** I come to the party?

Note: we use the verb **are**, and not **am**, with **I**:
- Why **aren't I** the winner? NOT ~~Why amn't I the winner?~~

use

We usually use a negative question to *check that what we think is correct*:
- **Aren't** you tired? (= *I think you are tired. Am I right?*)
- **Don't** you like Rob? (= *I think you like Rob. Am I right?*)
- **Wasn't** Sue in Bologna last year? (= *I think Sue was in Bologna. Am I right?*)
- **Aren't** they going to play tennis today? (= *I think they are going to play tennis. Am I right?*)

We can also use *question words* (**what, why, who** etc) with negative questions to *ask for new information*:
- **Why isn't** Yumi at school? (= *Yumi isn't at school. Why?*)
- **What haven't** we bought from our list? (= *We haven't bought something. What?*)
- **Who hasn't** arrived yet? (= *Some people haven't arrived yet. Who?*)

exclamations

We often use a negative question as an *exclamation with a positive meaning*. We usually use an exclamation mark (**!**):
- Aren't these chairs uncomfortable! (= *These chairs are really uncomfortable.*)
- Isn't Huang handsome! (= *Huang is very handsome.*)
- Aren't I silly! (= *I am silly.*)

EXERCISES

A
Use the words in the box to complete this conversation.

~~Isn't~~ Isn't Isn't Isn't Isn't isn't haven't aren't
aren't Wasn't don't hasn't Didn't didn't didn't

MAYA: Listen, darling, I have some amazing news. I have my own TV show. It's starting next week. ⁰ _Isn't_ that amazing!

ALISHA: That is amazing. But ¹ .... we in Italy next week for the Rome fashion show?

MAYA: ² .... the show next month?

ALISHA: No, it's next week. And, last week, ³ .... you promise to come with me to Rome and help me write my report on the show?

MAYA: But ⁴ .... you say yesterday that I didn't have to come to the show in Rome? And ⁵ .... you been a bit horrid to me? I have my own TV show! ⁶ .... that amazing news?

ALISHA: Sorry, sorry, yes, ⁷ .... I horrid! It is amazing news. But ⁸ .... you hate television?

MAYA: Yes, yes, I hate watching TV. But ⁹ .... it a lot of fun appearing on TV?

ALISHA: I don't know. I've never been on TV. ¹⁰ .... it hard work and very hot in a TV studio? But that isn't important. The important thing is – what do you do in your show?

MAYA: I interview famous fashion designers. My first interview is with Helmut String.

ALISHA: ¹¹ .... he a film star? ¹² .... he in that film about boxing that came out last year? ¹³ .... he get a special award – an Oscar?

MAYA: I don't know. I never go to the cinema. Why ¹⁴ .... anyone told me that he is an actor

B
Make negative questions that express the thoughts in brackets.

GUIDO: This is terrible, I can't find my wallet anywhere.

JACKY: (⁰ you usually put) _Don't you usually put_ it in that bowl on the table when you come into the flat?

GUIDO: Well, yes, when I am out, I always have my wallet in my jacket pocket and then I put it in that bowl when I come in. But, no, no, (¹ you remember) .... that, when we came in, the phone was ringing and I answered the phone and put my jacket on the sofa?

JACKY: So, (² your wallet is) .... still in your jacket?

GUIDO: No, I checked and it isn't there. This is terrible; it has my money and all my credit cards in it.

JACKY: (³ most people put) .... their credit cards in a different wallet from their money? (⁴ that is safer) ...., because then you won't lose your cards and your money at the same time?

GUIDO: (⁵ that is) .... a nuisance, because then you could lose two things and not just one?

JACKY: (⁶ you are) .... silly! You're always losing things. (⁷ you can stop) .... losing things?!

GUIDO: (⁸ you will stop) .... laughing at me and make some coffee?

JACKY: But (⁹ it's time) .... to leave? (¹⁰ Marco's party starts) .... in ten minutes?

139

RACHEL: Hi Karen. I'm a bit late.

KAREN: That's OK. **I was, too**. Have you brought the music?

RACHEL: **Yes, I have**. Here it is. Are we playing the Brahms today?

KAREN: **Yes, we are**. I really love this piece.

RACHEL: **So do I**, but it's quite hard to play. Is the 'cello part hard, too?

KAREN: **No, it isn't**. Actually, I thought the Mozart symphony was harder.

RACHEL: Oh, **so did I**! Some of it is so fast.

KAREN: Have you practised much during the week?

RACHEL: **No, I haven't**. I've been so busy I just haven't had time.

KAREN: **Neither have I**. Oh dear! Well, we'll just do our best.

short answers	When someone asks a simple question, you can answer **yes** or **no**, but it is more polite to use a *short answer*. When the question uses **be** (**is**, **am**, **are**, **was** etc) we repeat the verb in the answer: ■ '**Are** you ready to leave now?' 'No, I**'m** not. Sorry.' ■ '**Were** you in time for the show?' 'No, we **were**n't. We missed it.' If the question uses an *auxiliary* (**do**, **have** etc) or a *modal* (**can**, **would** etc), we repeat this verb in the answer: ■ '**Do** you like this cake?' 'Yes, I **do**, thank you.' ■ '**Did** Mr and Mrs Gopal visit you?' 'No, they **did**n't.' ■ '**Have** you ever tasted caviar?' 'Yes, I **have**. It's horrible!' ■ '**Can** you play the guitar?' 'Yes, I **can**.' ■ '**Would** you like to hear this CD?' 'No, I **would**n't, thank you.'
responding to positive statements	If someone tells us *what they do*, or *feel*, and *we do or feel the same*, we often say '**So do I**' or '**I do too**.' ■ 'I hate reggae music. '**So do I**! (= *I hate reggae too*.) ■ 'I often listen to jazz. '**I do too**.' If we are talking about someone else, we use **so do / does / did ...**, or ... **do / does / did too**: ■ Gavin often eats at the pizzeria. **So does Helen**. ■ Jane left early today. **Maria did too**. If the statement uses **be** or another *auxiliary* or a *modal*, we use *the same verb* in the response: ■ 'I**'m** really hungry!' 'I **am** too.' ■ 'I**'ll** go to the station with Cheung'. 'So **will** I.' But if someone suggests doing something together we say, '**Yes, let's**.' ■ '**Shall** we go to the park?' '**Yes, let's**!' NOT ~~Yes, we shall~~.
responding to negative statements	If someone tells us *what they do not do, or feel*, and the same applies to us, we say **neither + verb + I / you / he** etc, or if it is about another person, we say **neither + verb + name**... ■ 'Peter **doesn't** know how to knit.' '**Neither do I**.' ■ 'The teacher **didn't** understand Frank's answer'. '**Neither did we**!' ■ 'Olga **can't** run very fast.' '**Neither can Kim**.'

EXERCISES

A Read the conversation and choose the best short reply from the box.

No, I haven't	Yes, I would	~~Yes, I have~~	Yes, there was	Yes, it is	So do I
Yes, it was	Yes, there is	No, I wasn't	Yes, it is	No, I didn't	So do I

YUMI: I haven't seen you for ages! Have you been away?

MITSUE: 0 *Yes, I have* I was staying in Kyoto.

YUMI: Wow! How long did you stay there?

MITSUE: I was there for a week. Have you ever been there?

YUMI: 1 ...., but I have read about it. It's an amazing city!

MITSUE: 2 .... I really enjoyed my visit there.

YUMI: Were you staying in a hotel?

MITSUE: 3 .... I was staying with some old friends, near the Togetsukyo Bridge.

YUMI: Did you visit all the ancient temples?

MITSUE: 4 ...., there are so many of them! But I saw lots of wonderful places.

YUMI: It was the capital of Japan in ancient times, wasn't it?

MITSUE: 5 ...., until 1868.

YUMI: Isn't there a temple that is all covered with gold?

MITSUE: 6 .... It's called Kinkakuji. It's really stunning! And the gardens are incredible. I really love traditional Japanese gardens.

YUMI: 7 .... I love the cherry trees. Was there a lot of blossom?

MITSUE: 8 .... The city is full of flowers at this time of year.

YUMI: I think it's important to learn about our traditions.

MITSUE: 9 ...., but not many young people are interested now.

YUMI: It's very lucky that Kyoto wasn't destroyed during the war.

MITSUE: 10 .... Would you like to come and stay there with me next spring?

YUMI: 11 ....! That would be brilliant!

B Match the two sentences together.

0 I don't really like modern music.   a No, I haven't.

1 We often come to this folk music club.   b Yes, I would.

2 Have you heard the band called The Weavers? c No, I can't.

3 Would you like something to eat?   d So would I.

4 Shall we order some food now?   e Yes, it is.

5 This music is really nice.   f So do we.

6 Is Pete coming this evening?   g Neither do I.

7 Are the musicians from Ireland?   h Yes, let's!

8 Do you like Irish folk music?   i Yes, they are.

9 Can you play any instruments?   j No, he isn't.

10 I would love to play something.   k Yes, I do.

0 ......*g*......   2 ....   4 ....   6 ....   8 ....   10 ....

1 ....   3 ....   5 ....   7 ....   9 ....

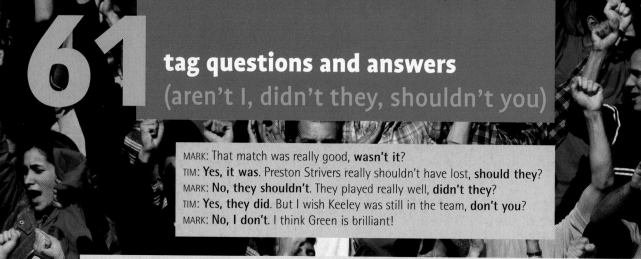

MARK: That match was really good, **wasn't it**?
TIM: **Yes, it was**. Preston Strivers really shouldn't have lost, **should they**?
MARK: **No, they shouldn't**. They played really well, **didn't they**?
TIM: **Yes, they did**. But I wish Keeley was still in the team, **don't you**?
MARK: **No, I don't**. I think Green is brilliant!

negative tags	Tag questions *make statements into questions*. They are asking for agreement or disagreement. In the tag, we use the same *auxiliary* (**have**, **was** etc), *modal* (**might**, **could** etc), or **be** *verb* that is in the statement. After a *positive* statement we use a *negative* tag question, with **not** or **n't**:
	■ It's really hot today, **isn't it**?
	■ There **was** a letter for me, **wasn't there**?
	■ You **could** stay for dinner, **couldn't you**?
	If the statement uses another verb, we use **don't**, **doesn't** or **didn't** in the tag questions:
	■ Charles **skis** very fast, **doesn't he**?
	■ Karl **played** in the hockey team last year, **didn't he**?
positive tags	After **negative statements** we use a *positive* tag question to make a question, using the same *auxiliary*, *modal*, or **be** *verb*:
	■ I **haven't** practised the music enough, **have I**?
	■ The sandwiches **didn't** taste very nice, **did they**?
	■ There **won't** be enough snow to ski, **will there**?
	■ The secretary **wasn't** at her desk, **was she**?
answering positive tags	If we want to *agree* with a *negative statement with a tag question*, we repeat the negative, with **No** and a *pronoun* (**I**, **you**, **we** etc):
	■ 'We **haven't** missed the lesson, have we?' '**No, you haven't**.'
	■ 'The students **don't** like this class, do they?' '**No, they don't**.'
	If we want to *disagree* with a negative statement with a tag question, we use a *positive* short answer:
	■ 'It **isn't** the right size for you, is it?' '**Yes, it is**.'
	■ 'Hari **couldn't** hit the ball, could he?' '**Yes, he could**.'
	■ 'The teacher **didn't** mark our homework, did she?' '**Yes, she did**.'
answering negative tags	If we want to *agree* with a *positive statement with a tag question*, we repeat the positive in the answer, with **Yes**:
	■ 'The house **is** lovely, isn't it?' '**Yes, it is**.'
	■ 'Mr Gardner **might** be the next chairman, mightn't he?' '**Yes, he might**.'
	■ 'Adrian and Lea **work** well together, don't they?' '**Yes, they do**.'
	If we want to *disagree* with a positive statement with a tag question, we use a *negative* short answer:
	■ 'This soup **is** salty, isn't it?' '**No, it isn't**.'
	■ 'You**'ve** forgotten your book, haven't you?' '**No, I haven't**.'
polite disagreement	If we disagree with someone's opinion, it is sometimes more polite to use a phrase beginning with **I think** ... or **I don't think** ....
	■ 'This film **is** really boring, isn't it?' '**I don't think it is**.'
	■ 'Tom **can't** play the piano very well, can he?' '**I think he can**.'
	■ 'We **won't** be able to finish this today, will we?' '**I think we will**.'

A

Read the conversation and write the verb, either negative or positive, in the gaps.

ANDY: Good morning! You're a bit late today, ⁰ ...*aren't*... you?

GINO: I know. I'm sorry. The traffic was really bad today, ¹ .... it?

ANDY: I don't know. I got here at 4.30 this morning! You'll stay until closing time today, ² .... you?

GINO: Yes, I ³ .... Those croissants smell lovely, ⁴ .... they?

ANDY: I don't know. I've got a cold. They look good, though.

GINO: Yes, they ⁵ .... Right, I'm making the sandwiches today, ⁶ .... I?

ANDY: Yes, please. There are plenty of fillings left from yesterday, ⁷ .... there?

GINO: Yes, there ⁸ .... I'll start straight away.

ANDY: And you have opened the shop, ⁹ .... you?

GINO: No, I ¹⁰ .... I forgot. I'll do that now.

ANDY: You'll forget your head next!

B **Circle the best short phrase in the following conversation.**

Mohammed and Sue are preparing for the parents' party at the school.

MOHAMMED: Sue, you sent all the invitations out, ⁰(didn't you)/ didn't they?

SUE: Yes, ¹ so do I / I did. And almost everyone replied. The food has been delivered, ² wasn't it / hasn't it?

MOHAMMED: Yes, ³ it has / it is. It's all in the kitchen. Gary can serve the food, ⁴ can't he / doesn't he?

SUE: Yes, ⁵ he can / he will. Now, I think I'll move these tables over here … There are twenty five people coming, ⁶ isn't it / aren't there?

MOHAMMED: Yes, that's right. So we'll need twenty five chairs, ⁷ won't they / won't we?

SUE: That's a lot! There are enough in the hall, ⁸ aren't there / isn't there?

MOHAMMED: We need the table cloths from the store room. You've got the key, ⁹ do you / haven't you?

SUE: No, ¹⁰ I didn't / I haven't. I gave it to you this afternoon. You remember, ¹¹ don't you / can't you?

MOHAMMED: Oh yes, now ¹² I do / I am. Sorry. Here it is. Oh, I hate these parties!

SUE: ¹³ So are they / So do I!

short questions (Have you? Don't they? Will she?)

AMANDA: Dad, I'm going up to London this weekend with Mike.
DAD: **Are you?**
AMANDA: Yes and I don't have very much money at the moment.
DAD: **Don't you?**
AMANDA: No. I was wondering if you could lend me some?
DAD: **Were you?**
AMANDA: Yes, I was. Well? **Will you?**
DAD: That depends. How much do you need?
AMANDA: Well, Mike wants to go to the opera ...
DAD: **Does he?** That's really expensive!
AMANDA: I know, but I've never been to an opera.
DAD: **Haven't you?** Oh well, all right, then. I could lend you fifty pounds.
AMANDA: Oh, Dad! **Could you?** That would be brilliant.

short questions	A short question is a *verb* and a *pronoun* (**I**, **you**, **he**, **they** etc). We often use short questions in conversation when we want to make sure we understand what someone has said. We also use them as a polite way of showing interest in what the other person has said: ▪ 'I'm going shopping this afternoon.' '**Are you?**' ▪ 'I think we should take Julie some flowers.' '**Do you?**'
after be, have (got) and modals	After **be**, and *modals* we repeat the verb used in the statement: ▪ 'I**'m** terribly late for the lesson.' '**Are** you?' ▪ 'The teacher **will** be very angry.' '**Will** she?' ▪ 'I**'d** love a cup of coffee.' '**Would** you?' When someone uses **has** or **has got** as the main verb in a statement, we can use **has** or **do / does** in the short question: ▪ 'Pino **has** very long hair.' '**Has** he?' or '**Does** he?' (= *does he have...?*) ▪ 'We**'ve got** plenty of time.' '**Do** we?' (= *do we have...?*) or '**Have** we?' Note: in American English, the response to statements with **have** is **do / does**. ▪ 'Carl **has** three daughters.' '**Does** he?'
after other verbs	After other single verbs we use **do / does / did**: ▪ 'Tim **works** in the theatre.' '**Does he?**' ▪ 'The bread rolls **tasted** delicious.' '**Did they?**' ▪ 'James often **goes** to the cinema. '**Does he?**'
after auxiliaries	When the speaker uses an *auxiliary verb* in a statement, we repeat it in the short question: ▪ 'Terry **has** just got back from Israel.' '**Has** he?' ▪ 'They **were** happy to see us again.' '**Were** they?' ▪ 'Mrs Sanchez **will** meet the visitors at the gate.' '**Will** she?'
after let's	After a suggestion with **let's** or **why don't you / we** ... we use **shall** in the short question: ▪ '**Let's** have some more ice cream.' '**Shall we?**' ▪ '**Why don't you** ask for promotion?' '**Shall I?**'
negative questions	After a negative statement, we use a negative short question: ▪ 'You don't need sugar on this cereal.' '**Don't you?**' ▪ 'We're not going to the party.' '**Aren't you?**' ▪ 'I couldn't understand that lesson.' '**Couldn't you?**'

EXERCISES

A Write the best short question in response to these sentences.

0 I'm not going to college today. ..... *Aren't you?* .....

1 No. I want to stay at home and do some work. ....

2 I can't work very well in the library. ....

3 No. It's often very noisy there. ....

4 Ben said he'd come over and help me revise. ....

5 Yes. He will be very useful. ....

6 Let's go out this evening. ....

7 Yes. But I might be too tired. ....

8 And we both need lots of sleep tonight. ....

9 Yes – the final exam is tomorrow! ....

10 Had you forgotten? Oh, you're useless! ....

B Read the conversation and correct the underlined short questions where they are wrong. If they are correct, put a tick (✓).

DAN: Hi Imran! We're all going to the beach tomorrow.

IMRAN: [0] <u>Will you</u>? I'm afraid I can't come. It's Eid.

DAN: What's that?'

IMRAN: The festival of Eid is really called Eid ul-Fitr.

DAN: [1] <u>Do they</u>? What does that mean?

IMRAN: Fitr means 'to break'.

DAN: [2] <u>Will it</u>? That's interesting.

IMRAN: Yes, Eid comes at the end of Ramadan. During Ramadan, we mustn't eat during the day.

DAN: Oh, [3] <u>must you</u>? That's hard.

IMRAN: And then at Eid we break the strict eating rules we kept during Ramadan.

DAN: [4] <u>Do you</u>?

IMRAN: Yes, and we can eat anything we want at any time.

DAN: [5] <u>Are you</u>? I bet you have a feast!

IMRAN: Yes, we do! The families all go to early prayers and then they go to visit their friends and families and have parties.

DAN: [6] <u>Have you</u>? That sounds great.

IMRAN: It's my favourite time. It's a time of peace and caring for each other, and we all wear brightly coloured clothes and give each other presents, and we say 'Eid Mubarak!', which means Happy Eid.

DAN: [7] <u>Does it</u>? Well, Eid Mubarak, Imran! Why don't you come round on Sunday, then?

IMRAN: [8] <u>Am I</u>? OK. That would be great. See you on Sunday. Bye.

0 ..... *Are you?* .....   2 ....   4 ....   6 ....   8 ....
1 ....   3 ....   5 ....   7 ....

145

review 9: questions (units 56–62)

A Read the answers to this health questionnaire and write the questions in the first box using the word(s) in brackets. Sometimes more than one answer is possible.

0	(name)	*What is your name?*	*Jasmine Burn*
1	(live)		*Birmingham*
2	(school or college)		*school*
3	(old)		*14*
4	(get to school or college)		*by bike or bus*
5	(favourite sports)		*swimming and athletics*
6	(times a week do sport)		*3 or 4*
7	(favourite activity)		*dancing*
8	(eat fresh vegetables)		*almost every day*
9	(vegetarian)		*No*
10	(smoke)		*No!*
11	(hours' sleep at night)		*usually about 10*
12	(often ill)		*No, almost never*
13	(last visit the doctor)		*Can't remember*
14	(weigh)		*52 kilos*
15	(tall)		*155 cm*

B Now look at the answers that Jasmine gave and answer the following questions using short answers:

0 Is she called Jasmine Burn? *Yes, she is.*

1 Does she live in London?

2 Is she at school?

3 Does she usually get to school by car?

4 Does she often do athletics?

5 Can she swim?

6 Is her favourite activity singing?

7 Does her diet include fresh food?

8 Does she only eat vegetables?

9 Is she a smoker?

10 Does she get too little sleep?

Continued

11 Is she often ill? ....

12 Can she remember when she last visited the doctor?...........................

13 Did she write her weight in pounds? ....

14 She's quite a tall girl, isn't she? ....

15 Should she change her habits to be more healthy? ....

C Read the dialogue and write the best word to go in the gaps.

TONI: Hello, please sit down. Are you Keith Unwin?

KEITH: Yes, I ⁰ ....*am.*..

TONI: And we have sent you some information about the job, ¹ .... we?

KEITH: Yes, ² .... right.

TONI: ³ .... you got any experience of baking?

KEITH: I'm afraid I ⁴ .... But I am very keen on cooking, and I'm a quick learner.

TONI: ⁵ .... old are you?

KEITH: I'm 23.

TONI: Right. And ⁶ .... are you working at the moment?

KEITH: At the moment I'm working in the video store on Stratford Street. ⁷..................... you know it?

TONI: Why ⁸ .... you looking for another job? ⁹ .... you like working at the video store?

KEITH: No, ¹⁰ .... don't. It's very dull. I'd like to start a real career.

TONI: ¹¹ .... you? Good. ¹² .... you got a reference from your employer?

KEITH: Oh yes, here it is. Oh sorry – I dropped it. I get really nervous at interviews.

TONI: Don't worry – so do ¹³ ....! Well, this reference looks fine. Would you ¹⁴ .... to come and have a look at the kitchen and try making some bread?

KEITH: Oh yes, I ¹⁵ .... That would be great!

D Something is wrong in each of these questions. Write them correctly.

0 What bought you in the supermarket? ....
   What did you buy in the supermarket?

1 Where supermarket did you go to? ....
   ....

2 Did we needed any more milk? ....
   ....

3 Have forgotten you the eggs? ....
   ....

4 We've got enough eggs, haven't us? ....
   ....

5 Wanted Jane some washing up liquid? ....
   ....

6 Are we have pasta tonight? ....
   ....

7 You really hate supermarket shopping, aren't you?
   ....

8 Which bus did take you to get home?
   ....

9 Where the peanut butter is?
   ....

10 You forgot that, too, doesn't you? ....
   ....

147

passive 1 (the room is being cleaned)

GEOFF: Hello. My name is Geoffrey Hardcastle. I think **a room is booked** in my name.

RECEPTIONIST: Ah, yes. Here it is. It's room number 206. Do you have any luggage?

GEOFF: My luggage **is being brought** to the hotel later this evening.

RECEPTIONIST: The room **is being cleaned** at the moment. Would you mind waiting for ten minutes?

GEOFF: That's fine. I'll sit in the lounge. Do you think a local newspaper and some tea **could be sent** to my room, when it's ready?

RECEPTIONIST: Of course, sir. When your luggage arrives, it **will be brought** to your room. I'm sorry for the delay.

present passive	We make the ***present simple passive*** by using the verb **be** + *past participle*. We usually use this form with a frequency adverb. ■ The old couple **are** often **visited** by their grandchildren. ■ Eagles **are** sometimes **seen** in the mountains. We make the ***present continuous passive*** by using the verb **be** + **being** + *past participle*: ■ The minister **is being driven** to the meeting. ■ The new CD **is being recorded** at the moment. Note: we often use the contracted form of the auxiliary (**'m**, **'re** etc) when we speak. ■ She**'s being given** a better job.
future passive	We make the future passive by using **will** (**'ll**), or **be going to**, + **be** + *past participle*: ■ I**'ll be shown** around the office first. ■ Patrick **is going to be helped** with his essay.
future passives with modals	We can make passives with other ***modal verbs*** (**could**, **would**, **might** etc) in place of will: ■ I **might be offered** a job in Spain. ■ Phoebe Tan **could be chosen** as the new head teacher.
negatives	To make a negative passive we add **not** (**n't**) after the first verb: ■ Mark **won't be trusted** by anyone any more. ■ The floor **is not being cleaned**.
use	We use the passive when we want to say *that something happens*, and *we may not know*, or *it is not important, who or what causes it*: ■ My house **is being burgled**! (= *I don't know who the burglar is*.) ■ The dog **is taken** for a walk every day. (= *It doesn't matter who takes him*.)
negative use	We use the negative passive when we want to say that *no-one does the action*: ■ Ewoud's **not being invited** to the wedding. (= *No-one is inviting Ewoud to the wedding*.) ■ Tara **isn't sent** the reports. (= *No one sends Tara the reports*.)
with by	We use **by** after a passive when we want to say who or what the cause (or agent of the action) is: ■ My tea is being brought **by** the waiter. ■ The garden is looked after **by** my son, Adam.
with with	We use **with** after a passive verb when we are talking about *a tool* or *material used to do something*: ■ The walls are being painted **with** a thick varnish. ■ Drums are usually played **with** wooden sticks.

A Look at the picture and choose the best verb from the box to put in the gaps, using passive forms. Be careful of the irregular past forms!

| hang | ~~sell~~ | clean | interview | eat | take | invite | fed | give | examine | steal | serve |

0 The red painting <u>is being sold</u> to the manager of the Fortescue Gallery.

1 It .... in his gallery.

2 Guido's agent, Marco, ... a cheque.

3 When his paintings .... away Guido is always very sad.

4 The small statue .... by the young woman.

5 Coffee .... by Tanya.

6 Guido .... by Marcey Swift.

7 The cheese biscuits .... by the dog.

8 Guido's food .... always by his dog!

9 The windows ....

10 I think Tanya .... out for dinner tonight to celebrate!

B Change the underlined phrases to passive forms.

MELISSA BURN: Now, Amanda, are you sure you don't feel [0] <u>we are abandoning you</u>? *you are being abandoned*

AMANDA: No, it's cool. I'll be fine! Oh, where [1] <u>do you keep the dog food</u>? ....

MELISSA: In the bottom cupboard. Well, we'd better get ready. [2] <u>The taxi is collecting us</u> at 4 o'clock.
....

AMANDA: Hurry up, then! Oh, and [3] <u>can I use the washing machine</u> for shoes? My trainers are all muddy.
....

MELISSA: Well, I suppose so, as long as [4] <u>you wash them alone</u>. Don't put anything in with them.
....

AMANDA: Fine. Off you go. And [5] <u>I will clean and tidy the house</u> before you get back, I promise. I'm asking some friends to stay so I won't be lonely. ....

MELISSA: Oh dear! How many people [6] <u>are you inviting</u>? ....

AMANDA: Only Sue and Kerry. And they might bring their boyfriends.

MELISSA: No, not their boyfriends too! [7] <u>You have never introduced me</u> to them ....

AMANDA: OK. Not their boyfriends. [8] <u>We will tell them</u> not to come. ....

MELISSA: Good. And remember, [9] <u>you must take the dog</u> for a walk every day, at least once.
....

AMANDA: I know. Remember, [10] <u>I'm giving you</u> the chance to have a complete rest. Just relax! ....

MELISSA: I know. Thank you, dear. Goodbye!

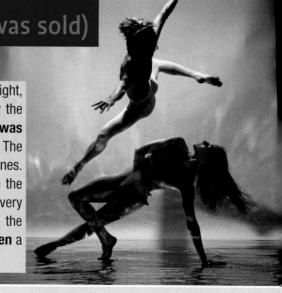

Frantic Dance Company appeared at the Open Space Theatre last night, performing a new piece which **was** specially **created** for them by the great Australian choreographer, Nickely Burke. The electronic music **was composed** by the artistic director of the company, Sergio Avalena. The costumes and set **were designed** by the famous designer, Astra Hines. The four dancers were brilliant, and the story **was explained** with the help of a video projected over the stage. The first performance **was** very well **received**, and while the dancers were **being applauded**, the designer and the composer also came on stage, and they **were given** a large bunch of flowers each.

past simple passive	To make the *past simple passive* we use the past of **be** (**was**, **were**) + *past participle* of the main verb:
	I **was given** we **were given** you **were given** you **were given** he / she / it **was given** they **were given**
past continuous passive	To make the *past continuous passive* we use **was** / **were** + **being** + *past participle*:
	I **was being asked** we **were being asked** you **were being asked** you **were being asked** he / she / it **was being asked** they **were being asked**
negatives	To make a *negative passive* we add **not** (**n't**) after the first verb: ■ Leo **wasn't given** a part in the play. ■ I'm sure we **weren't being told** the truth.
use	We use the *past passive* when we want to say that *something happened*, or *was happening* but *we don't know*, or *it is not important*, who or what caused it: ■ The house **was sold** for £150,000. (= *it doesn't matter who sold it*) ■ Maria was **being asked** to sing another song. (= *we don't know who asked*)
with a feeling or being verb	When we use the passive form with **be** or a *feeling verb* (**hope**, **want**, **like** etc), we use the past of the first verb + **to be** + *past participle*: ■ I hoped **to be given** a car for my birthday.
with by	We use **by** after a passive when we want to say *who or what made it happen*: ■ The bridge was built **by** Brunel. ■ The sea wall was being destroyed **by** the storm.
with with	We use **with** after a passive verb when we are talking about *a tool*, or *something used by someone*: ■ In the past, naughty children were hit **with** a ruler. NOT – … ~~by a ruler~~ ■ The tables were being covered **with** white table cloths. NOT – … ~~by white table cloths~~.
after frightened and scared	After **frightened** and **scared** we use **of** before the noun when we are talking about *a general feeling* or *an event that hasn't happened yet*: ■ Harry was frightened **of** the dark. He was scared **of** getting lost. ■ Don't be scared **of** sharks! There aren't any here. When we are talking about *a specific event* we use **by**: ■ Kofi was frightened **by** the customer shouting at him. ■ The girl was scared **by** a tree falling near her house.

EXERCISES

A Read the following text and write the correct passive forms of the verbs in brackets:

My daughter and I watched a live television programme about sharks last night. There was a diver in a cage who
0 (attack) ...was being attacked... by a huge shark. It
1 (call) .... a Great White Shark, and it was about 4 metres long! The man in the cage
2 (only protect) .... by some thin bars, and there were big gaps between them. The man was trying to 3 (bite) .... by the shark – well, he didn't actually want the shark to bite him, but to bite the fish that 4 (hold) .... on a stick, close to the cage. Inside the fish there was a sensor which measured the strength of the bite, so when the fish 5 (bite) ...., the scientists would know how strong the shark's jaws are. It took a long time, but finally the shark approached and we saw its teeth 6 (lower) .... into the attack position. My daughter and I 7 (really frighten) .... watching it! The shark bit the fish and shook it violently, and then tried to swim away with it. Of course, the stick 8 (break) .... immediately and the sensor 9 (take) .... down to the bottom of the sea, so the scientists couldn't measure the bite. Nothing 10 (learn) .... from the experiment, but it made wonderful, scary TV!

B Read the following letter, and then answer the questions, using the past passive.

Dear Lisa,

I had a horrible dream last night, and I know that you are interested in dreams, so I decided to ask you what it meant.

0 A big dog was chasing me. It was barking really loudly, but fortunately 1 a man was holding it on a lead. The man was quite small, so 2 the dog was pulling him along, but 3 the weight of the man slowed the dog down a bit. 4 The dog really frightened me, and I ran into a wood, where I climbed up a tree. 5 The leaves completely hid me. Suddenly, 6 something changed the dog into a squirrel, which ran up the tree. 7 The squirrel did not scare me, as it was very small. I tried to get down from the tree, but 8 a branch caught my foot, and I started to fall. Then 9 my own scream woke me up!

Isn't it strange? 10 A dog never bit me when I was a child, and I don't think I have ever fallen out of a tree, so I don't understand that dream.

Do tell me what you think it means!

Love,

Cindy

0 What was happening to you? _I was being chased by a big dog._

1 What was happening to the dog? ....

2 What was happening to the man? ....

3 What did the weight of the man do to the dog? ....

4 How did you feel? ....

5 What was it like in the tree? ....

6 What happened to the dog then? ....

7 What did you feel about the squirrel? ....

8 What happened to your foot? ....

9 What happened in the end? ....

10 Did a dog ever bite you as a child? ....

Calling all residents of Terence St!

The house at the end of Terence Street **has been burgled** again! It **has been broken into** three times now, and no-one **has been arrested** yet. A meeting **has been arranged** by the local residents, to see if they can help to protect the end house, and themselves. A man **has often been seen** walking around the area with a camera and a notebook. If you **have ever been worried** about someone behaving oddly in this area, please come to the meeting tomorrow evening in the church hall and give us a description of the person.

We need to work together to beat this criminal! This man **hasn't been found** yet – but maybe YOU can help!

Meeting: July 25th 7.30 p.m. St Nicholas Church Hall, Terence Street

present perfect passive	To make the *present perfect passive* we use the present of *have* (**'ve**, **'s**) + **been** + *past participle*:

singular	plural
I **have been seen**	we**'ve been seen**
you**'ve been seen**	you **have been seen**
he / she / it**'s been seen**	they**'ve been seen**

negative	To make the negative of the present perfect passive we add **not** (**n't**) after **has / have**:

- Julie **has not been sent** to the Birmingham office yet. (= *No-one has sent Julie …*)
- The keys I lost last week still **haven't been found**. (= *No-one has found them yet.*)

question	To make a question in the present perfect passive we use **have / has** + *object* + **been** + *past participle*:

- **Has the mail been delivered** yet?
- **Have you** ever **been interviewed**?

use	We use a present perfect passive verb when we want to say that *something has happened in the past*, and *we may not know*, or *it is not important, who or what caused it*, and *we don't know exactly when it happened*:

- The house **has been sold** to a couple from Frankfurt. (*We don't know who sold it, nor when it was sold.*)
- Ken and Jill **have been given** a new car. (*It is not important who gave the car to them, nor when it happened.*)

with by	We use **by** after a *present perfect passive* when we want to say *who* or *what did it*:

- Tom's puppy has been trained **by** his aunt.
- That book's been read **by** all the children.

with with	We use **with** after a passive verb when we are talking about *a tool*, or *something used by someone*:

- This picture hasn't been painted **with** a brush. NOT – … ~~by a brush~~
- His hair has been cut **with** a razor. NOT – … ~~by a razor.~~

with often, sometimes, never etc.	When we use a frequency adverb (**often**, **sometimes**, **ever** etc) we put it after **have / has**:

- This library book has **never** been borrowed by anyone.
- Voices have **often** been heard in the hall at night.

EXERCISES

Look at the picture and then make sentences using the words in brackets, using the present perfect passive.

0 (The shop / burgle) _The shop has been burgled._

1 (The window / break) ....

2 (The door / open) ....

3 (Something / write / on the wall) ....

4 (Some boots / take/ out of their box) ....

5 (The till / break open) ....

6 (The money / steal) ....

7 (Some footprints / leave / on the carpet) ....

8 (Some shoes / throw / on the floor) ....

9 (The police / call) ....

10 (Ismah / not rob / before) ....

B Put the verb phrases in brackets in the present perfect passive, putting the adverb in the right place.

Claudia 0 (recently catch) _has recently been caught_ taking some food from the supermarket.

She 1 (give) .... the chance to pay for it, if she apologises immediately.

She 2 (send) .... a letter about this. She 3 (tell) ....

that taking food is not allowed. We 4 (instruct) .... by head office to give her one

more chance, as she 5 (employ) .... by the supermarket for ten years.

It 6 (estimate) .... that the company loses ten million pounds a year from stealing,

but things 7 (mostly steal) .... by customers. We 8 (surprise) ....

by this event, as Claudia 9 (always trust) .... by the company.

We 10 (not give) .... any reason to suspect her before. We hope this will not be repeated.

A

Look at the picture and read the sentences, then write them as passive sentences.

0 Someone has wrecked the kitchen! _The kitchen has been wrecked!_

1 The cat has spilt the milk. ....

2 Someone has eaten the cake. ....

3 Someone has burnt the toast. ....

4 No-one has closed the fridge door. ....

5 Someone threw the fruit on the floor. ....

6 No-one has washed the dishes. ....

7 Someone has broken a cup. ....

8 Someone has left the kitchen in a horrible mess. ....

9 The children might have done it. ....

10 Their mother will shout at them. ....

B Read the text and put the best phrase from the box in each gap.

> have been changed   was built   are decorated   was covered   were constructed
> were given   were painted   was really amazed   has been made   was used
> were both developed   were not given   was first bought   be kept

My house ⁰ ...._was built_........... in 1865. It ¹ .... by a man who made

academic clothes for the university. It was a very wealthy time, when the town and the university

² .... very quickly. It was difficult to find information about the house, as the numbers

of the houses in this street ³ .... twice. At first, the houses ⁴ ....

numbers. They all ⁵ .... names, such as 'Isis Villas', and they ⁶ ....

in blocks of three or four, with gaps in between, so that the horses and carriages could ⁷ ....

off the street. At one time my house ⁸ .... as a school, and the walls of one of the

rooms ⁹ ...., probably by the teacher. They ¹⁰ .... with

pictures of flowers, trees and birds from the local area. I discovered this by accident, as the room

¹¹ .... with wallpaper and paint in the 1960s. I ¹² .... by the

discovery, and worked for weeks to carefully scrape off the paper. It is very romantic, and my house

¹³ .... very precious by that unknown teacher's painting.

C Read the conversation and change the underlined phrases into passive phrases.

DAVE: How are the hostel rooms? ⁰ <u>Have they given you</u> rooms with your friends?

0 *Have you been given* ....

ALICE: No. I wanted to be with Anisha, and ¹ <u>they've put me</u> in a room with Gina.

1 ....

DAVE: Well, I'll see if I can change the room for you. Now, ² <u>have they shown you</u> where the bathroom is?

2 ....

KURT: Yes. ³ <u>They have taken us</u> on a tour of the hostel. We've seen everything.

3 ....

DAVE: ⁴ <u>Did they serve you</u> breakfast in the dining room?

4 ....

ALICE: Yes. It was horrible. ⁵ <u>They didn't give us</u> any cereal. There was only bread.

5 ....

DAVE: Sorry, ⁶ <u>they didn't tell me</u> about the food. Maybe you can buy some cereal today.

6 ....

BILL: There isn't any shampoo in the bathroom. I didn't know ⁷ <u>they expected us</u> to bring our own.

7 ....

DAVE: I've got plenty. I'll give you some later. By the way, ⁸ <u>someone has left some dirty boots</u> in the hall. Do they belong to anyone here?

8 ....

KURT: I left mine there. ⁹ <u>They didn't tell us</u> where to put them.

9 ....

DAVE: Well, ¹⁰ <u>you should clean them all</u> when you get back from your trips, and put them in the shed by the front door. OK. Lunch time!

10 ....

66 make and do

The art class is **doing** pottery today. They are **making** clay mugs. The teacher showed them how to use the pottery wheel, and **made** an example for them to copy. Amanda is **doing** an evening class for the first time, and she is **making** a terrible mess!

'**Do** you want some help?' asks the teacher.

'Yes please. I'm not **doing** very well!' says Amanda. The teacher **makes** her start again with some new, drier clay.

'Who **does** the cleaning after the class?' Amanda asks.

'I'm afraid I **do**!' answers the teacher.

make	We use **make** to talk about *building or creating something*: ■ The children are **making** a sand castle. ■ Let's **make** some beautiful music. and when someone *forces someone to do something*: ■ Dad **made** Paul do his homework. and when someone *produces a change in something*: ■ I want to **make** my room look pretty.
do	We use **do** to talk about *general activity*: ■ Fatima is **doing** something very important. *work and jobs* (often with an -ing *form*): ■ Tara **does** the cleaning, and I **do** the cooking.
do + noun	We sometimes use **do** with a noun when we are talking about *something common*: ■ I forgot to **do my teeth** this morning. (= *clean my teeth*) ■ Melissa spent hours **doing her hair**. (= *brushing and arranging ....*)
do as auxiliary	We use **do** as an *auxiliary verb* in questions and short responses: ■ '**Do** you like classical music?' 'Yes, I **do**.' We also use **don't** / **doesn't** in *negatives*: ■ Peter **doesn't** often go to the cinema. ■ They **don't** enjoy helping in the kitchen
do not / don't as imperative	We use **do not** or **don't** to tell someone *not to do something*: ■ **Don't** speak to me like that! ■ **Don't** go yet! The party is just beginning.
so / neither with do	We use **so** + **do** / **does** to say *that you agree*, or *that someone does, or feels, the same*: ■ Priti shops in the market. So **does** Lakshmi. ■ 'Franz writes lots of emails.' 'So **do** I!' We use **neither** with **do** / **does** to say that someone *doesn't do, or feel, the same*: ■ 'I never shop at Frisco.' 'No, **neither do** I.'
phrases with do	**do up** = tie your shoes: ■ Cinzia hasn't **done up** her shoes. **do** (my / your / his etc) **best** = try very hard: ■ Don't worry if you can't finish the question. Just **do your best**! **do well** / **badly** = succeed or fail: ■ All my students **did** really **well** in the exam!
phrases with make	**make** (the, my, your, his etc) **bed** = tidy the sheets etc. ■ Erin never **makes her bed** in the morning. **make a mistake** = do something incorrectly ■ The secretary **made a mistake** in the letter. **make a mess** = be untidy or dirty ■ That dog has **made a mess** everywhere.

EXERCISES

A

Choose the right form of make or do to go in the gaps in the text.

Melissa Burn [0] (not) ....*doesn't*.... like cooking very much, but Bill really [1] .... He likes to [2] .... the Sunday lunch for the family. He is very good at [3] .... traditional British cooking, and he often [4] .... a special sauce for the meat. While he is [5] .... that, his wife Melissa usually [6] .... the beds or [7] .... some gardening, if the weather is nice. The children [8] (not) .... do very much on a Sunday morning! Amanda [9] (not) .... usually get up till midday, and then she [10] .... a lot of mess in the bathroom. Jasmine and Isaac usually help by [11] .... the washing up after lunch. Amanda [12] (not) .... eat very much, as she is always on a diet!

B

Look at the pictures and describe the situations, using the cues, and either make or do.

0 Julian / a big pile of cereal boxes. *Julian is making a big pile of cereal boxes.* ....

1 Paulette / a list of all the prices. ....

2 Kofi / an announcement. ....

3 Someone / a mess on the floor. ....

4 Charlie / the cleaning. ....

5 Caroline / the fruit look nice. ....

6 A customer / her shopping. ....

7 Leanne / a sandwich. ....

8 The little boy / a lot of noise. ....

9 The baker hasn't / any bread yet. ....

10 Louis (not) / anything! ....

C

Circle the best verbs in the text.

Matt is busy [0] doing / (making) the flat tidy, ready for the birthday party. This morning he [1] made / did a lot of shopping and [2] made / did a lot of nice food for the guests. He doesn't often [3] do / make a lot of work in the kitchen, but he loves [4] making / doing special meals for special occasions. He is [5] making / doing the dusting at the moment. It hasn't been [6] made / done for a very long time! The phone rings, and it is Dan, asking if he can [7] make / do anything to help. Matt asks him to bring some candles so he can [8] do / make the flat look nice and cosy, to [9] do / make the guests feel welcome.

67 get

Hi Jen, I've just finished my maths class, and I didn't **get** any of it! Mr Gopal **gets** worse every day! HELP! Did you **get** a message from Darren today? He texted me to say that he is **getting** a lift with his mum and will **get** to the swimming pool at 5. I can't **get** there till half past, because I have to do my homework when I **get** home. I'm really happy you **got** into the swimming team. It would be so cool if we **got** first prize this year! See you later, Bye!

Hi Yumi
Don't **get** stressed about your maths.
I must go and **get** a book from the library now,
CU L8er, Jen

receive	We often use **get** to mean *receive*: ■ Tom **got** 99% in the test today! ■ '**Did** you **get** my postcard from Tunisia?' 'Yes, I **got** it today.'
buy or obtain	We can use **get** to mean *buy* or *obtain*: ■ Remember to **get** some souvenirs for the twins while you are away. ■ **Did** you **get** anything for dinner when you were in town?
travel	We use **get** to mean *catch* or *take a bus / train / taxi / plane*: ■ I'm at the station. Don't come and meet me. I'll **get a taxi**. ■ Hamish **got the train** to Edinburgh.
arrive at	We use **ge**t + **to**, to mean *arrive at a place*. **get to + the / a + *noun*:** ■ We **got to the airport** before Mary's plane landed. ■ We need to **get to a garage** before we run out of petrol. **get to school, get to work** (without **the**): ■ The children **got to school** before the bell rang for assembly. ■ Bala doesn't usually **get to work** before eight in the morning. We say **get** + **here / there / home** (without **to**): ■ Jean and Helen went to the island. They **got there** by helicopter. ■ **Did** they **get home** before it was dark?
become	We use **get** + *adjective* (e.g. **cold**, **hot**, **angry**) to mean *become*: ■ I **get** really **cold** waiting for the bus in the morning. ■ Madeleine **got angry** because Martha was laughing at her. We can also use **get** with some **ed** *forms* (e.g. **engaged**, **married**, **bored**, **stressed**, **dressed**, **lost**), like *adjectives*: ■ Miss Simpson **gets** really **annoyed** when we are noisy. ■ Isaac had a shower, and **got dressed**.
get + into / out of etc.	We can use **get** with other *prepositions* (e.g. **in / into / on / out of / off**) to talk about *climbing or jumping*: ■ We **got into** the car and drove to the beach. ■ She **got out of bed** and looked for something to eat. ■ The robbers **got into** the bank through the window. (For more on phrasal verbs with **get**, see unit 81.)
idioms with get	**get a lift (with someone)** (= *someone drives you somewhere*): ■ I **got a lift** (with Jack) to the cinema. **get it / the message / the point** = *understand something*): ■ What is that man on the radio saying? I just don't **get the point!** **get into a team / a college** (= *be accepted into a team* etc) ■ Jane **got into** the basketball team. **get into something** (= *become interested in something*): ■ Kofi's **getting into** astronomy. He's just got a new telescope.

EXERCISES

A One of the verbs (or verb phrases) in each speech could be changed to the form of **get** in brackets. Underline the right verb.

0 FRAN: Let's <u>find</u> a table by the window. Look, what about this one? (get)

1 ZOE: Do they serve you, or do you have to fetch your coffee from the counter? (get)

2 FRAN: I think you have to carry it yourself. What do you want? (get)

3 ZOE: I don't know. I'm becoming tired of cappuccino. Maybe I'll have hot chocolate today. (getting)

4 FRAN: Good idea. With cream! I'll order them. (get)

5 ZOE: Thanks. Did you buy anything from the shop? You were in there for a long time. (get)

6 FRAN: Yes, I bought three CDs, and a poster of Spidereye. (got)

7 ZOE: Oh, I hate Spidereye. I used to like them, but I think they've become really boring. (got)

8 FRAN: What! Boring? I think they're brilliant! I received their video for my birthday. You should see it! (got)

9 ZOE: I'm becoming interested in Mathrock. Do you like it? (getting into)

10 FRAN: No. I just don't understand it at all. It's boring. (get it)

B Choose the best phrase from the box to put into the gaps.

got bored	got into	getting worse	get out of	got really	had got	go and get
	got angry	~~got home~~	got damaged	getting tired	get	

When Tim ⁰ _got home_ from work he found that someone had ¹ .... his room and taken some of his books and CDs.

He called Julian. 'Did you take my books and my CDs?'

Julian said, 'I ² .... and wanted something new to read.'

Then Tim ³ .... and said, 'You should never go into my room when I'm out. I'm going to ⁴ .... a lock to put on my door. Now go and ⁵ .... my things straight away. Anyway, I thought you ⁶ .... lots of new CDs the other day, so you shouldn't need to take mine.'

Julian said 'My Beyonce CD has ⁷ .... and I wanted to listen to it. I'm ⁸ .... of you being so mean, Tim, and I think you're ⁹ .... all the time'.

Tim said, 'Just ¹⁰ .... my room – and give me back all my things!'

have, have got, have got to

FELICIA: **Have you got** a spare pen? I need one for the lesson and I forgot to bring one.
RITA: No. I've only **got** one and it doesn't work very well.
FELICIA: I've really **got to** go and buy some pens and pencils. I've hardly **got** any left.
RITA: Well, I've **got to** go into the town centre this afternoon. Shall we **have a look for** some together?
FELICIA: Yes, that would be cool. Then maybe we could **have a coffee** in the Espresso bar.
RITA: Great. I'm going to **have a game of tennis** now, then I'll **have a shower** and I'll meet you at 2.
FELICIA: Well, I hope you **have fun**! I'm going to **have lunch**. See you at 2.

have got for possession

British English speakers often use **have got** like **have**, to mean *own* or *possess*, especially in informal speech. American English speakers do not use this form.

- Kerry **has got** a really nice sister.   ▪ **Have** you **got** a DVD player?

We make the negative with **not** or **'nt** after **have**:

- They **haven't got** enough money to go to Barbados.
- Wu Ying **hasn't got** a motor bike.

Note: we do not use **have got** in the past to mean *own*. We usually say **had**.

- I **had** a fast car when I was younger. NOT ~~I had got a fast car~~.

have (got) + to

We use **have to** or **have got to** + *infinitive* to mean *must* or *ought to*:

- You **have to see** the new video by the QTs!
- Hari**'s got to talk** to the boss.

We only use **have got to** in the present simple. For the past we say **had to**... and for the future, **will have to** or **be going to have to**...

- Tom **had to** write 3,000 words about Goethe. NOT Tom ~~had got to write~~...
- I**'m going to have to** do more revision. NOT I'm ~~going to have got to do~~...

other uses of have got

We use **have got** with *illnesses*:

- Jin**'s got** a bad cold, and Len**'s got** flu.

and with *personal features*:

- Paul has **got** big ears and curly hair.

have + noun

We often use **have** to talk about *doing certain activities*:

a **bath / shower**
- The children **have a bath** every evening.

a **meal (dinner, tea, supper** etc)
- We **had breakfast** at 6.30 a.m.

a **drink / sandwich** etc. (= *eat or drink*)
- Let's **have a cup of tea** before we go.

a **walk / dance / swim / trip / game** etc.
- Petra likes to **have a walk** before work.

a nice / horrible **time** (= *enjoy or not enjoy yourself*)
- Mr and Mrs Dalton **had a really lovely time** in Athens.

a **holiday / break**
- Kerry needs to **have a holiday** soon.

a **look (for)** (= *search for something*)
- Mark is going to **have a look** for his gloves at school.

a **look (at)** (= *look at something*)
- Did you **have a look at** the Louvre when you were in Paris?

fun (= *enjoy something*)
- Are you all **having fun**?

EXERCISES

A Rewrite the underlined phrases, using **have / has**, **have got** or **have got to**. As it is an informal conversation, use the contracted forms if possible. Sometimes more than one answer is possible.

KIERA: ⁰ <u>Do you have</u> the tickets?

SEAN: It's alright – don't panic! ¹ <u>I have</u> them. But don't forget, ² <u>we must</u> phone the airport to check whether the flight is delayed.

KIERA: OK. I'm so excited! ³ <u>I've looked</u> at the Ethiopia tourist guide, and there are so many things ⁴ <u>we must</u> see.

SEAN: I know – there are the lakes, and the ruined castles, and ⁵ <u>we ought to</u> visit the churches carved out of solid rock. Ethiopia ⁶ <u>possesses</u> such a fascinating history.

KIERA: I hope the hotel ⁷ <u>provides</u> air conditioning. It's going to be really hot.

SEAN: No it's not! Addis Ababa ⁸ <u>possesses</u> a very mild climate. It's a very modern city, and ⁹ <u>we have booked</u> rooms in a really lovely hotel. ¹⁰ <u>There is</u> a swimming pool!

KIERA: Brilliant. I love to ¹¹ <u>go swimming</u> before breakfast.

0 *Have you got*	6 ....
1	7 ....
2	8 ....
3	9 ....
4	10 ....
5	11 ....

B All the underlined phrases use **got**. If they are correct write a tick (✓) in the box, if not, cross out **got** (~~got~~) and put a cross (✗) in the box.

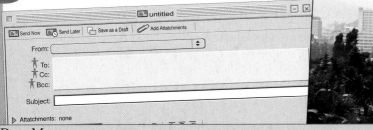

Dear Mum,

I am sitting in the hotel in Addis – yes, they ⁰ <u>have got an internet connection</u> ☑ in each room – and ¹ <u>I've got a beautiful view</u> ☐ of a huge fountain from my window. The flight was fine, and Sean and I ² <u>are having got a great time</u>. ☐ We ³ <u>had got dinner</u> ☐ in the hotel restaurant, which was lovely, and the hotel staff are really friendly. It's not too hot, and ⁴ <u>I haven't even got</u> ☐ a mosquito net. ⁵ <u>I've got to get</u> ☐ some clothes here as the fabrics are so beautiful. ⁶ <u>We had got a look</u> ☐ at the city from the taxi, but today we are going to ⁷ <u>have got a walk</u> ☐ around the centre. Sean's friend Addisu ⁸ <u>has got a flat</u> ☐ in the centre and we are going to visit him today. Then tomorrow ⁹ <u>we're going to have got a trip</u> ☐ out to Lake Tana. They say the country is very different outside the city as ¹⁰ <u>they haven't got enough water</u> ☐ and some people are very poor, so it may be a bit sad. ¹¹ <u>I've got my new camera</u> ☐ so I will take loads of pictures to show you when I get home.

Lots of love, Kiera

If I **could** fly, like those birds **can**, I'd fly to New York, so I **could** see you. But I **can't** fly, (except with an airline ticket, and I **can't** afford that). So what **can** I do? I **can** dream – so that's what I do. **Could** you be dreaming too?

can and could: form	**Can** and **could** are modal verbs. They are used like auxiliaries, to change the meaning of the main verb. They go before the main verb:

singular	plural
I **can** / **could** go	we **can** / **could** go
you **can** / **could** go	you **can** / **could** go
he / she / it **can** / **could** go	they **can** / **could** go

negatives	We make the negative by adding **not** or **n't** to can. There is no break between **can** and **not**: ■ Rajiv **can't** work on Saturdays. ■ We **cannot** hear the teacher very well. We make the negative of **could** by adding **not** or **n't**. There is a break between **could** and **not**: ■ The sea wall **could not** keep the waves off the road. ■ I **couldn't** eat all that rich food.
questions	To make questions we say **can** or **could** + **name or *pronoun*** + ***main verb***: ■ **Can Frank drive** a lorry? ■ **Could we have** some cutlery, please?
negative questions	We make a negative question with **can** or **could** by adding **n't**: ■ **Can't** you see the warning light? ■ **Couldn't** Charlie give you a lift?
n't or not?	We usually use the contracted form (**n't**) in speech and writing unless we are writing something formal, or if we want to *stress the negative*: ■ I just **could not** remember that man's name, though I tried really hard! ■ The manager **cannot** give you your money back, I'm afraid.
can and could for ability	We use **can** to say that someone *has the ability or skill to do something*: ■ Julie **can** dance better than Rachel. and we use **could** to talk about *what someone was able to do in the past*: ■ Ian **could** read when he was four.
can and could for permission and requests	We use **can** to *give, or ask for, permission*, often with an **if** *clause*. ■ You **can** have some more tea, if you want. We also use **could** to *ask for permission*, but it is more polite: ■ **Could we** use the sauna, please? We use **can you** to ask if something is *generally permitted*: ■ '**Can you** park on the yellow line?' 'No, **you can't**.' We use **can** and **could** to *ask someone to do something*. **Could** is more polite: ■ **Can** you tell me the time? ■ **Could** you pass me the sugar, please?
could for possibility	We use **could** to say that *something is possible*, often with an **if** *clause*: ■ Jacques **could** win the first prize. ■ It **could** be slippery on the path if it snows.

A Read the conversation and look at the underlined words, then write what kind of meaning they have: **A present or future possibility, B past possibility, C ability,** or **D permission or request.**

Maria and Frank ⁰<u>could</u> go anywhere this summer, but they ¹<u>can't</u> decide where to go.

MARIA: I think we ²<u>can</u> afford to go to Australia. What do you think?

FRANK: No, it's too far. I ³<u>can't</u> really enjoy a holiday if it takes so long to get there.

MARIA: OK. Well, we ⁴<u>could</u> go to Europe. We ⁵<u>can</u> get to France in a couple of hours.

FRANK: Yes, that's true. You ⁶<u>couldn't</u> get to France so quickly before they built the tunnel.

MARIA: ⁷<u>Could</u> you pass me the atlas? We ⁸<u>can</u> plan a route.

FRANK: Oh, ⁹<u>can</u> we go to Barcelona? I've always wanted to go there!

MARIA: Great! This ¹⁰<u>could</u> be a really exciting trip.

0   **A** ....
1   ....
2   ....
3   ....
4   ....
5   ....
6   ....
7   ....
8   ....
9   ....
10   ....

B Choose the best phrase from the box to write in the gaps on the following text.

| could stay | could have | Could we | can't do | can start | could be | could make |
| Could you | could go | can't decide | ~~Can you~~ | could help | can't earn |

SARAH: ⁰ ..*Can you*.. help me? I have to make a big decision and I ¹ .... what to do! I ² .... and work in the Stockholm office, or I ³ .... in my old job. I ⁴ .... much money here, but the work is quite interesting. If I went to Stockholm I ⁵ .... lonely and bored.

JOHN: I suppose I ⁶ .... you to make the choice. Maybe you ⁷ .... a holiday now, and give yourself time to think about it.

SARAH: No, I ⁸ .... that, because we are very busy in the office at the moment.

JOHN: Well, You ⁹ .... a list of all the things you want in life, and see which choice would make you happier.

SARAH: ¹⁰ .... do that together? That would be really helpful.

JOHN: Alright. ¹¹ .... get a piece of paper and a pen? Then we ¹² .... making the list.

TANYA: **May** I try on these trousers?

SHOP ASSISTANT: Of course, madam. But those are size 44. You **might** need a smaller size.

TANYA: Yes, I **may** have lost a bit of weight. I have been trying! I **might** be a 42 now.

JAKE: Mum, I want a drink!

TANYA: Don't be rude, Jake, I'm busy.

JAKE: Well, **may** I have a drink, then?

TANYA: No, you **may** not! You must wait till I've finished.

may and might: present forms	**May** and **might** are *modal verbs*, and are used, like *auxiliary verbs*, to change the meaning of the main verb. They go before the main verb, and do not change. *Present simple* (with present or future meaning): ■ I **may feel** too tired to go out this evening. (future) ■ Those boots **might be** too big for me. (present) *Present continuous* (with present or future meaning): ■ Phillip **may be coming** to stay next week. (future) ■ The company **might be having** financial difficulties. (present)
past forms	We make the *past simple* with **may** / **might** + **have** + *past participle*: ■ Lena **might have seen** the advert in the paper. ■ They **may have forgotten** the appointment. We make the *past continuous* with **may** / **might** + **have been** + **ing** *form*: ■ You **may have been having** a bath when I called. ■ We **might have been wasting** our time.
negatives	To make the negative of **may** we add **not**. To make the negative of **might** we add **not**, or **n't** in speech: ■ I **may not** have time to finish the report today. NOT ~~mayn't~~. ■ Mr Gopal said he **mightn't** arrive in time.
may and might for possibility	We use **may** or **might** to say that *something is*, or *was, possible*. The two verbs mean the same: ■ It **might** be snowing when you arrive. ■ He **may** have got lost in the fog.
may for polite requests and giving permission	We often use **may I** or **may we** to *ask for something*. It is used in the same way as **could**, and is more polite than **can**: ■ **May I** have your attention, please? ■ **May we** see that letter? We use **may** to *give permission*. It is *more formal* than **can**: ■ Tell the students they **may** leave when they have finished. ■ You **may** pay the bill at the end of the evening.
might for reported speech	When we want to say *what someone says or thinks is likely*, we use **might**: ■ Sheila said she **might** have lunch with Jim tomorrow. ■ I think you **might** like the film, 'Broken Flowers'.

EXERCISES

A

Rewrite the following sentences using the word in brackets.

0 It is possible that the Prime Minister will resign. (may) *The Prime Minister may resign.*

1 He says he is probably going to wait until the summer. (might)

....

2 His secretary said, 'Can I tell the Press?' (may)

....

3 He will possibly take a job as a company director… (may)

....

4 or possibly travel abroad, giving lectures, for a while. (might)

....

5 He has been a very good Prime Minister, but people possibly need a change now. (may)

....

6 He says he thinks he will enjoy having more free time. (might)

....

7 The Press thinks that the Deputy Prime Minister possibly will take his place. (may)

....

8 They asked him, 'Do you think you will be Prime Minister in the autumn?' (might)

....

9 He said he thought he possibly will be Prime Minister. (might)

....

10 Do you think you will vote for him to stay? (might)

....

B

Look at the picture and answer the questions, using the words in brackets.

0 Will the cereal boxes fall over? (may) *They may fall over.*

1 Is the woman buying some tea? (may) ....

2 Does the man at the till have enough money to pay? (might not) ....

....

3 Is Kofi working today? (may not) ....

4 Will the woman slip on the banana skin? (may) ....

5 Has the boy paid for the biscuits? (mightn't) ....

6 Is it raining outside? (may) ....

7 Have they got any oranges? (might not) ....

8 Is the man complaining about something? (might) ....

9 Has the fresh bread been delivered yet? (may not) ....

10 Will the little boy take a doughnut? (might) ....

165

71 would

Swinging on a Star

Would you like to swing on a star,
carry moonbeams home in a jar,
and be better off than you are?
Or **would** you rather be a mule?

would: present and future forms	**Would** (**'d**) is a *modal verb* and can be used in *conditional sentences* with an **if clause**. It goes before the *main verb* and does not change. We usually use the contracted form (**'d**) after words ending in a vowel sound when we speak, and in informal writing:

singular	plural
I**'d** / **would** read	We**'d** / **would** read
You**'d** / **would** read	You**'d** / **would** read
He**'d** / She**'d** / **It** would read	They**'d** / **would** read

To make the *present continuous* we use **would** + **be** + **ing** *form*:
- Greta **would be going** to school, if she wasn't ill.

past forms	To make the *past simple* with **would** we add **have** + *past participle*: - Gina **would have waited** for us, if she had known we were coming. To make the *past continuous* we add **have** + **been** + **ing** *form*: - Ivan **would have been sleeping** if that noise hadn't woken him.
negative	We add **not** or **n't** to make the negative. We do not use **would not** in negative questions: - **Wouldn't** you like to go out? NOT ~~Would not~~ you like …
would in requests	We use phrases with **would** to ask permission to do, or have, something, in a polite way. Common phrases are: Would it be alright if … + past verb: - **Would it be alright if** we stayed for dinner? (= *Can/May we stay…*) Would you / he / they etc. mind if … + past verb: - **Would your parents mind if** we didn't visit? (= *Will they be angry / sad etc. if …*) We also use **would** to *ask someone, politely, to do something*: - **Would** you give me that pen, please? We also say **would you** / **he** / **they** etc. **mind** + **ing** *form*: - **Would you mind taking** out the rubbish?
would for polite conversation	We use **would** or **'d** to say *what we want* or *what we would prefer to do* in a polite way. We often use it with **like** / **love** / **rather** / **prefer**: - I**'d like** some more coffee, please. - **Would** you **rather** be swimming or lying on the beach?
would for being willing or refusing	We use **would** to say that someone *wants*, or *wanted*, to do something, but they *don't* or *didn't do it*. We often add a **but** *clause*: - John **would** come to collect you, **but** his car is in the garage. - I**'d** have bought a ticket for the show, **but** it was too expensive! We use **wouldn't** to say that someone *refused to do something*: - Diana **wouldn't** help me with the filing today. Note: for the use of **would** in *conditional sentences* see units 83 and 84. For **will** and **shall** see unit 21.

EXERCISES

A
Read the conversation and write the words in brackets as polite

JULIE: ⁰ (you / like) to see the menu? __Would you like__

JURGEN: No thanks. I ¹(like) a tuna mayonnaise sandwich and a cup of coffee.

....

JULIE: ² (you / prefer) black or white coffee?

....

JURGEN: Oh – black, I think. ³ (you / mind) if I moved to that table by the window?

....

JULIE: No, of course not. The table is free now. I thought that customer
⁴ (never / leave)! ....

JURGEN: I'm a bit late for lunch. I ⁵ (have come) in earlier, but I had a long
meeting. ....

JULIE: Oh, it's not a problem. Anyway, at lunch time ⁶ (you / not / have got) a
table. ....

JURGEN: Oh, ⁷ (you / mind / taking) the dirty plates away?

....

JULIE: Sorry. ⁸ (I / do / it), but my hands are full. I'll come back in a minute.

....

JURGEN: Thank you. ⁹ (it be / alright) if I put my laptop computer here and did a bit of work while I wait?

....

JULIE: Yes, of course, sir. But ¹⁰ (you / not / prefer) to have a relaxed lunch?

....

JURGEN: Yes I would, but I have so much to do!

B
Read the text and correct the errors in the underlined would phrases.

MATT: ⁰ Would you liked to go to the theatre or the cinema tonight?

SUE: No. ¹ I'd preferring to stay in and watch television. It's too cold to go out.

MATT: OK. ² Would you mind to look at the TV guide to see what's on tonight?

SUE: No. Now, let's see … Oh, ³ I'd really love see the film at 8 – *Chocolat*. It's one of my favourites!

MATT: Great! ⁴ I would bought some popcorn if I'd known we were going to watch a film at home.

SUE: I can order some food to be delivered. ⁵ Would rather you have pizza, or a curry?

MATT: Hmm… I think ⁶ I am preferring a curry. Let's get an Indian takeaway.

SUE: Fine. But the local Indian restaurant isn't very good. It's a pity Hari isn't here. ⁷ He'd to make us a delicious, fresh curry.

MATT: ⁸ Would not you prefer to spend the evening with me?

SUE: Yes, of course! Sorry. ⁹ I'd just love have a good curry!

MATT: Well, ¹⁰ I would to try to make one, but I don't think ¹¹ it would be tasting very good!

0	_Would you like_	6	....
1	....	7	....
2	....	8	....
3	....	9	....
4	....	10	....
5	....	11	....

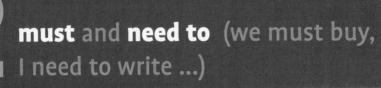

72   must and need to (we must buy, I need to write ...)

If you want to live a long and happy life, you **must** choose your food carefully. You **need to** eat lots of fresh vegetables and fruit, and you **mustn't** eat too much sugary, greasy food. You **need to** do some regular exercise, both for the body and the mind, but you **needn't** become an athlete! You **must** also try to smile and laugh! Happiness is the best medicine.

must	**Must** is a *modal verb* and goes before the infinitive of the main verb. The form does not change, and we don't need an *auxiliary verb* to make the negative or a question. We can use it with the *simple infinitive*: ■ We **must see** this film. the *continuous infinitive*: ■ Liam **must be arriving** in Lima now. or the *perfect infinitive*: ■ Mr Franks **must have given** Karen the job.
must: negative and question	We don't need an *auxiliary* to make a negative or a question with **must**: ■ Francis **mustn't be** late for the lecture. **Must** he **walk** so slowly?
need to	**Need to** is like a *modal verb* and goes before the infinitive of the main verb, but we add **s** for he / she or it, and **ed** for the past tense. We need an *auxiliary* to make questions and negatives: ■ I **need to have** a shower. **Do** you **need to use** the bathroom? ■ Michel **doesn't need to** fill in the form.
must: uses	We use **must** in the present simple (for present and future meaning) to talk about *obligation* or *necessity*: ■ Theo **must revise** for the exam tomorrow. (= *He has to revise.*) We use **must + be**, or a *thinking* or *feeling verb* to talk about something we *think is probably true*: ■ Lisa **must be** at work now. (= *I believe she is …*) ■ You **must trust** Guo a lot. (= *It seems you trust him.*) We use **must + have + *past participle*** to talk about something *we think happened in the past*: ■ The doctor **must have given** Magda an injection. (= *I am sure he gave …*) To talk about *obligation in the past* we use **had to** or **needed to**, and not **must have**: ■ Gianni **had to** leave his car at the station. NOT ~~Gianni must have left~~…
mustn't	We use **must not** and **mustn't** to say that *something is not allowed*: ■ You **mustn't** park your car there. We don't usually use **mustn't** in the past tense. We usually use **couldn't** to say that something was *not allowed in the past*: ■ We **couldn't** use the computers in the office. NOT ~~We mustn't have used~~….
need to: uses	We use **need to** to talk about something that is, or was, *necessary*: ■ I **need to** buy a new toothbrush. Do you **need to** buy anything?
needn't	We use **need not** or **needn't** without **to** for something that is or was *not necessary*: ■ You **needn't** write a very long essay. ■ Dylan **needn't** have done the washing up.

EXERCISES

A Rewrite the underlined phrases, using the verbs in the brackets.

0 When you go for an interview <u>it is important to make</u> a good impression as soon as you walk into the room. (need to)
...you need to make...

1 Your clothes are important, but <u>it is not necessary to wear</u> bright, fashionable clothes. (need)
....

2 <u>It is a good idea to give</u> the impression of being reliable and sensible. (need to) ....

3 <u>It is essential to choose</u> clean, neat clothes, that you feel comfortable wearing. (must) ....

4 <u>It is very important that your clothes give</u> the message that you are confident and mature. (need to) ....

5 <u>It is extremely important to make</u> eye contact with the person interviewing you! (must)
....

6 <u>It is important not to move</u> about in your chair too much. Sit still, relax, and smile! (must)
....

7 When you speak <u>it is necessary to speak</u> loudly and clearly. (need to) ....

8 <u>It is important not to talk</u> too much! Just answer the questions honestly. (must) ....

9 Remember, <u>it is not necessary to tell</u> them your life story! (need) ....

10 <u>It is important that you don't interrupt</u> when they are speaking. (must) ....

11 <u>It is necessary to listen</u> very carefully to the questions. (need to) ....

B Read the conversation and put the best phrase from the box in each gap.

> needed to have   must have read   must be   needed to buy   must feel   needed to know
> ~~must have been~~   must have thought   need to have   must go   need to find

SIDRA: Hi Julie! Wow, you look smart! You 0 *must have been* to the hairdresser!

JULIE: I've just had an interview for a job as a tourist guide in Toronto. I 1 .... and change my clothes.

SIDRA: Well, you 2 .... a haircut anyway. How did the interview go?

JULIE: Well, they 3 .... I was stupid, because I didn't know much about Toronto.

SIDRA: Do you know anything about Canada? You 4 .... something before you went for the interview!

JULIE: Well, I read some articles on the internet, but I didn't think I 5 .... very much. I thought I could learn all that later!

SIDRA: Oh dear! You 6 .... very depressed.

JULIE: Oh no. I don't mind very much. I didn't really 7 .... a new job.

SIDRA: You 8 .... crazy! Why did you go for the interview?

JULIE: Well, I 9 .... some new clothes, so it was a good excuse.

SIDRA: I don't 10 .... reasons to get new clothes. I just buy them when I want to.

MELISSA: Amanda! You **shouldn't** wear those high heels. They're bad for your back.
AMANDA: I know, Mum, but I love them. I think everyone **ought to** do things that are bad for you sometimes! Anyway, they say you **shouldn't** wear trainers all the time.
MELISSA: You **ought to** have a pair of good, leather, walking shoes.
AMANDA: Oh, Mum! You know I won't wear those. None of my friends wear them.
MELISSA: You **shouldn't** care so much about what other people think.
AMANDA: You're always telling me what I **should** and **shouldn't** do! I am 18 and I **ought to** be able to decide for myself what I wear.
MELISSA: You're right. But if you change your mind, I'll buy them for you.

should and ought to	**Should** and **ought to** are *modal verbs* and go before the *infinitive* of the main verb.
	We can use them for the present:
	■ Lacho **should be working** now.
	■ You **ought to be having** a holiday this week.
	or for the future:
	■ I **should clean** my oven.
	■ Tim **ought to buy** some new shoes.
	or for the past (simple and continuous):
	■ The government **should have voted** against that bill.
	■ They **should have been studying** harder.
	■ We **ought to have won** the competition.
	■ Jen **ought to have been playing** in the team.
negatives	We make the negative by adding **not** in writing, or **n't** when we speak, or in informal writing.
	■ You really **shouldn't talk** so fast.
	■ Paul and Helen **ought not to have bought** that car.
questions	We don't usually use **ought to** in questions. We make questions with **should + subject + verb**:
	■ **Should Elmer send** the letter today?
	■ **Shouldn't we have given** the employees a pay rise?
for advice	We often use **should** and **ought to** when we are *giving advice*:
	■ You **ought to** have a rest now.
	■ I think you **should be** more polite to the teacher.
for expressing an opinion	We use **should** and **ought to** when we want to say what we, or someone else, thinks is *the best thing to do*:
	■ Pu Li thinks you **should** apply for the job.
	■ I think Mr Khan **ought to** take a day off.
should for expectation	We use **should** with the *simple infinitive* to talk about things we *expect to happen in the future*:
	■ Tom **should arrive** at six. (= *I think he will arrive at six.*)
	We use **should** with the *continuous infinitive* (**be** + **ing** *form*) to talk about things we *think are happening now*:
	■ Yuri **should be taking** his driving test right now. (= *I think he is taking it now.*)
	We use **should** with the *past infinitive* (**have** + **ed** *form*) for things that *we expected to happen in the past, but didn't*:
	■ The carrots **should have been** ready in September. (= *They weren't ready.*)
	■ Karen **should have phoned** you yesterday. (= *She didn't phone.*)

EXERCISES

A Read the description and write sentences about each point, giving Andy advice about his life, using the correct form of the verb in brackets. Sometimes more than one answer is possible.

0. Andy is very unhappy. He doesn't like his job. (should) *He should find another job.*

1 He has worked very long hours for years. (should not) ....

2 He is overweight. (ought to) ....

3 He doesn't eat very healthy food. (should) ....

4 He doesn't take much exercise. (ought to) ....

5 His desk is very untidy. (should) ....

6 He owes a lot of money to his friends. (shouldn't) ....

7 He wanted to go skiing this winter but he didn't book the holiday in time. (ought to) ....

8 He would like to get a dog to keep him company. (should) ....

9 He is in love with Claire, but he doesn't dare to tell her! (should) ....
.... *(Give your own opinion.)*

B Andy invited Claire for dinner. Things went wrong! Write what he says to his friend Wasim, using the verb in brackets.

0 He wanted the flat to look nice and tidy. It didn't. (should) *The flat should have looked nice and tidy.*

1 She asked for some fruit juice. He didn't have any. (should) ....

2 He cooked meat. She is a vegetarian. (shouldn't) ....

3 He played jazz music on his stereo. She hates jazz. (shouldn't) ....

4 He served a big chocolate pudding. She is on a diet. (ought not to) ....

5 They watched the football match after dinner. She was bored. (shouldn't) ....

6 He couldn't remember her second name. (ought to) ....

7 He smoked a cigar after dinner. She is allergic to tobacco smoke. (shouldn't) ....

8 She brought her sister, Alice! (shouldn't) ....

9 The girls talked to each other all evening. (ought not to) ....

10 But Alice ate the meat and the chocolate pudding and smoked a cigar! He really liked her! (should) ....

171

uses	present	past
ability	can	could
requests and preferences	will/shall, would	would have
possibility and permission	may, might, can, could	may have, might have could have
expectation and advice	must, should, ought to	must have, should have, ought to have
intention and promises	will / shall	would, would have
obligation and necessity	must, need to (have to)	needed to (had to)

Note: for more on **have to**, see unit 68, and for **will** and **shall**, see unit 21.

A Read the text and add the best modal verb from the box.

needs to	couldn't	will	must	~~would have~~	might
ought to have	would	must	can't	will	

Tanya is going on holiday with her two little boys. She ⁰ ...... *would have* ...... left them with her mother, but

she was too busy. Jake ¹ .... like to do his own packing, but Tanya says she is going to

help him. He ² .... take warm clothes, but if she lets him pack he ³ ....

only take toys. Sam was very excited, so Tanya ⁴ .... get him to sleep last night. Now he's

fallen asleep in his buggy and Tanya is in a hurry. They ⁵ .... leave now or they

⁶ .... miss their train! She ⁷ .... afford to use a taxi, so they

⁸ .... take the bus to the station. She really ⁹ .... booked seats on the

train! She worries that the train ¹⁰ .... be very crowded.

B Read the letter and circle the best modal in each sentence.

Dear Gaby,

I ⁰(need to)/ will do something about my boss, but I don't know what to do. My problem is that he is a bully and I ¹ should / would protect the employees he is bullying. I ² shouldn't / can't decide what is the best thing to do. My wife says I ³ must / will report him to a senior manager, but I ⁴ could / need to lose my job. I know I ⁵ ought not to / wouldn't ignore the situation. I work in a travel agents, and I ⁶ have to / would be friendly and cheerful with the customers, but it's very difficult. I ⁷ would / will talk to him about it, but then he ⁸ should / might start bullying me, too. I ⁹ can / will be going on holiday this month and I really ¹⁰ might / should do something before I go. ¹¹ Shall / Could you give me some advice about what I ¹² have to / can do, without risking my own situation?

Yours desperately,

Peter

C Read Gaby's reply, and choose the best phrase from the box for each gap.

ought to be	may be able to	should be	have to work	need to take	won't be able to
should talk	could write	~~must be~~	should do	having to go	might suggest	might feel

Dear Peter,

I feel really sorry for you and your colleagues. It ⁰ ___*must be*___ difficult to ¹ _____ _____ with a man like that. I understand that you ² _____ _____ responsible for your colleagues, but are you really? I'm not suggesting that you ³ _____ nothing, but I think there ⁴ _____ a way for you all to act together, so he ⁵ _____ _____ blame you individually.

I think you ⁶ _____ to the other employees and decide, together, what action you ⁷ _____ . You ⁸ _____ a letter to the manager signed by all of you, for example. Or you ⁹ _____ _____ inviting your boss to a meeting with his staff to discuss the problem in person. You ¹⁰ _____ resolve the problem without ¹¹ _____ to senior management.

Rather than losing your job, I think you ¹² _____ promoted! Good luck.

Yours truly,

gaby

TIM: I had a phone call from the garage. They say they've **finished repairing** your car. They say they've put on new tyres. I'm afraid you're not going to **like getting** the bill.

IMRAN: Oh no! I haven't got any money at the moment. I don't **remember asking** them to put on new tyres. I wonder if I can **delay paying** until next month.

TIM: You shouldn't have **risked having** the car repaired yet. It's always expensive.

IMRAN: I wish I could just buy a new one, but I can't **imagine** ever **earning** enough money to do that if I stay in my current job!

TIM: Well you can't **avoid paying**. What are you going to do?

IMRAN: I don't know. I could **delay collecting** the car till I get a pay rise!

TIM: Don't be stupid! I **don't mind lending** you the money, if you really think you will be able to pay me back next month.

IMRAN: That would be great! Thanks, Tim.

When we want to use two verbs together we use either **to + infinitive** or the **ing form** of the main verb in the sentence. The first verb usually tells us about our *attitude* to the action or situation. Some verbs can be followed by either form, but some can only be used with the **ing form**. These are:

some *action verbs* which are connected with *not doing something*:

finish
- I've **finished writing** my essay.

deny
- Vassily **denied telling** a lie.

risk
- They didn't think they should **risk giving** John so much responsibility.

delay
- The engineers **delayed starting** the building.

avoid
- We often **avoid taking** difficult decisions.

admit
- Guo **admitted spending** too much money.

and some *thinking* and *feeling* verbs:

imagine
- Can you **imagine owning** a yacht?

not mind (= *not feel negative about*)
- Karen does**n't mind working** late today.

miss (= *feel the lack of something you had before*)
- I really **miss driving** my old tractor!

enjoy
- I'm **enjoying working** for the local council.

suggest
- Grazia **suggested sharing** the room with her sister.

Some verbs, like **start**, can be used with the **ing form** and the **to + infinitive**, but some verbs change meaning when we use them with **ing form verbs**:

remember
- Do you **remember telling** me about your holiday? (= *You already told me about it.*)

forget (about)
- Diane **forgot** (about) **paying** the phone bill. (= *She forgot that she paid it.*)

stop
- I wish David would **stop** smoking. (= *I wish he would not smoke any more.*)

(Note: for verbs with **to + infinitive forms** see unit 76.

A

Write what Matt and Sue might say, using the verbs in brackets.

0 Matt says he did not eat the last piece of chocolate cake. (deny) *'I deny eating the last piece of chocolate cake!'*

1 Matt says to Sue he saw her eat it earlier. (remember) 'I .... ,

2 Sue said she took it. (admit) 'I .... ,

3 She said eating it was really nice! (enjoy) 'I .... ,

4 She is going to buy some more after she cleans the kitchen. (finish) .... ,

5 Matt is sad he can't have another piece of cake with his coffee. (miss) 'I .... ,

6 He told her not to continue to clean the kitchen. (stop) 'I .... ,

7 Sue wanted to go to the shop later. (delay) 'I .... ,

8 He thinks she's trying not to buy another cake. (avoid) 'I .... ,

9 She tells him not to be so childish. (stop) .... ,

10 He says he is not behaving in a childish way. (deny) 'I .... ,

B

Read the text and choose the best phrase from the box to go in each gap.

| stop being | regret missing | admit doing | enjoy spending | start choosing | stop working |
| avoid risking | delay starting | value working | remembers thinking | ~~remember noticing~~ |

Do you ⁰ *remember noticing* that someone has treated you badly because of your age, race, or sex? I think almost everyone ¹ .... that at some time. In many countries now, it is against the law to refuse someone a job because of any these things. Most companies won't ² .... it, but discrimination still continues. In the past it was normal. Many people don't want to ³ .... when they are 60, but it is difficult to get a new job at that age. Older people don't ⁴ .... useful – in fact, they often have special skills which young people don't have. Women sometimes ⁵ .... a family because they are afraid of losing their jobs if they take a few years at home to ⁶ .... time with their children. Even though they ⁷ .... their jobs, they often ⁸ .... the chance of having children when they are young.

Employers must ⁹ .... people just because they are good at the job, and ¹⁰ .... with a group of people of all kinds. Variety is the spice of life!

verb + ing forms with and without the
(start the cleaning, stop cleaning)

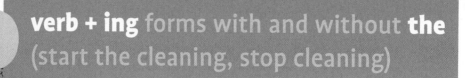

VAL: Our first guests are arriving tomorrow, and we haven't even **finished the painting**! John, you can **start the cleaning** while I **do the decorating**. And Hassan can **do the shopping**.

JOHN: Oh no, he hates **doing the shopping**.

VAL: Alright. I'll do it after I've **finished the ironing**. I've got to do all the curtains and sheets. He can **start cleaning** the kitchen.

JOHN: But Rita has already **started the cleaning** downstairs. Shall I tell her to **stop working** and help you?

VAL: No – oh, I'm getting so confused! Why don't you **do the organising**, and I'll get on with the work!

We often use verbs like **start**, **finish**, **do** etc. with **the / this / that / some** + **ing** *form* when we are talking about *a specific job that needs to be done*. Some **ing** *forms* we use like this are:

verbs connected with the house and garden:

the washing (= *laundry*)
- I **did** all **that washing** yesterday.

the cooking
- Aziz **did some cooking** last night.

the ironing
- Valerio hasn't **started the ironing** yet.

the washing up (= *washing dishes after a meal*)
- Shall we **start the washing up** now?

verbs connected with building and decorating:

the painting (= *of walls etc*)
- Let's **finish the painting** in the morning.

the decorating (= *painting and wallpapering a room or house*)
- We need to **start the decorating** before we move into the house.

the plastering
- Yemi's going to **finish the plastering** this afternoon.

verbs connected with the office:

the filing (= *putting documents in the correct places*)
- Mr Grant has **done the filing** already.

the typing
- Can you **do some typing** for me now?

the photocopying
- I've **begun the photocopying**, but there's a lot to do.

and some verbs describing other kinds of jobs:

the driving
- Lily usually **does all the driving**.

the packing
- You haven't **started the packing** yet. Hurry up!

the talking
- In our English lesson, the students **do most of the talking**.

We use **ing** *forms* without **the / this / that** when we want to talk about *general jobs or activities*
- Wayne likes **washing** his car, but he hates **washing** floors!
- Sobhana does **photocopying** and **filing**, but she doesn't do **typing**.
- **Ironing** sometimes takes a long time.

Sometimes we use **the** + '**ing** form to talk about *the objects involved*, and not the activity:
- **The washing** is in the basket. (= *the clothes etc*)
- **The shopping** on the table is mine. Don't eat my biscuits!
- **The painting** was really beautiful! (= *a finished work of art*.)
- **The writing** on the envelope is very neat.

A Decide if you need to add **the** in the gaps.

Dear Mum,

I'm having a great time here.

In the camp site, each group of campers have to do ⁰ .*the*. cooking in turn.

When it is our team's turn, we have to decide who is going to do ¹ ...... cooking and who is going to do ² ...... washing up. When we have finished ³ ...... serving the meal, we ring the bell to tell everyone the meal is ready.

Each group has to take a turn at doing ⁴ ...... cleaning. Everyone must keep their own tent tidy. We have to finish ⁵ ...... tidying up the camp site before we start ⁶ ...... eating breakfast. I hate ⁷ ...... working so hard at home, but here it's quite fun!

This evening, I have to finish ⁸ ...... drawings I started yesterday. I'm drawing pictures and writing about the plants we have found.

We have built a wooden hut by the river, and the leader has chosen me to do ⁹ ...... sanding. I really hate ¹⁰ ...... sanding wood, as the dust gets in your hair and everywhere. We are going to use the hut for ¹¹ ...... bird watching.

See you on Friday.

Lots of love, Josh

B Matt and Sue are going to have a party. Finish the sentences.

0 Sue has started .*the cleaning*. (She is cleaning the flat.)

1 Matt has finished .... the furniture. (The furniture is polished.)

2 Matt has already done .... (The carpet is swept.)

3 Sue did .... yesterday. (She's already been to the shop and bought the food.)

4 Matt and Sue are going to do .... (The food must be cooked.)

5 Matt did .... after lunch. (The dishes are washed.)

6 Sue hasn't finished .... the floor. (The floor is not washed yet.)

7 Matt has nearly finished .... everyone. (He has nearly emailed everyone.)

8 Sue probably won't dust the sitting room because she doesn't like .... (She doesn't want to dust the sitting room.)

9 They will start .... the furniture when she has finished cleaning. (The furniture is not moved yet.)

10 When they have finished .... everything for the party, they're going to sit down with a nice cup of tea! (When the preparations for the party are done, they're going to rest.)

177

RAJIV: Hello, Mr Jennings. You're going to be interviewed by Baz Harrington, aren't you? I'm going to try to **help you to prepare** for the interview. Now, I **want you to relax** and think about how you want to appear in the interview. **Would you like the audience to respect** you, or **would you prefer them to feel** sympathy for you? If you want to **persuade the viewers to support** your point of view you must believe in it yourself, and then just be honest. I'm going to **teach you to speak** slowly and clearly, because you **can't expect anyone to agree** if they can't understand you. Well, let's make a start...

verb (+ object) + to *infinitive*	Some verbs can have an *object* before a **to *infinitive***, but we can also use them without, depending on the meaning. These are verbs which refer to *how we feel about something in the future*.

want
- Joe **wants to come** to London next week.
- Tim **wants Joe to come** to London tomorrow.

expect
- Sarah **expects to arrive** at 7.
- Sarah **expects her dad to meet** her at the airport.

need
- Yuko **needs to have** a holiday.
- Yuko **needs Mr Gomez to let** her have a week off work.

would prefer
- **Would you prefer to travel** by car?   ■ **I'd prefer you to walk.**

would like / love / hate / prefer
- **I'd love to come** to your birthday party.
- **We'd prefer the children to go** to bed earlier.
- **I would hate to be** late.   ■ I **would hate you to miss** the concert.

Note: we can use **ask** and a **to *infinitive*** with or without an *object* when we are talking about *requests or permission to do something*:
- Jenny **asked to go** home. (She said, *'Can I go home?'*)
- Mrs Downs **asked Igor to help** her. (She said, *'Help me, please, Igor.'*)

influence verbs	After verbs which we use to talk about *influencing the future*, we need an *object* before the **to *infinitive***:

tell
- My teacher told **me** to stop talking.

teach
- Mr Jardine taught **his son** to ride a bicycle.

encourage
- Bill is going to encourage **Jasmine** to clean her room.

force
- I forced **the horse** to jump over the fence.

help
- Shall I help **you** to write the application?

remind
- Please remind **Gary** to bring his sports equipment tomorrow.

send
- Mrs Forest sent **Yuko** to buy some more printer paper.

EXERCISES

A

Choose the best phrase from the box to put in each gap.

> ~~want me~~   tell the school   remind you   ask the teacher   expect me
> force you   'd love you   encourage you   prefer you   want them   need you

JASMINE: Don't you ⁰ _want me_ to learn to ride properly? I really need to have some lessons.

MELISSA: Of course ¹ .... to become a good horsewoman. I didn't want to ² .... to have lessons, but if you're keen….

JASMINE: Great! So I can start next week? I ³ .... to teach me to jump, and do all those things they do in the competitions.

MELISSA: Yes but you have to start with the basics. I'll ⁴ .... to book you into the beginner's course.

JASMINE: But won't that be boring? I'd ⁵ .... to book me into a higher level. I already know how to ride, a bit.

MELISSA: But you haven't ridden in years. I really think it would be better to start at the beginning. You need someone to ⁶ .... how to do it properly. If you do really well it will ⁷ .... to continue.

JASMINE: Oh, alright then. But I'll ⁸ .... to buy me some riding clothes. They will ⁹ .... to have proper boots and those special trousers. I think they're called jodhpurs…

MELISSA: I know. Maybe I can get them second-hand. I'll phone the school and ¹⁰ .... to recommend a good shop.

B

Read the conversation and then answer the questions, using phrases from the text.

POLLY: We're opening for business next week and I think we should ⁰ invite some important people to come and celebrate with us. We could tell the local newspaper to ¹ send someone to take some photographs of the party.

HENRY: Oh, I don't know. I think I'd ² prefer us to concentrate on the business. ³ A party would cost an awful lot.

POLLY: But it would be worth it. You can't ⁴ expect people to make bookings if they don't know anything about the new hotel. We really ⁵ need the press to take an interest in us, and this would be a good way to do it.

HENRY: Well, yes, I suppose so – but wouldn't it be cheaper to ⁶ ask the local paper to put an advertisement in the next edition?

POLLY: Maybe, but it wouldn't be as much fun. But I'm not going to ⁷ force you to have a party, if you really don't want to.

HENRY: It's not that I don't want us to celebrate. But people will ⁸ expect us to provide champagne and expensive food, and we really don't have the money.

POLLY: But that will help us to make the money, don't you see? Oh, come on, darling! I'd ⁹ hate us to think we'd wasted an opportunity for free publicity.

HENRY: But it's not free! Oh – alright, if you insist. I'll ¹⁰ ask Lord and Lady Hampton-Grieves to come, and to bring all their smart friends. You contact the photographer.

0 Who does Polly want to invite to the celebration? _some important people._

1 What does she want to tell the local paper to do? ....

2 What would Henry prefer to do? ....

3 Why? ....

4 What can't you expect people to do? ....

5 What does she need to the press to do? ....

6 What does he want her to ask the local paper to do? ....

7 Is Polly going to force Henry to have a party? ....

8 What does Henry think people will expect? ....

9 What would Polly hate to think? ....

10 Who is Henry going to invite? ....

Leila **brought her husband, Hamid, some water**. He handed her the spade, and said, 'I think you should **show Ahmad how** to prepare the ground for planting. We will **leave him the farm** one day, and he must know how to run it. He's old enough now.'

Leila sighed. 'But Hamid, our son doesn't want us to **teach him anything**. He is much more interested in studying from books. He even **wrote his teacher a letter** asking her to **send him some books** during the holidays.'

Hamid smiled. 'Yes, he is a clever boy. But he can study in the evening, and we can **teach him everything** he needs to know about farming during the day. Go on, **give him the spade!**'

'Alright, Hamid. Now, Ahmad my dear, put that book away and listen to me....'

After some verbs we can use two *objects*:

subject	verb	object	object
■ Danila	writes	Graham	emails. (= *Danila writes emails to Graham.*)
■ I	sang	the baby	a song. (= *I sang a song to the baby.*)

We can use two *objects* after verbs when we want to talk about *communicating something to someone*:

read
- ■ Bogdan **told Marya some exciting news**.

teach
- ■ Mr Holt **teaches the children music**.

read (aloud)
- ■ Their teacher usually **reads the children a story** in the afternoon.

ask (for information)
- ■ I **asked the inspector the time**.

write (a letter, an email etc)
- ■ We **wrote Jim letters** while he was away.

or *giving something to someone or doing something for someone*:

give
- ■ Junani **gave Steve some more paper**.

offer
- ■ They **offered all the employees a pay rise**.

send
- ■ The bank **sends the customers statements** every month.

get/buy
- ■ I've **got you a present! I bought you a box of chocolates**.

order
- ■ Will you **order me a cheese salad**, please?

sing/play (a musical performance)
- ■ Ros **sang us a beautiful song**, and Richard **played us some jazz**.

pass
- ■ **Pass me the sugar**, please.

bring
- ■ The postman **brought me a parcel**.

sell
- ■ My grandfather **sold the tourists all his old tools** when he retired.

pour/cut
- ■ Lucy **poured Simon some coffee**, and **cut him a slice of bread**.

serve
- ■ They **served us potato soup** for lunch.

Note: we don't usually use a *pronoun* for the *second object*. We usually use a preposition (to, for):
- ■ David sent **it to Paul**. NOT ~~David sent Paul it~~.

When we talk about *doing something for ourselves* we use the *reflexive pronoun* (**myself, yourself, himself** etc) as the first *object*:
- ■ I bought **myself** some new shoes. NOT ~~I bought me some new shoes~~.

A Read the sentences and write what each person says, using the verbs in brackets and with two objects.

0 Phil needs Jack to give the sugar to him. Phil says:
'Will you pass me the sugar, please,'
Jack? .... (will, pass)

1 Phil wants him to pass the salt to him, too. Phil says: ....
.... (give)

2 Yung needs some water. Phil asks Jack: ....
.... (could, pour)

3 Bill would like a slice of bread. Bill asks Phil: ....
.... (cut)

4 Jack thinks they will bring some soup for them next. Jack says: ....
.... (will, serve)

5 Jack knows Bill doesn't want any soup. Jack says to the waiter: ....
.... (not, offer)

6 Yung wants to know what the main course is. Yung asks the waiter: ....
.... (could, tell)

7 Phil sees that the waiter has forgotten to bring any spoons. Phil asks the waiter: ....
.... (bring)

8 Bill would like to know the recipe for this soup. Bill asks the waiter: ....
.... (can, teach)

9 Phil doesn't want the waiter to take his bowl away. Phil says to the waiter: ....
.... (will, leave)

10 Jack thinks it is time to pay the bill now. Jack asks the waiter: ....
.... (could, bring)

B Read the conversation and rewrite the underlined phrases, using the verb and two objects.

TIM: Hi Matt. Hi Zara. Have you [0] ordered anything for me?

MATT: No. I didn't know if you were coming. I just [1] got a sandwich for myself.

TIM: That's OK. I'll [2] buy something for myself later. Has Don [3] sent a letter to you?

MATT: Yes! I was just [4] reading what he wrote to Zara.

TIM: When did Don [5] write that letter to you?

MATT: It was when he was in Botswana. They've [6] offered a job to him, in a hospital there!

TIM: Did he accept it? I thought he was back in England.

MATT: Yes, I think he is, but I haven't seen him yet. He says he's [7] bought presents for us all in Africa.

ZARA: Great! He said he was going to [8] bring an African drum for me.

TIM: He's accepted the job, but he's not starting till September. Let's [9] give a big goodbye party to him.

ZARA: Good idea! But I'm going to miss him.

0 *ordered me anything*
1 ....
2 ....
3 ....
4 ....
5 ....
6 ....
7 ....
8 ....
9 ....

78

verb + what, where, that etc.
(Do you know where Tom lives?)

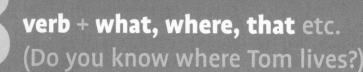

GUIDO: Do you **remember when** you first came to work for me?

TANYA: Yes. I **thought that** you were very frightening. I didn't **know how** I could clean this studio. I couldn't **tell what** was rubbish and what was valuable art!

GUIDO: I know. I didn't **know why** you seemed so unfriendly. But then I **realised how** difficult it was for you. It wasn't an ordinary cleaning job.

TANYA: No, that's true. And I didn't **understand what** you were trying to do. But now I can see which paintings are important. And I really **like what** you are doing.

GUIDO: Good. And fortunately the art dealers agree with you. Thank you, Tanya.

After *feeling* and *thinking verbs* we can use a *question word*. The phrase beginning with this word is the *object* of the first verb, and is a statement, not a question.

subject	verb	object
Olga	saw	**who** you were talking to. (= *Olga saw **the person** you were talking to.*)
Marcus	likes	**what** Dina is wearing. (= *Marcus likes **the clothes** Dina is wearing.*)

After *feeling* verbs we can use **where** (*the place*), **what** (*the thing or things*), and **how** (*the way*):

feel
- I'm sure Brad feels **what** you feel.

love
- Maria loves **what** her mother gave her for her birthday.

prefer
- Jamila prefers **where** she lives now.

like
- Andy didn't like **how** Yumi was behaving.

hate
- Mr Gupta hates **what** the local council has decided to do.

After *thinking verbs* we can <u>also</u> use **who** (*the person*), **which** (*a choice of thing or person*), **when** (*the time*), **why** (*the reason*) and **that** (*followed by a fact*). For example:

know
- I **know why** Julia is phoning Juan.

learn
- Ahmad must **learn that** farming can be very interesting.

hear (= *learn*)
- Have you **heard which** candidate has won the election?

forget
- Bob has **forgotten when** he's going to the theatre.

understand / say
- Shane can't **understand why** he didn't pass his exam.
- He wouldn't **say why** he failed

realise / discover
- Guido realised **why** Tanya was so nervous.

guess
- Geraint tried to **guess which** bus to catch.

see (= *perceive*)
- The referee **saw which** footballer touched the ball.

remember
- Do you **remember how** to do quadratic equations?

tell (= *perceive, know*)
- You can't **tell that** the actor is German.

- Guido realised **that** Tanya was nervous.

Note: after these verbs we can omit **that**:
- I know **that** you are right. (= *I know you are right.*)

Note: we can also use **how + long** (*time*), **much / many** (*quantity*), **good / bad** (*quality*), **big / small** (*size*) etc, but the phrase after it must be a statement (*subject + verb*), not a question (*verb + subject*):
- Lars forgot **how long** the journey was. NOT ~~Lars forgot **how long** was the journey~~.

EXERCISES

A

Read the text and choose the best item from the box to go in each gap.

| ~~that~~ | how big | which | why | what | which | that | where | how | that | what |

Watching English language television or listening to the radio is very useful for students. You will quickly discover
⁰ _that_ there are many different ways to pronounce English words. If you watch a lot of television you will begin
to understand ¹ .... people are saying, and you will realise ² .... you can guess ³ ....
someone comes from by the way they speak. It is fun learning ⁴ .... to recognise accents from different
nationalities and regions. It is often difficult to tell ⁵ .... country pop singers come from, because they
usually sing with an American accent, even if they are not American. Some people used to think ⁶ .... it was
more 'cool', but that is changing now.

Students usually study either British or American English, and it is helpful to understand ⁷ .... you don't
understand something. One English speaker sometimes find it difficult to understand ⁸ .... an English
speaker from another area is saying. Students need to learn ⁹ .... the regional differences are. Even different
parts of Britain and America have different pronunciation. It doesn't usually matter ¹⁰ .... type of English you
use, as long as people can understand you!

B

Look at the underlined phrases, and replace them with that, what, where, when, why or how.

SERGEANT AHMED: Mrs Burn, can you remember ⁰ <u>the reason</u> you called the police?

MRS BURN: Because I have been robbed. But I have forgotten exactly ¹ <u>the place</u> I was when the man attacked me. I am too shocked!

SERGEANT AHMED: Never mind. I'm sure some other people saw ² <u>the thing that</u> happened. Can you remember ³ <u>the clothes that</u> he was wearing?

MRS BURN: Yes — I know exactly ⁴ <u>the way</u> he was dressed, because it was so strange. He was wearing a panda suit! I don't know ⁵ <u>in what way</u> he managed to run so fast!

SERGEANT AHMED: A panda suit? Do you know ⁶ <u>the reason</u> he was wearing a panda suit?

MRS BURN: I suppose so he couldn't be recognised. But I could see ⁷ <u>the fact</u> he was a young, white man, from his hands.

SERGEANT AHMED: And do you know ⁸ <u>the amount</u> he stole from you?

MRS BURN: Well, he took my bag, and I think there was about £25 in it, and my driving licence and everything. He shouted something, but I couldn't hear ⁹ <u>the thing that</u> he said, because of the mask on his face.

SERGEANT AHMED: Could you see ¹⁰ <u>the place</u> he ran to?

MRS BURN: Yes — he ran off through Kennet's Park. I really hope you catch him!

0 _why_	1	2	3 ....
4	5	6	7 ....
8	9	10	

A lot of wild boar have been released from a farm in the west of England. The farmer was not **responsible for** the escape. It was animal rights protesters, who felt **sorry for** the wild animals and thought it would be **kinder to** them to let them go free. Local people have been quite **frightened by** these animals, which can be **dangerous to** people if the animals feel threatened. The press have been very **interested in** the story, as several people have been **surprised by** the sight of wild boar walking about the English countryside. The farmer says he is very **angry with** the protesters. He says it was **stupid of** them because now many of the boar have been shot. But the protesters are **not ashamed of** what they did, as they say the boar would have been killed for meat, anyway.

adjective + of

We use *adjective* + **of** to talk about *how someone feels about something*:
- Dagmar is **afraid of** mice.
- Roxanna seems very **fond of** shopping.
- Jamie feels **ashamed of** his old car.

We often use **it** + **be** (am, was etc) + *adjective* + **of** to talk about *someone's behaviour*:
- It was very **kind of Sylvie** to lend me her brush.
- It's **nice of you** to talk to Dennis.
- It would be **rude of Jarred** not to reply to the invitation.

We also use **of** after **short**, **full**, and **capable**:
- I'm a bit **short of** money. (= *I don't have much money*.)
- The bath is **full of** bubbles.
- Pietro isn't **capable of** being cruel.

adjective + to

We use *adjective* + **to** to talk about *someone's behaviour to someone*:
- Sylvie was **kind to** me.
- You are very **polite to** Dennis.
- Jarred wasn't **rude to** anyone.

We use *adjective* + **to infinitive** to talk about *something leading to an action*:
- We are all **ready to leave** now.
- Pablo was **able to read** Arabic script.
- The horses were **keen to start** the race.

We also use **to** after **married** and **engaged**:
- I thought Pat was **married to** Jim, but she's just **engaged to** him.

After **different** we can use **from** or, **to** with the same meaning:
- Your house is very **different from** / **to** mine.

adjective + with

We use *adjective* + **with** to talk about *someone's emotional response to something*:
- The managers are very **pleased with** the staff.
- Fidor is **angry with** his landlord.
- Soo Li was **happy with** the result of the test.

We also use **with** after **bored** and **crowded**:
- Ling is **bored with** watching television.
- I hate it when the train is **crowded with** people.

adjective + by

We use *past participle* + **by** to talk about the *cause of someone's feelings*:
- I hope you're not **depressed by** the bad news.
- The audience was **excited by** his brilliant performance.

but after **interested** we use **in**:
- Are you **interested in** nuclear physics?

adjective + at

We use **at** after **good** / **bad** etc. to talk about *abilities*:
- The students are **brilliant at** grammar.
- Riva is really **bad at** sports.

adjective + for

We use **for** after **responsible** and **famous**:
- The dog's owner is **responsible for** its behaviour.
- Natalia is **famous for** her role in the film 'Grace'.

EXERCISES

A

Circle the best preposition in the dialogue.

TONI: It was Keith's first day today and I am quite pleased ⁰ (with) / at him. He is not very good ¹ at / for baking yet, but he is very nice ² to / of the customers. He said he was really bored ³ with / of his old job, and he's much happier ⁴ by / with this one. He learnt how to make the sandwiches and I was impressed ⁵ of / by the way he worked. He was very polite ⁶ to / at me, and he seems to be really interested ⁷ at / in the business. I think I'll make him responsible ⁸ by / for serving the customers and making the sandwiches. I'll soon find out if he's good ⁹ at / with getting up early, and if he is, I'll teach him how to do the baking.

GINA: Oh good! By the way, did you know he's engaged ¹⁰ with / to Carol Harris, that nice girl from the bank?

B

Read the text and choose the best preposition from the box to write in the gaps.

| in | ~~by~~ | for | with | of | by | with | for | with | at | by | of | with |

The world has been surprised ⁰ ...by... the election of Ellen Johnson Sirleaf as President of Liberia. When she started in politics, no one thought she could become president, but the people have become very fond ¹ .... her, and trust her to improve things in their country. The most popular candidate was a younger man, who was famous ² .... being a football star, so she had to find something that would make the people interested ³ .... her.

When the result was announced, George Bush telephoned to congratulate her, and said he was surprised ⁴ .... the result and happy ⁵ .... with it. The country was created by freed American slaves in 1822. The Liberian people were very excited ⁶ .... the fact that Condoleeza Rice, the secretary of State for the USA and a black American woman, was present at the inauguration ceremony.

Things have been very bad ⁷ .... the Liberian people for a long time, and they have been very unhappy ⁸ .... the amount of corruption in their government, but now they are full ⁹ .... hope.

She is very good ¹⁰ .... communicating with the women voters, and she believes that education is the most important thing for the country. She is also comfortable ¹¹ .... the ordinary people of the country, and they feel safe ¹² .... her.

KEITH: I'm so lucky to have found this job! I've been **looking for** a better job for months. I **applied for** loads' before I found this one.

MUM: Yes, I really must **congratulate** you **on** getting it. And Mr Cavalliere is so nice. I always **talk to** him when I go into the shop. He **reminds** me **of** Robert de Niro. Does he pay you well?

KEITH: The pay isn't very high, at least not at first, but I can **live on** it while I'm still living at home, and I'm sure he'll give me a pay rise when he knows he can **rely on** me.

MUM: It won't be so easy when you have to **leave for** work in the middle of the night to go and do the baking.

KEITH: No. I won't be able to go out in the evenings, but the good thing is that then I won't have to **spend** so much money **on** taking Rachel out. I'm going to have to **tell** her **about** that....

verb + at	We use **at** after some verbs to say *doing something towards something*:
	■ Donald **smiled at** the customs man, who was looking at him suspiciously.

verb + to	We use **to** after some verbs to talk about *communicating with someone*:
	■ Tomas **wrote to** the Prime Minister. ■ We often **talk to** the Imam.
	■ Can I **introduce** you **to** Mr Hannigan?

verb + for	We use **for** after **leave** (*to go somewhere*), **apply**, **look** / **search**, **wait**:
	■ Imogen is **leaving** London **for** Singapore next Tuesday.
	■ I'm looking for the form because I'd like to **apply for** a driving licence.
	■ Are you **waiting for** the number 29 bus?

verb + on	We use **on** after **spend** (+ money or time), **congratulate** (+ someone), live (= *survive by means of*), rely / depend (= *need support from someone or something*):
	■ I would like to **congratulate** you **on** your promotion.
	■ Can you **live on** 20 euros a week? Sharon **spends** that **on** makeup!
	■ Oonagh **relies on** her sister to help her.

verb + of	We use **of** after **take care, remind, dream, hear, think**:
	■ Makosi **takes care of** her grandmother. (= *Makosi looks after her.*)
	■ Phil **reminds** me **of** Olivier. (= *He makes me think of Olivier.*)
	■ Laura **dreams of** winning the lottery. (= *Laura wishes to win it.*)
	■ She has **heard of** Stanislavski. (= *She knows of his existence.*)
	■ What do you **think of** it? (= *What's your opinion of it?*)
	■ I can't **think of** the number. (= *I can't remember the number.*)

verb + about	We use **about** after some verbs to talk about *the subject of the event*:
	■ Daniela **heard about** the party.
	■ Last night I **dreamed about** Scotland.

verb + in / into	We use **in / into** after **bump / crash** + **cut / divide / break** and:
	■ The bus **crashed into** the fence.
	■ Why don't you **break** the chocolate **into** pieces?
	■ The baker **cut** the large loaf **in** half.

verb + from	We use **from** after **suffer**, to talk about *an illness or other problem*, and **retire**:
	■ Janet's daughter is **suffering from** earache
	■ Tina is **retiring from** the organisation next year.

EXERCISES

A

Choose the best preposition from the box to go in the gaps in the conversation.

to ~~of~~ of to from for of at into for from to for

JULIE: Have you met the new accounts clerk, Imran? He reminds me ⁰ ....*of*.... that Bollywood star – I can't think
¹ .... his name – anyway, he's gorgeous. I always smile ² .... him when I go past his desk, but I
haven't spoken ³ .... him.

SIDRA: No, I haven't been introduced ⁴ .... him yet.

SAM: I have. I talked ⁵ .... him yesterday when I was looking ⁶ .... the Thompson file. I bumped ⁷ ....
him in the corridor, and asked him if he was enjoying his new job. He said he was suffering ⁸ .... jet lag, as
he had just arrived ⁹ .... Pakistan. He said he had applied ¹⁰ .... the job in Islamabad, and he had left
¹¹ .... England just two weeks after that! He says he's always dreamed ¹² .... working in London. He's
really nice.

B

Circle the best preposition.

Mr Martinez retired (⁰ from)/ at his job at the end of last month. He used to take care ¹ from / of all the foreign
accounts, and the company relied ² of / on him for years. He has always dreamed ³ at / of visiting China, and he
heard ⁴ about / to an interesting job teaching English there, so he has written ⁵ to / with the school, applying
⁶ for / at the job. At the moment he is waiting ⁷ of / for his visa to arrive, as he plans to leave ⁸ for / to Nanking in
March. When he retires, the company will give him some money, which he will spend ⁹ for / on the flight. He also
has some money saved, which he will be able to live ¹⁰ at / on for a few months before he starts work. He plans to
see all the interesting tourist sites in China.

187

JASMINE: Hi, Sarah. No, I'm afraid you can't **come round** today. I've been studying so hard that I need to **get out** of the house, so I'm **going out** with Rahida this afternoon. I'm fed up with **sitting down** all day. We're going to go to the park, and then to the library to **go through** our history notes together. I'm finding the work really hard, but I'm not going to **give up**. I failed the history exam last term because something **came up** at home and I couldn't revise. My grandmother died, and I just couldn't **carry on** working. I had to **get away** for a while, but I've **got over** it now and I'm ready to try again.

Phrasal verbs are idiomatic phrases, and can be made with a *verb + an adverb*. We don't put an *object* between the *verb* and the *adverb*. Here are some useful phrasal verbs of this kind:

get	get back = *return*	■ Did you see Guo when he **got back** from the office?
	get away = *leave, have a holiday*	
		■ I'm so tired I really need to **get away** for a while.
	get off = *climb down from, finish work*	
		■ We should **get off** work at 5.30 today.
	get out = *leave somewhere*	■ Dean **got out** of work at 6.30.
	get in = *arrive in a building*	■ It's nearly 10 and Theo hasn't **got in** yet.
	get up = *get out of bed*	■ Paulette usually **gets up** before her sister.
	get over = *recover from*	■ Shuren hasn't **got over** flu yet.
come	come in = *enter*	■ Shut the door when you **come in**, please.
	come out = *exit*	■ Delia **came out** of the cinema with Emma.
	come up = *happen unexpectedly*	■ I can't talk to you now, because something has **come up**.
	come round/over = *visit someone*	■ What time is Mara **coming round**?
go	go out = *leave, or have a date with someone.*	
		■ Rahida is **going out** with Ahmed this evening.
	go through = *experience*	■ Imagine what those children **went through** during the war!
	go off = *become rotten or explode* (of a firework or a gun)	
		■ Don't put that milk in the coffee, it's **gone off**!
	go over = *check, or study carefully*	
		■ Larry needs to **go over** the list of members.
give	give in = *accept that you have lost*	■ The boxer was tired, and soon **gave in** to the stronger man.
	give up = *decide to stop doing something*	
		■ Anthony is trying to **give up** smoking.
stand / sit	stand up = *rise to standing*	■ Everyone must **stand up** when the President arrives.
	sit down = *be seated*	■ The choir must **sit down** quietly at the end of the song.
carry	carry on = *continue*	■ Shall we stop, or **carry on** walking?

EXERCISES

Circle the best verb to make a phrasal verb in this conversation.

CAROLINE: [0] Give / ⟨Come⟩ in, Leanne, and [1] sit / stand down. Now, I've called you here to talk to you about your work. What time did you [2] go / get in this morning?

LEANNE: Oh, I don't know. I [3] got / went out of bed a bit late today. And then the bus was stuck in traffic so I had to [4] go / get off and walk…

CAROLINE: In fact it was 10.30. And that's not all. You haven't been checking the fruit properly. You have been selling strawberries that have [5] gone / been off.

LEANNE: Oh, I'm so sorry! I thought I [6] went / came over them carefully. I will be more careful in future.

CAROLINE: Although you have [7] gone / got through a thorough training, I think you should [8] come / go over your instructions again when you [9] go / get off work today.

LEANNE: I will, definitely. I'm really sorry about today. I'm going to stay at home this evening and read my job description again, instead of [10] going / coming out.

Choose the best preposition from the box for each gap.

> over   out   back   in   ~~back~~   off   up   down   out   up   on   over   away

BILL: Why don't you come [0] ....*back*.... to my flat after the rehearsal? We could go [1] .... our lines for the play.

SIMON: Alright. I'm having problems with the scene where I have to carry [2] .... talking while I come [3] ...., sit [4] .... in the armchair, drink a cup of tea, and then stand [5] .... and go [6] .... again. It's a huge, long speech, and I always forget it.

BILL: I know. That scene's really hard. I have problems with the scene where the gun suddenly goes [7] .... It always surprises me and all my lines go [8] .... of my head. I'd really like to go [9] .... that part again.

SIMON: Of course, if that would be helpful. I won't be able to stay long as I have to get [10] .... early tomorrow to catch a train. Simona and I are getting [11] .... for a few days.

BILL: Lucky you! I hope you will get [12] .... in time for the next rehearsal.

Tanya ordered Jake a bicycle on the internet, but when it arrived he saw the parcel, and the shape of it **gave the secret away**. She tried to **make a story up** about it, but she couldn't **take him in**. She **sent Jake and Sam away**, and took the paper off, but it was the wrong colour! He didn't want a pink bicycle, so she had to **send it back**. When the new, silver bike arrived, Jake was really happy and **tried it out** straight away. It was perfect.

get	get something back = *have something again* ■ Bronwen has **got** her old room **back** now. get something off = *remove* ■ I'm trying to **get** the sauce **off** my tie.	get something out = *take from somewhere* ■ The students **got** their books **out** and started work.
send	send something away = *make something go* ■ Zane wanted to talk to the Principal but he **sent** Zane **away**. send something back = *return* ■ The college **sent** all the exam papers **back** to be marked again.	send something in = *send to an organisation* ■ Have you **sent** your application **in** yet?
make	make something up = *invent* something ■ If you don't know the answer, **make** something **up**.	make something out = *see or hear, with difficulty* ■ It was so dark, Ivan couldn't **make** the road signs **out**.
put	put something back = *replace* something ■ Tao Ping **put** the pans **back** on the shelf. put something out = *extinguish, turn off* ■ We must **put** the candles **out** before we go to bed.	put something on = *dress in something* ■ Deven forgot to **put** his gloves **on** before he left.
give	give something back = *return something to someone* ■ Max **gave** Jacob's tie **back** to him. give something away = *let a secret be known* or *donate* ■ I told you not to **give** the secret **away**.	give something in = *give something to the right place* ■ Umer found some money and **gave** it **in** to the office.
take	take something away = *remove* something ■ The men **took** all the furniture **away**. take someone in = *deceive* ■ Tanya thought she could **take** Jake **in**.	take something off = *remove (of clothes)* ■ Sally **took** her hat **off** and hung it up.
try	try something on = *put something on to see if it looks good or fits* ■ **Try** this skirt **on**. I think it will suit you.	try something out = *test something* ■ Mr Arden **tried** the car **out** before he bought it.
pick	pick something up = *take in your hand, collect, or learn* ■ Heinz **picked** Swedish **up** in Stockholm.	pick something out = *choose* ■ Now, what shall I read? Will you **pick** a book **out** for me?

EXERCISES

A Circle the best preposition in the dialogue.

JULIAN: Have you sent your essay ⁰(in)/ away yet?

GUSTAV: Yes, the teacher has marked mine, and I've already got it ¹ back / in. I gave it ² up / in last week.

JULIAN: I'm finding it really hard to find enough information. I think I'm going to have to make some of it ³ off / up.

GUSTAV: Maybe I can help you. I've given the books ⁴ away / back to the library, but I might be able to remember.

JULIAN: Did you get a good mark?

GUSTAV: I think so. I could hardly make the teacher's writing ⁵ out / off, but I think he's written 75%.

JULIAN: Really? Are you sure? Get it ⁶ on / out and let's have a look.

GUSTAV: Look, there. Can you make it ⁷ up / out?

JULIAN: No. The writing is too messy. You'll have to send it ⁸ back / off. I'll do that for you.

GUSTAV: What are you doing? Give my essay ⁹ back / in to me! I didn't say you could read it!

JULIAN: I'm only kidding. I thought I'd taken you ¹⁰ out / in for a moment!

B Circle the best verb in this story.

The circus master was preparing a new act with a dog. He ⁰took /(put) a hat on the dog, and it kept trying to ¹ put / get it off again. He had to keep on ² putting / picking it back. Then it ³ picked / got the hat up in its mouth, and the circus master couldn't ⁴ put / get it out. The dog just growled at him, and wouldn't ⁵ give / send it back. He thought he would ⁶ make / try another dog out, so he ⁷ tried / sent the first one back to the kennel and ⁸ picked / gave another one out. The second dog ran round and round the ring, barking, and he had to ⁹ put / send that one away as well.

He decided he was going to ¹⁰ give / try the dogs away, and ¹¹ send / make something else up for the new act!

If you **like** sweet-scented flowers, you **will love** narcissi. There are many different colours and shapes, but my favourite is the Paperwhite. If you **plant** the bulbs indoors in the autumn, you **will have** a beautiful display of scented, white flowers in the middle of winter. There is one problem with them, however, and that is that the stems are very long and the flowers **fall over, unless** you **support** them with sticks. But gardeners have recently discovered an interesting fact. **If** you **put** a little alcohol in the water you feed them, the stems **don't grow** so tall, and **when** the stems **are** shorter, they **don't need** support. I think they look nicer without sticks, so I am going to try this method this year.

general conditional	

Conditional sentences often have two parts, or clauses – the *condition clause* and the *consequence clause*. The condition clause usually has **if** at the beginning.

condition clause	consequence clause
If you heat wax,	it melts.
If Jack doesn't eat,	he gets angry.

In the *general conditional* we are talking about *something that is generally true*, and we use the *present tense* in both clauses (this may be a *present perfect*):

- Cats **purr** if you **stroke** them.
- If the weather **is** warm, the harvest **should be** good.
- I **feel** more confident if I **have researched** my subject.

Note: we can also use **when** at the beginning of a condition clause in a general conditional sentence.

- **When** you heat wax, it melts.
- Jack gets angry **when** he doesn't eat.

particular conditional	

We use the *particular conditional* to talk about a particular situation, and we *predict something will happen*:

condition clause	consequence clause
If Han wins,	we will celebrate.
If the engine is damaged,	I'll buy a new car.

The condition clause is in the *present tense* and we use **will** ('ll) in the consequence clause. The consequence clause can be first or second. If the *condition clause* is first, we use a comma after it:

- Paolo will be upset if Jan doesn't come. = If Jan doesn't come, Paolo will be upset.
- If the waitress doesn't serve us soon, I will have to leave. = I'll have to leave if the waitress doesn't serve us soon.

unless	

If we want to say that something *will happen if something else doesn't*, we can use **unless** in the *condition clause*.

- You may miss the play **unless** you buy tickets now. (= *If you don't buy tickets now, you may miss the play.*)
- **Unless** she hurries, Rani will be late . (= *If Rani hurries, she won't be late.*)

even if	

We can begin the *condition clause* with **even if**. This means that *something will happen anyway*.

- **Even if** Seema finishes her tasks early, she'll have to stay till 5.30.
- Tan won't take the job, **even if** they offer it to him.

EXERCISES

A Read the text below and underline the *condition clauses*. There are eight of them, including the example. Then find the eight *consequence clauses* in the same text, and circle the *main verb* of each one.

Bill Burn is a pessimist. <u>If he has a holiday,</u> he always (thinks) something will go wrong. If he doesn't leave for the airport at least three hours before the flight, he is terribly anxious. He usually takes all the family's documents in his jacket pocket, because he is afraid that, unless he looks after them, they will get lost. This makes Melissa Burn very cross. The children get really bored if they have to wait at the airport for hours.

If there is any turbulence while they are flying, Bill believes the plane is going to crash. Melissa is much calmer, and she has discovered that, if she talks to him all the time during the flight, he isn't so nervous. She really hopes the hotel is nice because, if it isn't, Bill will get really upset. When they have been on holiday for a few days, he always calms down, until it is time to go home again!

B Make sentences from the two clauses, using either the general or the particular conditional. Use the right form of the verbs in brackets.

0 Takis (want) to be a footballer – he (have to) practise all the time.

If Takis wants to be a footballer, he will have to practise all the time.

1 Someone (want) to be the best – they (must) live and breathe football, day and night.

....

2 Takis (should) join a club – he (be) not already a member.

....

3 He (can) contact the local sports council – he (have) not found a local club. ....

4 He (watch) the great footballers play – he (learn) some good techniques. ....

5 Footballers (get) advice from their coaches – their diets (be) not perfect. ....

6 Young footballers (like) to party until dawn – they (have to) change their habits. ....

7 They (not warm up) before a match – they easily (get) injured…

....

8 …and no-one (be) allowed to play – they (have) an injury.

....

9 Takis (become) a professional footballer – his training (be) not easy. ....

10 He (succeed) – his life (be) very exciting. ....

193

SALESMAN: Good morning, sir. **Would you like** to test-drive the new Amicon hatchback?

KOFI: Well, I **would, if I had** enough time. I was just looking, and I'm in a bit of a hurry.

SALESMAN: You **could** come back later, **if you don't have** time now. It's a great car, and, **if you bought** it before the end of the month, **you'd get** a 20% discount.

KOFI: I need to get a new car, and I **would buy** a hatchback, **if the price was** right ...

SALESMAN: **If you want**, I **could make** you an appointment later today.

KOFI: Can I come back at five o'clock? If **I'd known** about this, I **would have arranged** my meeting for later today.

SALESMAN: Five o'clock **would be** fine. I'll see you later, then.

imaginary conditional: form	We make the imaginary conditional with a **past form** in the **condition clause**, and **would** + **infinitive** in the **consequence clause**:

condition clause	consequence clause
If Robin **had** enough money	he **would buy** a new suit.
If my car **wasn't** so old	we **would get** home quicker.

use	We use the **imaginary conditional** when we want to talk about *something which might happen*, and the *imaginary consequences*: ■ If the weather **got** colder, the river **would freeze**. ■ Morris **would be** happy if Raquel **agreed** to marry him.
without a condition clause	We often use a **would clause** without a condition clause when we are talking about what someone *chooses* or *wants* (often with **would like / love**): ■ I **wouldn't like** to lose my job. (= *I don't want to ...*) ■ Pat **wouldn't give** Marya flowers. (= *He doesn't choose to ...*) and when it is clear what the condition is: ■ Dev **wouldn't have** time to talk to you. (*if you went to see him.*)
could	We can use **could** in the consequence clause if we are talking about *being able to do something*, or *if something is possible*: ■ If you missed the bus, you **could** stay at Jim's house. ■ Honorata **could** speak better if she was more confident.
with continuous forms	As with all conditionals, we can use the **simple** or the **continuous** form in either, or both, clauses: ■ Bob would **be earning** more if he **wasn't having** so many holidays. ■ If Hanna **was trying** harder, she would **be doing** better.
imagined past conditional: form	We make the imagined past conditional with **had** + **past participle** in the **condition clause**, and **would / could** + **have** + **past participle** in the **consequence clause**:

condition clause	consequence clause
If Robin **had had** enough money	he **would have bought** a new suit.
If my car **hadn't been** so old	we **could have got** home quicker.

use	We use the **imagined past conditional** when we want to talk about something *which might have happened but didn't happen*, and the *imagined consequences*: ■ If the river **had frozen** we **would have gone** skating. (*the river didn't freeze.*) ■ Morris would **have been** happy if Raquel **had agreed** to marry him. (*she didn't agree to marry him.*)

EXERCISES

A

Write the correct form of the verb in brackets in each gap. Sometimes you need to add would.

Rachel loves music, and she plays the violin. If she ⁰ (practise) ....._practised_..... more she ⁰ (be) ....._would_.....
....._be_.... better. When she was a child, Rachel ¹ (learn) .... to play the piano, if her parents ² (have)
.... enough money to buy one. Her friend, Jacques, ³ (play) .... the cello in the
Canberra college orchestra if he ⁴ (be) .... good enough, but he isn't. He ⁵ (like) .... to
join. If he ⁶ (play) .... in the orchestra, he ⁷ (be able to) .... make some new friends.
He is looking for a better job, and if he ⁸ (find) .... one he ⁹ (start) .... having cello
lessons. His cello is not very good, but if he ¹⁰ (earn) .... more money he ¹¹ (buy) ....
a better instrument. Nadhir had a beautiful old cello at home in Tunisia, and if he ¹² (know) .... that
Jacques wanted to play, he ¹³ (bring) .... it to Australia when he came.

B

Read the descriptions of a situation and look at the pictures, then write a sentence saying what would have happened if ... :

0 The man didn't buy any sugar. There wasn't any.
   The man would have bought some sugar if there had been any.

1 The tins didn't fall over. The woman didn't take the bottom tin.
   ....

2 The door wasn't open. The dog didn't run into the shop.
   ....

3 The man didn't steal the meat. The guard was watching him.
   ....

4 The boy didn't eat the apple. His mother stopped him.
   ....

5 The girl had lost her purse. She didn't buy the chocolates.
   ....

6 Kofi didn't help the new employee. She didn't ask him to.
   ....

7 The pile of baskets didn't fall over. Leanne took some of them away.
   ....

8 She didn't walk on the wet floor. The old lady didn't slip.
   ....

85 mixed conditionals etc. (If you had got the job, you would work with me)

If Grazia Falludi **hadn't bought** a copy of *Fresh Start* she **would still be** a 'Desperate Housewife'! Since she appeared on the front cover of our magazine, her life has changed completely. Doesn't she look great? (Turn to page 15 to see how she used to look.) But if she **hadn't entered** our competition, she **wouldn't be** on the cover of the magazine this week. She used to be an ordinary housewife, and if she **hadn't had** the professional makeover she **wouldn't be feeling** so confident and optimistic.

Do you feel a bit bored and depressed? Why not go in for this week's competition (see page 34), and you too could have a Fresh Start!

use	When we want to talk about *the possible present consequences of something that might have happened, but didn't*, we use a *mixed conditional*. ■ Boris **wouldn't be** here if he **hadn't seen** the advertisement for the course. (= *He did see the advertisement. He is here.*) ■ If the children **hadn't had** a sleep after lunch, they **would be** tired now. (= *They did sleep. They aren't tired.*)
form	A mixed conditional uses the condition clause of an imagined conditional (**had + *past participle***) with the *consequence clause* of an imaginary conditional (**would + *infinitive*** of **be** or a *thinking or feeling verb*): condition clause consequence clause If we **had missed** the bus we **would be** late. If Guo **hadn't read** the letter he **wouldn't know** what had happened.
with a present continuous	We can also use a *continuous infinitive* (**be + ing** *form*) in the *consequence clause*: ■ Renata wouldn't **be working** now if she hadn't had an operation. ■ If we hadn't bought these skates, we wouldn't **be having** so much fun!
'If I were you …'	We often use the *subjunctive form* of **be** (**were**) in the expression **If I were you …** We use this phrase sometimes when we are *giving someone advice*: ■ If I **were** you, I wouldn't buy that hat. ■ I wouldn't speak to Kjeld again, if I **were** you.
with a modal	We can use a *modal verb* (e.g. **could / might**) in place of **would**, if the consequence is *probable or possible*: ■ If Nadia had taken her medicine, she **might** feel better today. ■ If it had snowed last night, we **could** be skiing now.

A Match the consequence clause with the condition clause.

0 If the car tyres hadn't been so old   a the tree would still be standing.

1 If the wind hadn't been so strong   b she wouldn't be able to pay for the repairs.

2 If Tammy had been wearing her seat belt   c the car might not be so badly damaged.

3 She would be paralysed now   d if he hadn't had his mobile phone switched on.

4 If the car had not been insured   e if she hadn't decided to go out last night.

5 She wouldn't be feeling so comfortable   f he wouldn't know where she was.

6 She would still be safe at home   g if the surgeon hadn't been so clever.

7 If Tammy hadn't phoned Carlos   h she might not be in the hospital.

8 Carlos would not be visiting her in the hospital   i if the nurses hadn't been so kind.

B Read the two sentences and put them together, using a mixed conditional. The beginning of the sentence is given.

0 Karen chose box number 8. She has one thousand Euros.

If she hadn't _chosen box number 8, she wouldn't have one thousand euros._

1 She got the answer to her question right. She is playing this round of the game.

If she hadn't ....

....

2 Aziz got the answer wrong. He is out of the game.

Aziz wouldn't ....

....

3 He is feeling very cross. He made a stupid mistake.

If he hadn't ....

....

4 Karen knows a lot about the subject. She studied it before the competition.

She wouldn't ....

....

5 She studied a lot. She is feeling relaxed.

If she hadn't ....

....

6 She bought some new clothes. She looks really good.

She might not ....

....

7 She took some time to think of the answer. She is winning.

If she hadn't ....

....

8 The host gave her some advice before the show. She feels confident.

She might not ....

....

9 Her husband sent in her entry form. She is in the show.

If her husband hadn't ....

....

10 She decided to do the show. She is one thousand euros richer.

She wouldn't ....

....

general conditional	**if + present … present** We use this to talk about *the inevitable consequences of something*: ■ **If** the curtains are open, the sun shines in. ■ Doxa forgets everything **if** you don't remind her.
particular conditional	**if + present … will + infinitive** We use this to talk about *a particular situation that might exist now, and what the consequences will be*: ■ **If** the curtains are open, the sun **will** shine in. ■ Doxa **will** forget about it **if** you don't remind her.
imaginary conditional	**if + past … would / could + infinitive** We use this to talk about *things that might happen now and what the consequences might be*: ■ **If** the curtains were open, the sun **would** shine in. ■ Doxa **would** forget about it **if** you didn't remind her.
imagined conditional	**if + had + past participle … would / could + have + past participle** We use this to talk about *things that didn't happen in the past*, and *what the consequences might have been*: ■ **If** the curtains **had** been open, the sun **would have** shone in. (= *The curtains were not open.*) ■ Doxa **would** have forgotten about it **if** you **hadn't** reminded her.

A Choose the best word or phrase from the box to go in the gaps in this text.

> didn't have   would have   would have   ~~had been~~   works   would like   will feel
> will be ready   would be   had finished   spoke   studies   would manage

Although Tanya adores her sons, she finds it hard being a single mother. She sometimes thinks that, if
things 0 ....*had been*.... different, she probably 1 .... got a well-paid job
by now, like her friends. She left university half-way through the course, but if she 2 ....
.... the course and got a degree, she 3 .... more likely
to get a good part-time job now. She is thinking of starting some evening classes, and finishing her degree.
Her mother is very happy to help her to look after the boys. She doesn't know how she 4 ....
.... if she 5 .... such a kind mother. Tanya is looking through
some course brochures now. She 6 .... to work for an international
organisation, as she is very keen to travel. If she 7 .... another language
fluently, she 8 .... a better chance of getting the job she wants. If she
9 .... a language and some business skills, she 10 ....
.... better prepared for the working world. If she 11 .... really hard,
she hopes she 12 .... to apply for some jobs in a year. She is very excited
about her plans.

B Look at the pictures, and make conditional sentences starting with **if**, using the clues in brackets (don't change the order of the clauses).

0 (The cat climbed the tree. It is stuck.)
If the cat hadn't climbed the tree it wouldn't be stuck.

1 (Captain Splendid put on his special suit. The old lady asked him to help her.)

....

....

2 (Captain Splendid isn't very strong. He can't save the cat easily.)

....

....

3 (The cat was so frightened. It has scratched him.)

....

....

4 (The cat scratched him. He has torn his suit.)

....

....

5 (He has torn his suit. He didn't carry the cat down.)

....

....

6 (The lady found a ladder. She was able to get Captain Splendid down.)

....

....

7 (She gave him her coat. He didn't feel more embarrassed.)

....

....

8 (The lady didn't get the ladder earlier. She couldn't save the cat herself.)

....

....

9 (The lady didn't wait a while. The cat didn't come down anyway.)

....

....

10 (Captain Splendid is going out again tomorrow. He won't be wearing his special suit!)

....

....

86 relative clauses (That's the dog which bit me!)

Have you ever tried any of the extreme sports **which are so popular nowadays**? Quite well known is hang-gliding, **which involves flying in a frame attached to a small glider**. Another very popular one is bungy-jumping. You are tied to a long, strong, elastic cord, **which is attached to a high platform**. You then jump off, fall a long way, and bounce up and down in the air. You really have to trust the equipment **that you are using**, and the person **who is organising the event**. A new sport, **which is a combination of snowboarding and water skiing**, is called wakeboarding. A very familiar extreme sport is rock climbing. Normally, climbers use ropes, **which are attached to the rock face**, but in deep water soloing you don't use ropes. If you fall off, you land in the deep water **that is below you**. People seem to love the excitement, **which gives them a big adrenaline rush**.

relative clauses	A relative clause is usually the second clause in a sentence, and gives us more information about the *object* of the first clause. It often begins with **which**, **that**, **where**, **when**, **who** or **whose**. **Which** and **that** are used for *things*, and mean the same. **Where** is used for *places*. **Who** and **whose** are used for a *person*, or the *thing someone possesses*. ■ Give me the *card* **that** you are holding in your hand. ■ Sajida was talking to *Marya*, **who** comes from Poland. ■ John is *the man* **whose** car is parked outside. ■ That's the *house* **where** I used to live. ■ Do you remember *last June*, **when** we had our holiday? There are two kinds of relative clauses.
adding clauses	Adding clauses add more information about the *object* of the first clause. We put a comma after the first clause. We use **which** for *things* in adding clauses: ■ Jo made £50 for her story, **which** appeared in the magazine this month. ■ The council are building a new shopping centre, **which** Conrad will design. ■ Baz is interviewing the lead singer in Trash, **who** Kirsty likes.
specifying clauses	A specifying clause tells us more about **who** or **what** the *object* of the main clause is. In this kind of relative clause, we can leave out **that**, **which**, **when**, **who** *when they are the object of the clause*. We can't leave out **whose** and **where**: ■ That's the coat **that** Emile wants to buy. (= *That's the coat Emile wants to buy*.) ■ Tim phoned me at the time **when** I usually leave for work. (= *Tim phoned me at the time I usually leave for work*.) ■ There is the boy **who** Dana talked to this morning. (= *There is the boy Dana talked to this morning*.) ■ I really like the girl **whose** pen you borrowed. ■ Rowena visited the island **where** her mother was born
in the middle of a sentence	We often use relative clauses beginning with **which / that**, **where** or **who** in the middle of a sentence. The *verb* of the first clause comes after the *relative clause*. When we are using a *specifying clause* we don't need to use commas. With an *adding clause*, we use a comma after the first part and after the relative clause: ■ The person **who is speaking when the whistle goes** loses the game. ■ My aunt, **who is nearly 100**, lives in Germany.

EXERCISES

A Read the text and look at the underlined relative clauses. Write a pronoun (**which**, **where** or **who**) in the gaps.

73,000 people died in the terrible earthquake in Kashmir, 0 *which* took place on 8th October 2005. After it, there were 3.5 million people 1 _____ had lost everything. The snows, 2 _____ come every winter, fortunately started late that year. There are several hundred aid agencies trying to help the people from Bagh, Muzaffarabad and Balakot, 3 _____ the earthquake was most severe. It is very difficult to get aid through to them, as the road system, 4 _____ was never very modern, is not adequate for the lorries and vans 5 _____ need to use them. There have been lots of accidents involving lorries 6 _____ were overloaded. Many of the roads have become cracked and broken, and the drivers find it hard to drive on the winding roads 7 _____ climb up the mountain sides. Some bridges are still standing, but the authorities have closed those 8 _____ are not strong enough to support the heavy lorries. The months ahead look bleak for many of the homeless people, 9 _____ have very little food and shelter. Fortunately, the Indian and the Pakistani governments, 10 _____ were in conflict over the area of Kashmir, are now working together to help the refugees. It is very difficult for charities, 11 _____ are receiving big donations from people all over the world, to get the aid to the people 12 _____ need it.

B Read the dialogue and rewrite the two sentences to make one long sentence with a relative clause. Sometimes you won't need to use **which**, **that**, **where** or **who**.

ROB: I got a letter in the post this morning. Have you seen it?

0 *Have you seen the letter (that) I got in the post this morning?*

TIM: I only saw one letter. It was addressed to me.

1 _____

ROB: It was an important letter. I have been waiting for it.

2 _____

ROB: It was from a company. The company has invited me for an interview.

3 _____

TIM: There was a phone call yesterday from a man. He wanted to speak to you.

4 _____

ROB: A man phoned. Do you know what he was called?

5 _____

TIM: He had a strange accent. I couldn't really understand it.

6 _____

ROB: I bought some coffee yesterday. Where is it?

7 _____

TIM: You buy a special kind of coffee. I don't like it.

8 _____

ROB: Strong coffee will wake me up. I really need some.

9 _____

TIM: I think it's all these late nights. They are making you forgetful.

10 _____

> My dearest Grace,
> By the time you read this letter, I will be far away. I have decided that
> it is best for us to be apart. As soon as I realised how much I loved
> Katerina, I knew that I had to go. I know that you will be very angry with
> me when you read this, but I think it is better to tell the truth. When she
> asked me to go to Frankfurt to be with her, I couldn't refuse. I hope you
> are not too unhappy.
> When I arrive in Frankfurt, I will write you another letter, explaining why I
> did this terrible thing. I hope, when you read it, you will be able to forgive
> me. While we were together, I promise you, I was never unfaithful to you.
> Yours affectionately, William

future time clauses	To talk about something happening *at a particular time in the future*, we use a *present tense* in the time clause and a *future* in the other clause. We don't use a *future verb* in a time clause: ■ **When** the train **arrives**, we **will have to** run. NOT ~~When the train will arrive...~~ The time clause can come first or second. If it is first, we use a comma after it: ■ Paulette will have dinner ready **when** Marie gets home. (= *When Marie gets home, Paulette will have the dinner ready.*) We can also use a *modal* in the second clause: ■ **When** the sun is strong, you **must** wear sun cream.
present time clauses	To talk about *something that is always true*, we use the *present* in both clauses: ■ **When** the spring **comes**, the daffodils **appear**. ■ The tourists **go** home **as soon as** the snow melts.
past time clauses	After a time clause with a *past verb*, we use a **past verb** in the second clause: ■ **As soon as** the door **opened**, Pierre **saw** the lovely new carpet. ■ The class **learned** a lot **when** Mr Porter **was teaching** them.
as soon as	We can use **as soon as** at the beginning of a time clause. It means *immediately after*: ■ **As soon as** Damien gets the text, he will phone Marc.
while	We use **while** at the beginning of a time clause, to mean *during the time that*. It is often followed by a *continuous* verb. We can also use a *simple present* with the same meaning: ■ **While** the kettle **is boiling**, I will make the sandwiches. (= *While the kettle **boils** ...*) ■ Harry is writing an email **while** Charlotte **photocopies** the invoices. (= ... **while** Charlotte **is photocopying** the invoices.)
before / by the time / since / until	When we want to say that *one thing happens earlier than another*, we use a time clause beginning **before**: ■ I'm going out to buy some milk **before** the shop shuts. (*future*) If we want to say that *something has happened before something else has been done*, we use **by the time (that)**: ■ **By the time** the hall was built, the cost had doubled. (*past*) When we start the time clause with **since**, we use a *perfect verb* (**have / had +** *past participle*) in the second clause: ■ Phil **had been working** very hard **since** he got his new job. To say that *something will stop when something else happens*, we use **until**: ■ Lily ran **until** she was exhausted. (= *then she stopped running*)

EXERCISES

A Choose and circle the best time word or phrase in each sentence.

0 (Before) / As soon as you begin installing your new wireless internet connection, you must turn off the computer.

1 Don't turn it off <u>until / by the time</u> you have saved and closed all your files.

2 <u>While / When</u> this is done, you can connect the mains cable to the wireless transmitter.

3 You should see a green light on the box <u>as soon as / since</u> it is connected.

4 <u>Since / After</u> about one minute, you should also see a yellow light on the box.

5 <u>Before / By the time</u> you start connecting to the computer, you must make a note of the code on the transmitter.

6 You will need this <u>when / until</u> you start the installation process.

7 <u>Since / As soon as</u> you see the yellow light, you can connect the wireless transmitter to the computer and start the computer again.

8 The installation program should start automatically <u>before / when</u> you restart the computer.

9 <u>While / Since</u> the installation is in progress, you must follow all the instructions carefully.

10 <u>By the time / While</u> installation is complete, you will see three green lights on the box.

11 <u>Before / As soon as</u> you see the three green lights you will be able to go online.

Happy surfing!

B Choose the best word from the box to go in the gaps.

> until   while   Before   while   soon   until   ~~since~~   By   since   soon   When

ISMAH: Hi Adnan. I've been so busy! I have sold 26 pairs of shoes ⁰ ......*since*...... I started work at eleven!

ADNAN: That's good. ¹ .... you arrived, I hadn't had any customers at all!

ISMAH: No-one came ² .... I got back from my lunch break – then it was crazy. I'm exhausted.

ADNAN: I'll make you a cup of tea as ³ .... as I have put these boxes in the store room.

ISMAH: Oh, that would be lovely. There was a group of about ten people, and, ⁴ .... I was serving them, Mrs Duval came in wanting school shoes for her three children. ⁵ .... the time I had finished serving them all, there were two more customers waiting! I've never known a Saturday like it.

ADNAN: Did any customers walk out ⁶ .... you were serving other people?

ISMAH: I don't think so, because as ⁷ .... as I saw a new customer come in, I went and welcomed them and asked them to wait a few minutes. They were very patient.

ADNAN: Well done! ⁸ .... I get a rush of people like that, I'm not usually so patient!

ISMAH: Well, what have you been doing ⁹ .... you left?

ADNAN: Well, ¹⁰ .... a few minutes ago I thought I had been very busy, but, compared to you, I've had an easy day!

The new health centre opened this morning, **and** all the employees were very excited. The old health centre was not really big enough for all the services they offer, **so** the new, bigger building is much better. There is even a well-equipped dentist's office, **but** they haven't employed a dentist yet. **Although** the new centre has much more space and better equipment, some employees say they will miss the friendliness of the old place. The staff members used to work very closely together, **but** now all the departments are separate. **In spite of** the clean, modern environment, some patients say they miss the old familiar centre. The project has taken three years to complete; **even though** it has been a long wait, it is a wonderful achievement.

adding clauses: and, and … also	When we want to *add more information* to something we start the clause with the conjunction **and**. We don't usually begin a sentence with **and**:
	▨ The house was empty, **and** someone had broken the windows.
	▨ Mouttou went to Spain **and** the weather was lovely.
	Note: we don't usually use **also** at the beginning of a clause, but we can use it with **and** when we want to stress the addition. It goes after the subject of the verb:
	▨ …, **and** Irina **also** served couscous. ~~NOT …, also Irina served couscous.~~
contrasting clauses: but	When we want to give some information which is *in contrast* to the first clause, we use the conjunction **but**. We don't usually begin sentences with **but**:
	▨ Dina looked through the window, **but** it was too dark to see.
	▨ He stayed in an expensive hotel, **but** it wasn't very nice.
although / even though	We use **although** when we want to say that *something is unexpected and in contrast with the first clause*. It can also go at the beginning of the sentence. **Even though** is used in the same way, but the meaning is stronger:
	▨ Mr Chan was very strong, **although** he was 86.
	▨ **Even though** he ate a lot, he was very slim.
even if	We use **even if** to say that *something will not change a situation, though we might expect it to*. It can also go at the beginning of the sentence:
	▨ Janice won't be promoted, **even if** she does well.
	▨ **Even if** Juanita wants to stay, she has to go.
in spite of / despite	We use **in spite of** or **despite** before a *noun clause* or an *ing form* to say that something happens, when *something in the other clause says that it is unlikely*:
	▨ **In spite of** the rain, the students went for a picnic.
	▨ Gary went to the party **despite** having a cold.
	Before a full *verb clause* we say **in spite of / despite + the fact that** … It can go at the beginning, too:
	▨ Jan bought a car, **in spite of the fact that** she couldn't drive.
	▨ **Despite the fact that** Dinah didn't like fish, she ate some salmon.

EXERCISES

A

Read the story and circle the best word to use.

It was a bright spring day, ⁰ but /(and) the spring flowers were coming out. ¹ Even though / But it was April, it was still very cold. Dan and Narciso were walking in the woods ² and / although Dan was enjoying the fresh air, ³ and / but Narciso was not. He was complaining about the cold, ⁴ although / despite he was wearing two sweaters and a coat. Dan didn't feel very cold, ⁵ and / though he was tired of Narciso's complaining. He offered to lend him his hat and scarf, ⁶ but / and also his gloves, if he would promise to stop moaning! Narciso took the hat and scarf, ⁷ and / but he didn't take the gloves.

'I'm sure you will need them, ⁸ in spite of / even though you don't feel cold now,' he said. 'Remember, I've just arrived from Spain, ⁹ in spite of / and it's much warmer there!'

'That's true,' said Dan. 'I hope you are enjoying the English countryside, ¹⁰ and / even though it is a bit cold.'

'Oh yes, it's really beautiful, ¹¹ in spite of / even though the weather,' said Narciso.

B

Show with an arrow where the word or phrase in brackets should go in the sentence. Sometimes there is more than one correct answer.

HOROSCOPE FOR THIS WEEK

Leo

0 ↓ Leos are usually good at making decisions, this week you will have trouble making up your mind about something very important. (although)

1 the influence of the new moon the power of Mars will make you feel a bit confused. (and)

2 there are some difficult times ahead, you will succeed, … (even though)

3 … if you trust your inner voice follow your instincts. (and)

4 the problems you are facing, you should be feeling energetic and positive. (despite)

5 you think you should delay making a decision, don't! (even if)

6 you must act now, be sure your decision is the right one for you. (but)

7 one of the greatest qualities of a Leo is self-confidence, this sometimes looks like arrogance. (but)

8 don't be afraid of the opinion of others, some people may be upset by what you do. (even if)

9 they will understand in the end, you should be prepared for some arguments! (although)

Darren woke up in the middle of the night **because** he heard a loud noise downstairs. He was frightened, **as** his wife was away on a course and no-one else was in the house. He thought that **either** it could be a cat that had got in through the window, **or** it could be a burglar. He didn't hear anything else, **so** he tried to go back to sleep. He couldn't sleep **because** he was too nervous, **so** he got out of bed **so that** he could go downstairs to check. He put on his bathrobe, **as** it was really cold. Darren went quietly down the stairs and picked up an umbrella, **in case** he had to defend himself. His wife came out of the kitchen and started laughing **because** he looked so funny, holding an umbrella, in his bathrobe. She had come home unexpectedly **because** the course had finished early.

explaining clauses: because	When we want to add a clause with information which *explains another clause*, we use **because**. We can begin a sentence with the conjunction **because**: ▪ The bus broke down **because** oil was leaking from the engine. ▪ **Because** it was so hot, everyone was wearing sandals.
as	The meaning of **as** is very similar to **because**. We use it to say that something is *the reason for something else*. **As** can go at the beginning of a sentence: ▪ Pablo went to bed, **as** he was very tired. ▪ **As** the train was delayed, they were late for the appointment.
so	When we want to say that something is *the consequence of something else*, we use the conjunction **so**. **So** doesn't go at the beginning of a two-clause sentence: ▪ Pablo was very tired, **so** he went to bed.
so that	When we want to say that *something is done to make something else happen*, we use **so that**, usually with **would** or **could**: ▪ Judith bought some wool **so that** she could knit a jersey. ▪ Hari rocked the baby **so that** he would sleep.
in case	To say that someone has done something *because of something that might happen*, we use **in case**. **In case** can go at the beginning of a sentence: ▪ Han carried an umbrella **in case** it rained. ▪ **In case** you forget, I've written it down.
alternative clauses: or	To *suggest an alternative* to the first clause, we start the second clause with the conjunction **or**. We don't begin two-clause sentences with **or**. We don't need to repeat the subject and the verb if they are the same as the first clause: ▪ Shall we have lunch here, **or** shall we eat in the park? ▪ The children could play cricket **or** (*they could play*) football.
either ... or	We use **either** to say that *there is more than one alternative*. We begin the second clause with **or**: ▪ Sam works **either** for IBM, **or** for Intel – I can't remember which. ▪ **Either** you could go for a swim, **or** you could try a yoga class.
neither ... nor	We use **neither ... nor** with a positive verb when we are talking about *two negatives*: ▪ Jacob can **neither** play the guitar **nor** sing very well. (= *he can't play the guitar and he can't sing*.) ▪ **Neither** Assefa **nor** Peter wanted to go to the cinema.
unless	We use **unless** to say that *something will happen if another thing does not happen*. **Unless** can also go at the beginning of a sentence: ▪ Akiko will be cold **unless** she gets another blanket.

EXERCISES

A Choose the best word or phrase from the box to go in the gaps in the text. Notice the number of letters in each gap!

either   as   because   Because   unless   as   so   ~~because~~   so   or   so that   in case   or   because

Mary Blandy was hanged in 1752 ⁰ ..... *because* ..... she poisoned her father.

She wanted to marry a captain called Cranstoun, but her father didn't like him, ¹ _ _ she couldn't marry him. Her father said she must never see him again, ² _ _ _ _ _ _ _ he didn't trust him. At her trial, Mary said that Cranstoun had told her to put a love potion ³ _ _ _ _ _ _ in her father's food ⁴ _ _ in his tea, ⁵ _ _ _ _ _ _ her father would like him. He said that, ⁶ _ _ _ _ _ _ she did it, he would leave her, ⁷ _ _. Mary did it. Her father died, ⁸ _ _ the potion was, in fact, arsenic.

The jury had the choice of hanging her as a murderer ⁹ _ _ letting her go free, to marry Cranstoun. ¹⁰ _ _ _ _ _ _ _ her father had been an important man locally, the members of the jury were not very sympathetic to her. Even though they were not sure, they decided to hang her, just ¹¹ _ _ _ _ _ _ she was lying. Cranstoun was not prosecuted, ¹² _ _ he had escaped to France.

The case was also interesting ¹³ _ _ _ _ _ _ _ it was the first legal case to use medical evidence as proof of poisoning.

B Read the two parts of these sentences, and choose the best word or phrase to join them.

0 When you are choosing a holiday, it is best to use a travel agent. ((because)/ so) holidays are very expensive.

1 The agent may have personal experience of the place (or / as) they should have reports from other clients.

2 You shouldn't book a holiday without being sure it is what you want, (unless / in case) you like taking risks.

3 Some tourists have found that the hotel is not yet built (because / or) it is miles from the sea, for example.

4 Your holiday must be insured (or / so) you can get your money back if anything goes wrong.

5 It is always worth getting travel insurance (in case / either) you lose your suitcases.

6 You can _ _ _ _ _ _ book your holiday on the phone (either … or / neither … nor) you can go into the office.

7 Don't use an unknown agent (in case / unless) you know they are reliable.

8 It is a good idea to check the agent's reputation online (or / as) look in their brochure.

9 It is easier to book through a travel agent (so / because) they do all the work for you.

10 A travel agent will do their best for you (so / as) they want you to use them again next year.

A

Circle the best conjunction at the beginning of these clauses:

Canada is an enormous country, ⁰ that /(though) it has a small population for its size. The majority of the population lives in the area around the Great Lakes, ¹ which / where are on the border with the USA, ² because / in case it is very fertile and the land is fairly flat. There is also a heavily-populated area around Vancouver, ³ which / but is on the Pacific coast. The north western part of Canada, ⁴ where / as there are enormous forests and mountains, is very wild and beautiful. ⁵ Unless / Although Canada has a very cold winter, the summer is very hot in the south of the country.

⁶ Until / During the Conservatives won the election in 2006, there had been a Liberal government for many years. The Liberals lost the election ⁷ because / in case there were some problems with corruption in the previous government.

There are a lot of fascinating wild animals in Canada, such as bears, racoons, skunks and chipmunks, ⁸ who / which are all quite common in the forests.

Canada is a great place for a sporting holiday, ⁹ as / though you can do all kinds of sports there, from skiing to canoeing, ¹⁰ and / or the people are very welcoming.

CANADA

USA

B

Choose the word from the box to go in the gaps in this dialogue. Some of the words can be left out. If they can, put the word in brackets ( ).

| who   so   where   or   that   Because   Although   ~~who~~   Either   that   When   which   which   when |

BAZ: This evening I'm interviewing Jerry Thompson, the famous comedian ⁰ ...*who*.... won the Golden Pineapple award this year.

JERRY: Hi. Go on then. Kill me.

BAZ: No, no! We want to keep you alive, ¹ .... you can go on making us laugh for as long as possible! I just loved the show ² .... I saw in Toronto this September. Are you touring with that show?

JERRY: No. The Toronto show was all about the political situation at the time, ³ .... isn't funny any more. ⁴ .... my comedy has to be fresh, I write a new show every few weeks.

BAZ: Are you still working with the woman ⁵ .... acted with you in Toronto? Liz Durham, wasn't it?

JERRY: Yes, that's right. No, Liz has gone to the States, ⁶ .... she's working now. She's too expensive for me now! ⁷ .... I worked with her, she was much cheaper.

BAZ: How did you feel about the award ⁸ .... you won recently?

JERRY: I had mixed feelings. ⁹ .... it's nice to be respected, it's always a problem for a radical comedian ¹⁰ .... you are accepted by the public. But, ¹¹ .... you survive as a comedian, ¹² .... means earning money, ¹³ .... you have to get a day job. I'm too lazy to work!

C Join the two clauses of these sentences with an arrow.

0 Before they started the expedition
1 Even though the snow was falling,
2 The weather was worse the next morning
3 But in the afternoon
4 They decided to start the climb
5 A local man was leading the climb
6 No foreigner had climbed this route
7 The leader had a cell phone
8 Everything went very well
9 One of the climbers suddenly slipped
10 Fortunately, she was attached to the next climber,
11 They decided to stay where they were

a before this expedition.
b although the wind was still very strong.
c until about 8 p.m.
d in case they needed to be rescued.
e they managed to set up the tents.
f the team planned everything carefully.
g who pulled her up again.
h when they woke up.
i and slid over the edge of a ravine.
j the sky cleared.
k until the weather improved.
l because he knew the mountain well.

Well, Leonard announced that he **had written** a new play for the company, but Justin said he **wouldn't** even **audition** for it, because he **didn't like** Leonard's plays! Then Maria **said**, 'I think Leonard is a great playwright, and I really like working with him.' So Leonard thanked her, and said that if they **weren't** sure, they **could decide** after they **had read** the script. So Justin agreed that that **was** a good idea, and that they **could take** a vote on it. So now Justin is telling everyone that they **must vote** against the play! I think he**'s** just **jealous** because Maria says she **won't go out** with him any more. He says he**'s going to write** a letter to the company manager, saying that Leonard's behaviour **is** unprofessional! Are you **going to say** you **will work** with him, or not? I can't make up my mind. I don't like him, because he once **said to me**, 'Darling, you needn't audition for the main part, but I'd love you to do our costumes!' I think I **might say** I**'m** too busy at the moment ... '.

direct speech	When we want to write what someone *says*, *thinks* or *writes*, we can use speech marks (also called inverted commas) ('') around *exactly what they say*:

- Rob **said**, 'I've finished now.'

We can put the ***reporting clause*** before or after the speech, but we usually put it after. When we put it after the speech, we usually put the verb first:

- 'I've finished now,' **said** Rob.

There are lots of verbs we can use to report speech, e.g.: shout, answer, mumble, wonder etc. If we use an ***adverb***, it goes after the subject:

- 'I've finished at last,' sighed Rob, **happily** – not ~~sighed happily Rob~~

We can use any appropriate tense in the reporting clause. The speech clause stays the same (it keeps the speaker's exact words):

- When he finishes, Rob **is going to shout**, 'I've finished now!'
- Rob **whispers**, 'I've finished now.'
- 'Have you finished?' **asked** Omar.
- 'I have finally completed my work,' wrote Rob in his email to Omar.

Note: for more on **ask** see unit 91.

We often use direct speech to *write* about what someone thinks, but we don't usually use it when we're *talking* about what they think.

- 'I hope Rob has finished,' **thought** Omar.
- Rob **thought**, 'I hope this is finished.'

indirect speech: change of perspective	To report what someone says, writes or thinks, using ***indirect speech***, we use the tense *appropriate to the time we are reporting the speech*, and we don't use speech marks. We often need to change the ***verb tense***, ***pronouns*** and ***time clauses*** in the speech to *our own perspective*. We often use **that** before the speech clause, especially when writing:

- (*him to me, yesterday*) '**I am** really tired **this evening**.' → (*me to you, today*) 'He said **he was** really tired **that evening**.'
- (*Helmut to Lorna, last week*) '**Olaf beat me** at chess.' → (*Lorna to Olaf, today*) 'Helmut said **you beat him** at chess.' OR 'Helmut said **you had beaten him** at chess.'
- (*Dian to Mo, on Tuesday*) '**We'll leave tomorrow**.' → (*Jack to Paolo, on Thursday*) 'Dian said that **they would leave yesterday**.'

reporting present speech	When we report *what someone says, writes or thinks*, we don't have to change the tense of the verb in the speech: ▪ Ulrike: 'I**'m** still on the train.' → Ulrike **says** that she**'s** still on the train. ▪ Nils: 'I **have spent** too much.' → Nils is thinking that he **has spent** too much. ▪ Petra: 'Kika **will phone** later.' → Petra says that Kika **will phone** later.
reporting future speech	When we report *what someone will say, write or think in the future*, we don't have to change the tense of the verb in the speech: ▪ Han: 'I**'m going** to fail my test.' → Han **will say he's going** to fail **his** test. ▪ Shuren: 'You **were** right!' → Shuren **is going to think** that we were right. ▪ The journalist: 'Rio **is** busy!' → The journalist will write that Rio **is** busy.
reporting past speech	When we report *what someone said, thought or wrote in the past*, we often need to change the tense in the speech to show *the present perspective of what they said*: ▪ Jamil: 'I **am** bored at school.' (*we don't know if he is still bored*) → Jamil **said** that he **was** bored at school. ▪ Jorg: 'I **am** bored at the office.' (*we think he is still bored now*) → Jorg **said** that he **is** bored at the office. ▪ Jurgen: 'Tan **is going to enjoy** the film.' → (*we report after Tan saw the film*) Jurgen **thought** that Tan **was going to enjoy** the film. ▪ Emil (*on Monday*): 'The letter **will arrive** on Friday.' → (*we report on Tuesday*) Emil **said** that the letter **will arrive** on Friday. ▪ Emil (*on Monday*): 'The letter **will arrive** on Friday.' → (*we report on Saturday*) Emil **said** that the letter **would arrive** on Friday. If the speaker used a *present perfect* (**has** + ed *form*), we must use the *past perfect* (**had** + ed *form*) *when reporting it*. If the speaker used a *past tense* (*continuous* or *simple*), when we report it we can use either the *past tense*, or the *past perfect*. The meaning is usually the same. ▪ Lafia: 'You**'ve given** me the wrong tool, Bouba.' → Lafia **muttered** that Bouba **had given** him the wrong tool. ▪ Jenny: 'Jamil **was** bored at school.' (*Jamil was bored at a time before Jenny spoke*) → Jenny **said** Jamil **had been** bored at school. OR Jenny **said** that Jamil **was** bored at school. ▪ Dave: 'I **did**n't **bring** anything to the party.' → (*we report after the party*) Dave **admitted** that he **had**n't **brought** anything to the party. OR … that he **did**n't **bring** anything …'. ▪ Raoul: 'Donna **was**n't **driving** the car.' → Raoul **said** that Donna **had**n't **been driving** the car. OR … that Donna **was**n't **driving** the car. Note: for using **ask** and **tell** to report speech, see unit 91.
with modals	When the speaker used **will**, **can** or **may**, we can use **would**, **could** or **might** when we report it later: ▪ 'We**'ll** send the goods next week.' → She said that they **would** send …. ▪ 'Tina **can** speak Urdu.' → She said that Tina **could** speak Urdu. ▪ 'I **may** come round this evening.' → He said he **might** come round …. When the speaker uses a *modal* (**might**, **could**, **should** etc), we use the *same form* when we report it: ▪ 'I **should** buy a new pen.' → He said that he **should** buy a new pen. ▪ 'Naeem **could** win the competition.' → They said Naeem **could** win ….

A Read the conversation between Sir James Murray (the first editor of the *Oxford English Dictionary*) and his wife, and then look at the underlined words and report what was said. The beginning of each sentence is given. Remember to change the pronouns (**you, my** etc) to **her, his** etc.

SIR JAMES MURRAY: [0] I'm going to the hut to start work, dear.

MRS MURRAY: [1] I wish you didn't work in that miserable hut. It's so cold!

SIR JAMES: True. However, unfortunately [2] there's no room in the house for all my documents.

MRS MURRAY: Yes, I know. [3] You've been working on the dictionary for 34 years. [4] I think it's time you retired!

SIR JAMES: But, my dear, [5] the dictionary is nearly finished. [6] I'm working on the Y words. It's fascinating! [7] We've found references to the word 'yellow' in the year 1160.

MRS MURRAY: That's wonderful, dear, but [8] I hardly ever see you.

SIR JAMES: I know, and I promise that [9] I will stop soon, but we have to finish the work.

MRS MURRAY: When I married you in Scotland 40 years ago, when you were a humble school teacher, I never thought you would be so famous. Of course, I am very proud of you. But [10] we could be enjoying our old age together.

SIR JAMES: I look forward to that too, my dear. [11] You won't have to wait for very long.

MRS MURRAY: But [12] you've been saying that for years!

SIR JAMES: Well, [13] we should talk about it this evening. [14] I must get on with my work.

0 He said that *he was going to the hut to start work.*

1 She said she wished that ....

2 He replied that she knew that ....

3 She said that ....

4 She said that she thought that ....

5 He said that ....

6 He said that ....

7 He explained that ....

8 She complained that ....

9 He promised that ....

10 She wished that ....

11 He promised that ....

12 She said that ....

13 He suggested that ....

14 Then he said that ....

EXERCISES

B Read the interview with Adam Twine, and then answer the questions, using **He said** (with or without **that**) at the beginning of your answers.

ADAM: I am a farmer, and I am building a wind farm on my land. I also grow organic crops and produce organic milk and beef. I think wind farms are very important because they are much better for the environment than most other ways of producing electricity. The world needs more technologies for making electricity that are less damaging to our planet – clean, safe energy.

At first, I wanted to build a group of small turbines, but the bank didn't think that was economically efficient, so then I put in a new planning application for some larger turbines, as they produce more electricity, and I managed to get funding for a larger project.

Some local people were afraid that the wind turbines would be ugly and noisy, but the local council did a study and decided that my plans were acceptable. I got planning permission last summer. I did a lot of research and set up a web site, and I finally persuaded people to accept my plan. I got a lot of help from environmental organisations like Friends of the Earth and Greenpeace.

It has been a long battle, but we won in the end.

  0 What did Adam say he was building? *He said he was building a wind farm (on his land).*
  1 What else did he do on his farm? ....
  2 Did he think wind farms were good for the environment? ....
  3 What did he think the world needed? ....
  4 What had he wanted to build at first? ....
  5 What did he manage to get funding for? ....
  6 What were some local people afraid of? ....
  7 What had the local council done? ....
  8 Has he got planning permission? ....
  9 What did he do to persuade people to accept his plan? ....
 10 What had happened in the end? ....

JASMINE: Have you seen Susanna? Has she **told** you **what** happened to her?

CHERYL: I saw her just now but she didn't **tell** me **anything**.

JASMINE: Well, I saw that she was upset this morning so I **asked** her **if** I could help. Then she **told** me **that** she had been moved to another class! She was **asked to** collect her things and move.

CHERYL: No! Did she **tell** you **why**?

JASMINE: She **told** me **that** the teacher said she wasn't good enough to stay in this class. He **told** her she should have worked much harder.

CHERYL: Oh, that's not fair! Did she **tell** you **which** class she is going to?

JASMIN: Well, I **asked** her **where** she was going, and ... sshhh, here comes Gareth. Don't **tell** him **anything** about it!

reporting questions ask if / whether	When we want to report someone *asking for a yes or no answer*, we use **ask (someone) + if** or **whether**. We use the same verb patterns as in reporting statements: ■ Rose **asked if** we were going to the pool. ■ She **asked** us **whether** the water was warm.
reporting requests: ask to, ask if	To report someone *asking someone to do something in a polite way*, we use **ask ... to + infinitive** or **ask ... *pronoun* + would + *infinitive*** ■ Sahida **asked** Imran **to lend** her a pen. ■ Sahida **asked** Imran **if he would lend** her a pen. ■ Sahida **asked** Imran **if she could borrow** his pen.
ask where, what etc	If we are *asking for information*, we use **ask + question word** (**what**, **where**, **how**, **which** etc). We put the verb that was said after its *subject*: ■ Then she **asked where** the changing rooms **were**. ■ She **asked** us **how much** it cost and **what** the pool **was** like.
reporting instructions: tell ... (not) to	When we want to report *what someone instructed someone to do*, we use **tell ... to + infinitive**. To make the negative instruction we say **tell ... not to ...**: ■ Gustav **told** the secretary **to** write down the client's details. ■ I **told** the woman **not to** speak so quickly.
giving information: tell someone + noun	To report *someone or something giving information*, we use **tell ... + *noun clause***: ■ Laurence **told** Olaf his name. ■ The schedule **tells** us the time of each event.
tell + that, what, where etc.	To talk about *giving specific information about something that happens*, we use **tell .... + that / what / where** etc. + ***verb clause***. ■ Suhrud **told** everyone **where** the fire was. ■ The instructions **tell** you **how** to connect the hardware. ■ I'll **tell** you **when** to start the test. Note: we can leave out **that** after **tell**: ■ The article **tells** us **that** they have discovered a new planet. (= *The article tells us they have discovered a new planet.*)
tell + about	When we are talking about *giving general information on a subject*, we use **tell ... about + *noun clause***. ■ Professor Jesira Kone **told** us **about** her new discovery. ■ He always **tells** everyone **about** his children. To say that someone *gives us all the information*, we say **tell ... all about ...** : ■ Chaim **told** us **all about** his family.

EXERCISES

A Read about the interview with the organiser of the Watoto Children's Choir. Choose the best word from the box to go in the gaps. Sometimes, if the word is in brackets, it can be left out.

> what (that) if about ~~where~~ when (that)
> to about (that) when where

Sally Gomez, of the *New Zealand Times*, asked the organiser ⁰ ....*where*.... the children come from.

He told her ¹ .... the children come from Uganda.

She asked him ² .... they all live together.

He told her ³ .... they live in a community, because they have no parents.

She asked him ⁴ .... the choir started.

He told her ⁵ .... it started in 1944.

She asked him ⁶ .... kind of music the choir sings.

He told her all ⁷ .... their music, which is a mixture of Gospel and traditional African songs.

She asked him to tell her ⁸ .... their tour.

He told her ⁹ .... they were going, and ¹⁰ .... they are next performing in New Zealand.

Finally, she asked them ¹¹ .... sing something for us.

B Last summer, Nuru and Zeenat were arguing. Report what was said, using the clues in brackets.

NURU: Where is my towel, Zeenat?

  0 (ask – where – towel)

    Nuru asked Zeenat where her towel was.

ZEENAT: It's in the bathroom.

  1 (tell – in the bathroom)

    ....

NURU: No, it's not. I've looked everywhere.

  2 (tell – looked everywhere)

    ....

ZEENAT: You put it in the washing basket.

  3 (tell – where – put it)

    ....

NURU: Oh, yes, Here it is.

  4 (tell – found it)

    ....

NURU: Have you been using my towel?

  5 (ask – been using – towel)

    ....

ZEENAT: I haven't touched your towel.

  6 (tell – not touched – towel)

    ....

ZEENAT: I've got three of my own.

  7 (tell – got three of her own)

    ....

NURU: Who has been using it, then?

  8 (ask – been using it)

    ....

ZEENAT: I don't know. Go away and stop shouting at me.

  9 (tell – go away and stop shouting at her)

    ....

NURU: Why are you getting so angry?

  10 (ask – getting so angry)

    ....

A

Look at the picture and complete the sentences using indirect speech. Sometimes more than one answer is possible.

0 Mrs Shaw is asking Agnes .... *which doctor she usually sees.*

1 Agnes is saying ....

2 Karen is asking Sam ....

3 Sam is saying ....

4 Omar is asking ....

5 Mr Patel is telling Omar ....

6 The doctor is asking Mr Patel ....

7 Gino is telling Frank ....

8 Frank is asking Gino ....

9 Barry is telling the receptionist ....

10 The receptionist is asking Barry ....

B Last winter, Tanya and Jake were talking about hedgehogs. Complete the sentences below to report their conversation.

TANYA: ⁰ Have you seen the hedgehog in the garden?

JAKE: ¹ What is a hedgehog?

TANYA: ² It's a little, brown animal with spikes all over it.
³ Hedgehogs curl up into a ball when they are frightened.

JAKE: Oh, yes, I know. ⁴ Was it running about?

TANYA: No, ⁵ it was sitting in the flower bed.

JAKE: ⁶ Do they eat flowers?

TANYA: No, I don't think so. ⁷ They eat worms and insects, I think.

JAKE: ⁸ Bring it into the house, Mummy!

TANYA: No. ⁹ It will be too frightened. ¹⁰ Put on your coat and gloves and ¹¹ we can go out and give it some food.

0 Tanya asked Jake *if he had seen the hedgehog in the garden.*

1 Jake asked Tanya ....

2 Tanya told Jake ....

3 She told him ....

4 He asked her ....

5 She said ....

6 He wondered ....

7 She thought ....

8 He told her ....

9 She said ....

10 She told him ....

11 She said they ....

C Read the conversation and put in the right form of **say, tell,** or **ask** in the gaps.

MATT: Rachel ⁰ *told* me you were leaving tomorrow.

DON: Yes, that's right. I ¹ (not) .... anything to the others as I didn't want a big fuss.

MATT: Oh, but we wanted to have a party for you! You should ² .... us!

DON: I hate that kind of thing. Rachel ³ .... me if I wanted to go to the party on Saturday, so I had to ⁴ .... her.

MATT: Were you ⁵ .... anything before you left?

DON: I was going to ⁶ .... everyone this evening. John ⁷ .... we were going to have dinner at the Pizzeria tonight.

MATT: Well, I'm really glad you've got a good job back in Botswana. What did your mother ⁸ .... about it?

DON: Well, my mother is really excited. She ⁹ .... when I was arriving, so my brothers could all come to meet me at the airport.

MATT: We're really going to miss you! I hope you ¹⁰ .... us all about your new life.

DON: Of course I will! And you must come and stay with me there.

TABLE 1   **types of words and their use**

1 nouns and pronouns

A **noun**, or naming word, has a singular and a plural form. A noun can be one word or it can be made of two or more words. Usually the plural has a final **s**, but there are many irregular plurals:

> house, houses   party, parties
>
> koala bear, koala bears   running track, running tracks

(For more on nouns, see units 22–23, and for irregular noun plurals, see Table 3.)

There are two different kinds of nouns:

> **proper nouns** (which start with a capital letter) are names of places, people, or unique things:
>
> Hawaii   Mount Kilimanjaro   Karen   the Crown Jewels   Saturn
>
> **common nouns** are all the other nouns:
>
> book   river   man   window   science   light

Pronouns are words which are used in place of nouns. There are four different kinds of pronoun:

> **subject pronouns** – I, you, he, she, it, we, you, they:
> - The bird is in the back garden. **It** is singing.
>
> **object pronouns** – me, you, him, her, it, us, you, them:
> - Mrs Grant sent **me** an email.
>
> **possessive pronouns** – mine, yours, his, hers, its, ours, yours, theirs:
> - That coat is **hers**.
>
> **reflexive pronouns** – myself, yourself, himself, herself, itself, ourselves, yourselves, themselves:
> - The cat is washing **itself**.

(For more on pronouns, see units 27, 28 and 39.)

2 articles and other determiners

The **indefinite article** (**a** or **an**) before the noun tells us that *it doesn't matter*, or that *we don't know, which person or thing it is:*

> - **A** bird is singing. (*It doesn't matter which bird.*)
> - I heard **an** awful noise. (*I don't know what made the noise.*)

If we use the **definite article** (**the**) before the noun, it can tell us that *we already know which one it is:*

> - **The** bird is singing. (*The bird I told you about before.*)
> - I heard **the** awful noise of hammering. (*A noise I recognised.*)

(For more on articles, see unit 24.)

In addition to articles, there are other types of words that come before a noun, or **adjective** + **noun**. They are all called **determiners**, and they are:

> **demonstratives** – this, these, that, those (See unit 29.)
>
> **possessives** – my, your, his, her, its, our, your, their (See unit 28.)
>
> **quantifiers** – some, any, every, each, enough (See units 30, 32–35.)

3 main verbs and auxiliary verbs

A *main verb* comes immediately, or very soon, after the subject and tells you what the subject does or what the subject feels:

subject	verb
■ The lion	roars.
■ I	understand.

Each of these examples is a *sentence*. A basic sentence has all the information needed to communicate a simple idea.

Verbs have four possible forms:

an *infinitive*:

paint, look, offer, rain etc. (often with **to**)

a *third person singular* ending after **he**, **she**, **it** etc:

paints, looks, offers, rains

an **ing** *form*:

painting, looking, offering, raining

a *past* (**ed**) *form*:

painted, looked, offered, rained

Most verbs have the same form in the infinitive and present simple, but **be** is *irregular*:

be – am, are, is

A lot of common verbs have different past participle and past simple forms:

go – been, went

(For a list of irregular past forms, see Table 2.)

To add meaning to the main verb, we can add an *auxiliary verb* (**do**, **have**, **will**, **be**).

We use the auxiliary **do** to make questions and negatives, and as a substitute for other verbs:

■ '**Do** you like rock music?'   'Yes, I **do**.'

■ We **don't** know how to make chapattis.

We use the auxiliary verb **have** with a past participle (**ed** *form* of the main verb) for the perfect forms:

■ I **have worked** for Gargantuan for three years.

We use the auxiliary verb **be** with the present participle (**ing** *form* of the main verb) to indicate that something continues for some time:

■ Sheila**'s playing** tennis at the club.

Main verbs can be either *passive* or *active*. We make the passive form with **be** and the past participle:

■ Harry **is given** a lot of encouragement.

■ Don't **be tricked** by anyone!

(For more on passive verbs, see units 63–65.)

TABLE 1: types of words and their use in sentences

4 modal verbs

Modals are like auxiliary verbs, but they tell us different types of things about the main verb. They have only one form. Examples of modals are **must**, **might**, **may**, **should**, **ought to**, **will**, **have to**. After a modal verb we use the main verb in the infinitive. We use modals to say:

whether something is *necessary*:
- I **must** go now.
- They **must** pay for their meal.

whether something is *right or wrong*:
- Students **shouldn't** copy other people's work.
- Jack **ought to** stop laughing at Gail.

how *probable* something is:
- This book **will** help you pass the exam. (Note: **will** *is an auxiliary <u>and</u> a modal*.)
- **Shall** we try again?

how *possible* something is:
- I **might** not finish the paper in the time.
- Ahmed **may** get here this evening.

that someone is *capable of* doing something:
- Philip **can** do the tango!
- He **can't** make very good coffee.

that we are *asking permission or offering* to do something:
- **May** I talk to you for a minute?
- **Would** you like another piece of cake?

(For more on modal verbs, see units 69–73.)

5 describing words: adjectives and adverbs

To *describe* things and situations we use **adjectives**. These usually go before the noun:
- Jeffrey bought Sue a **beautiful** handbag.

We also use adjectives to *describe how something is or seems*. They usually go after the verb:
- The flowers were **bright orange**.

(Look at units 40 and 41 for more on adjectives.)

We also use the adjectives **my**, **your**, **his / her / its**, **our**, **your**, **their**, to talk about *possession*. They go before the noun:
- Where is **your** wife?

We can give more information about actions and states with **adverbs**. They may be one word or a phrase. There are several different categories of adverbs:

adverbs of manner (or comment) – These often end in **-ly** and go after the verb:
- The British gymnast landed **awkwardly**.

adverbs of time – These usually go at the end of the sentence:
- Tom always goes to bed **very late**.

adverbs of place – These usually go after the verb:
- A large black cat ran **across the bridge**.

adverbs of frequency – These usually go before the verb:
- The prime minister **usually** has a body guard.

adverbs of probability – These usually go before the verb:
- It's **definitely** going to rain.

adverbs of focus (or emphasis) – These usually go before the verb:
- Lucy has **only** been here for two days.

adverbs of quantity (intensifiers or diminishers) – These usually go before an adjective:

- You are **totally** wrong!

(For more on adverbs, see units 45–47.)

6 prepositions

To say *where* or *when something happened* we need to use *prepositions* (**in**, **at**, **on**, **under**, **through** etc). They are at the beginning of the phrases they refer to. These phrases are called *prepositional phrases*. Usually the prepositional phrase goes after the verb, but we also sometimes put it at the beginning of the sentence, especially in written English:

- There was a shed **in** the back garden. = **In** the back garden, there was a shed.

Sometimes we use a preposition on its own at the end of a sentence, especially if it is part of a *phrasal verb*:

- Maria told me to put my coat **on**.

(For more on prepositions, see units 48–54, and for phrasal verbs, see units 81 and 82.)

7 subjects

The *subject* of a clause or sentence is the person or thing who does the action or is the agent of the main verb. A subject may be:

a noun or noun phrase:

- **The old house next door** is empty.

a determiner:

- **That** smells nice!

or a pronoun:

- **We** have finished our homework.

In questions the subject goes after the auxiliary verb or **be**:

- Have **you** seen my file?
- Is **it** on the table?

8 objects

The *object* of a clause or sentence tells you who or what the subject acted on. The object may be a noun, or a phrase made up of a noun and other words, and it usually comes after the verb:

- Nabila picked **some flowers**.
- Imran watched **the grass moving in the wind**.

Not all verbs take objects:

- The train left at six o'clock.

Often there are two objects in a sentence. The main object is called the *direct object* and comes after the verb. The second object is called the *indirect object* and usually comes before the direct object:

	subject	verb	indirect object	direct object
■	David	is giving	the baby	a bottle of milk.
■	Ian	threw	Jeremy	the ball.

When the indirect object goes after the direct object we add **to** / **for** etc:

	subject	verb	indirect object	preposition	direct object
■	David	is giving	a bottle of milk	to	the baby.
■	Ian	threw	the ball	for	Jeremy.

TABLE 2

irregular past forms

1 irregular past participles ending in **en**, **n** or **ne**

infinitive	past simple	past participle
be	was/were	been
beat	beat	beaten
bite	bit	bitten
break	broke	broken
choose	chose	chosen
do	did	done
draw	drew	drawn
drive	drove	driven
eat	ate	eaten
fall	fell	fallen
fly	flew	flown
forbid	forbade	forbidden
forget	forgot	forgotten
freeze	froze	frozen
give	gave	given
go	went	gone
grow	grew	grown
hide	hid	hidden
know	knew	known
lie	lay	lain
ride	rode	ridden
rise	rose	risen
sew	sewed	sewn
shake	shook	shaken
show	showed	shown
speak	spoke	spoken
steal	stole	stolen
swear	swore	sworn
take	took	taken
tear	tore	torn
throw	threw	thrown
tread	trod	trodden
wake	woke	woken
wear	wore	worn
write	wrote	written

2 irregular past participles ending with a final syllable vowel change

infinitive	past simple	past participle
become	became	become
begin	began	begun
come	came	come
dig	dug	dug
feed	fed	fed
find	found	found
get	got	got
hang	hung	hung
light	lit	lit
meet	met	met
read /riːd/	read /red/	read /red/
ring	rang	rung
run	ran	run
shine	shone	shone
shoot	shot	shot
shrink	shrank	shrunk
sing	sang	sung
sink	sank	sunk
sit	sat	sat
spring	sprang	sprung
stand	stood	stood
stick	stuck	stuck
sting	stung	stung
stink	stank	stunk
strike	struck	struck
swim	swam	swum
swing	swung	swung
understand	understood	understood
win	won	won

3 irregular past participles ending in **t**

infinitive	past simple	past participle
bend	bent	bent
build	built	built
deal	dealt	dealt
feel	felt	felt
keep	kept	kept
learn	learned / learnt	learnt
leave	left	left
lose	lost	lost
mean	meant	meant
send	sent	sent
sleep	slept	slept
spend	spent	spent
spill	spilled	spilt
sweep	swept	swept

4 irregular past participles ending in **ught**

infinitive	past simple	past participle
bring	brought	brought
buy	bought	bought
catch	caught	caught
fight	fought	fought
seek	sought	sought
teach	taught	taught
think	thought	thought

5 irregular past participles with no change

infinitive	past simple	past participle
bet	bet	bet
burst	burst	burst
cost	cost	cost
cut	cut	cut
hit	hit	hit
hurt	hurt	hurt
put	put	put
set	set	set
shut	shut	shut
split	split	split
spread	spread	spread

TABLE 3

1 nouns with no change in the plural

Some nouns have the same form in the singular and the plural:

sheep	crossroads
fish	series
deer	gasworks
craft	grouse
dice	data
species	aircraft
means	salmon / trout / cod etc.
barracks	

2 en plurals

Some nouns coming from Old English have an **en** ending in the plural:

child → children
woman → women
man → men
ox → oxen

3 ouse singular → ice plural

Some nouns change from the singular **ouse** to the plural **ice**:

mouse → mice
louse → lice

4 oo singular → ee plural

Some nouns change **oo** + *consonant* to **ee** + *consonant*:

foot → feet
goose → geese
tooth → teeth

5 Latin and Greek endings

Some words coming from Latin and Greek have a different system of plural endings:

analysis → analyses
antenna → antennae (or antennas)
appendix → appendices (or appendixes)
automaton → automata
cactus → cacti (or cactuses)
crisis → crises
criterion → criteria
curriculum → curricula
fungus → fungi
medium → media (news, TV, radio etc)
nucleus → nuclei
phenomenon → phenomena
stratum → strata
thesis → theses

6 plural nouns with no singular

Some nouns are only used in the plural:

arms (weapons)	outskirts
belongings	remains
clothes	surroundings
congratulations	thanks
contents	trousers
earnings	scissors
goods	glasses (spectacles)

These plural nouns have a singular form:

police	youth
cattle	people

7 singular nouns ending in **s**

Some nouns have an s ending but are only used in the singular:

mathematics	politics
physics	gymnastics
billiards	measles
ethics	mumps

8 singular **o** → plural **oes**

hero → heroes
potato → potatoes
tomato → tomatoes

9 **fe** singular → **ves** plural

calf → calves
knife → knives
leaf → leaves
life → lives
loaf → loaves
self → selves
shelf → shelves
thief → thieves
wife → wives

TABLE 4 pronunciation

1 vowels, consonants, and phonemic symbols

The vowels of English are written as **a**, **e**, **i**, **o** and **u**. There are more vowel sounds than vowels, and some vowel sounds have more than one possible spelling. We use different phonemic symbols for each vowel sound. Dictionaries use these to help you to pronounce a new word. Here is a list of the phonemic symbols for English vowels.

/ə/ – op<u>e</u>n	/ɒ/ – h<u>o</u>t
/ɜː/ – b<u>ir</u>d	/ɑː/ – p<u>a</u>th (southern British)
/ʌ/ – t<u>u</u>g	/æ/ – b<u>a</u>d
/uː/ – sp<u>oo</u>n	/e/ – t<u>e</u>n
/ʊ/ – p<u>u</u>t	/ɪ/ – h<u>i</u>t
/ɔː/ – f<u>our</u>	/iː/ – f<u>ee</u>t

When two vowel sounds work together, they are called a *diphthong*. There are phonemic symbols for each diphthong:

/əʊ/ – s<u>o</u>	/ɔɪ/ – r<u>oy</u>al	/aʊ/ – t<u>ow</u>n
/eɪ/ – s<u>ay</u>	/ɪə/ – h<u>ere</u>	/ʊə/ – f<u>ewe</u>r
/aɪ/ – cr<u>y</u>	/eə/ – f<u>air</u>	

Each consonant sound also has a phonemic symbol:

/b/ – <u>b</u>old	/l/ – <u>l</u>emon	/ʒ/ – mea<u>s</u>ure
/k/ – <u>k</u>idney, <u>c</u>ar	/m/ – <u>m</u>ood	/t/ – <u>t</u>en
/tʃ/ – <u>ch</u>urch	/n/ – <u>n</u>othing	/ð/ – <u>th</u>is
/d/ – <u>d</u>oor	/ŋ/ – si<u>ng</u>	/θ/ – <u>th</u>in
/f/ – <u>f</u>ine	/p/ – <u>p</u>it	/v/ – <u>v</u>owel
/g/ – <u>g</u>ood	/r/ – <u>r</u>ight	/w/ – <u>w</u>in
/h/ – <u>h</u>air	/s/ – <u>s</u>un	/j/ – <u>y</u>es
/dʒ/ – <u>j</u>ust	/ʃ/ – <u>sh</u>ore	/z/ – <u>z</u>en

Note the sounds of the consonants **q** and **x**:

/kw/ – <u>q</u>ueen	/ks/ – e<u>x</u>it

2 intonation

Intonation is the rise and fall of the voice in speech. In English the voice is usually high on the most important words in a sentence, and falls at the end of a statement:

Karen likes water skiing

In questions the intonation usually starts high, and then falls and rises at the end:

Would you like a newspaper?

3 pronunciation of s endings

We add **s** to the end of nouns and verbs. The pronunciation of the **s** depends on the sound at the end of the word:

1 /k, f, p, t/ + /s/:
   pic<u>ks</u>, laug<u>hs</u>, ta<u>ps</u>, pu<u>ts</u>
2 /b, d, g, l, m, n, ŋ/ + vowel sounds + /z/:
   ro<u>bs</u>, ad<u>ds</u>, ba<u>gs</u>, b<u>oys</u>
3 /tʃ, s, ʃ, z/ + **es**, pronounced /ɪz/:
   pushes, fetches, passes, faxes

4 pronunciation of the **ed** ending

There are lots of irregular **ed** verb endings. The pronunciation of the regular endings depends on the sound of the previous syllable:

      1 unvoiced consonant (/k, f, p, t, s/) + **ed**, pronounced /t/:
         missed   tapped   picked   puffed
      2 voiced consonant (/b, d, g, m, n, ŋ/) + **ed**, pronounced /d/:
         robbed   praised   admired   nagged
      3 vowels and liquids (**l, w, y, r** etc) + **ed**, pronounced /d/:
         pulled   bored   prayed   sewed
      4 /t/ or /d/ + **ed**, pronounced /ɪd/:
         batted   padded   lasted   attracted

5 pronunciation of **r**

There are different pronunciations of the letter **r** in different parts of the English-speaking world. In 'standard' Southern British English we pronounce the **r** after a consonant very short and forward in the mouth, more with the lips than the tongue. We do not roll the tongue. A final **r** is not pronounced. In other regions, such as Scotland, the tongue is rolled, and in American English and the southwest of England, the **r** is 'dark', and made at the back of the mouth with the lips rounded.

Before a consonant, or between two vowels, we do not pronounce the **r**. It changes the pronunciation of the previous vowel:

park – /pɑːk/	sore – /sɔː/
port – /pɔːt/	care – /keə/
hurt – /hɜːt/	here – /hɪə/

6 weak and strong forms

Many common one-syllable words are pronounced very quickly in spoken English, and the pronunciation is different than when they are spoken slowly and clearly. The vowel is weakened, often to become /ə/ or /ɪ/. This is called the **weak** form of the word. The following is a list of some of the most common weak forms used in everyday speech:

a / an – /ə, ən/	will – /wəl/
the – /ðə/	would, could, should – /wəd, kəd, ʃəd/
some, come – /sʌm, kəm/	can, had, have – /kən, həd, həv/
at, as, am, that, than – /ət, əz, əm/	from, of, was – /frəm, əv, wəz/
you, to, should – /jə, tə, ʃəd/	them – /ðəm/
been – /bɪn/	shall – /ʃəl/
for – /fə/	

When a syllable is not stressed in a word with more than one syllable, the unstressed vowel is weakened. /iː/ becomes /ɪ/ and all the other vowels become /ə/:

part<u>ner</u> – /pɑːtnə/	b<u>e</u>lieve – /bɪliːv/
b<u>e</u>come – /bɪkʌm/	s<u>u</u>cceed – /səksiːd/
r<u>e</u>cov<u>er</u> – /rɪkʌvə/	<u>a</u>pply – /əplaɪ/

INDEX

ACKNOWLEDGEMENTS

with thanks:

to my best friend and editor, Ros Bell;

to my mother and Bill, my beautiful daughters, and friends Keith, Ken and John, who all helped to get me through the process a second time;

to all those fellow-teachers and authors who set me a good example;

to the illustrators who contributed so much to the book;

and, of course, to my publishing team, Simon Ross, Lucy Brodie and Carol Goodwright, and project manager Cathy Willis and designer Jo Barker, for realising my ideas better than I thought possible.

Photographs

p.6 ©Dynamic Graphics Group/IT Stock Free/Alamy; p.7 ©Warren Faidley/Oxford Scientific Photo Library; p.9 l ©Tom & Dee Ann McCarthy/Corbis, c ©BananaStock /Alamy, r ©Royalty Free/Corbis; p.13 ©Emma Thaler/Taxi/Getty Images; p.17 ©Getty Images Sport/Getty Images; p.19 ©James D. Morgan/ Rex Features; p.22 t ©Andy Cotterill, used with kind permission, b ©Ingram Publishing/Alamy; p.24 ©Ian M Butterfield/Alamy; p.25 l ©Bettmann/Corbis, r ©Popperfoto/Alamy; p.29 t ©Lee Krystek, b ©Authors Image/Alamy; p.30 ©Jack Sullivan/ Alamy; p.33 ©Redferns Music Picture Library/Alamy; p.36 ©Sipa Press/Rex Features; p.39 ©Rob Wilkinson/Alamy; p.40 ©Bill Miles/Corbis; p.43 ©Rex Features; p.44 ©Organic Picture Library/Rex Features; p.45 ©Mary Evans Picture Library; p.51 tl ©Peter Dazeley/Alamy, tr ©Steve Bloom Images/ Alamy, b ©Reuters/Corbis; p.53 ©Yann Arthus-Bertrand/Corbis; p.58 ©Svend and Carl Freytag/ NOAO/AURA/NSF/Science Photo Library; p.60 ©Andre Jenny/Alamy; p.61 ©Oxford Picture Library; p.64 ©Steven May/Alamy; p.67 ©Robbie Jack/ Corbis; p.72 ©Visualsafari/Alamy; p.74 ©Danita Delimont/Alamy; p.75 t ©Images of Africa Photobank/Alamy, b ©Dallas and John Heaton/Free Agents Ltd/Corbis; p.76 ©Tony Wilson-Bligh/Alamy; p.88 ©Brand X Pictures/Alamy; p.89 ©The Garden Picture Library/Alamy; p.93 ©Ross Nicholas; p.94 ©EuroStyle Graphics/Alamy; p.95 l ©Yang Liu/ Corbis, r ©Steve Allen/Alamy; p.96 ©The Image Bank/Getty Images; p.97 t ©The Image Bank/Getty Images, c ©WorldFoto/Alamy, b ©Gary Cook/Alamy; p.98 ©Alaska Stock LLC/Alamy; p.99 ©Royalty Free/Corbis; p.100 ©David Robertson/Alamy; p.102 ©Stock Works/Corbis; p.105 ©Ace Stock Limited/Alamy; p.106 ©Ark Religion/Helene Rogers; p.110 ©Blinkstock c/o Blink Enterprises, LLC/Alamy; p.111 ©Reza; Webistan/Corbis; p.112 t ©John Springer Collection/Corbis, bl ©Bettmann/Corbis, br ©Najlah Feanny/Corbis Saba; p.116 ©Detlev Van Ravenswaay/SPL; p.120 ©Smiley N. Pool/Dallas Morning News/Corbis; p.122 ©Dennis Cooper/ Zefa/Corbis; p.124 ©Charles Stuge/Alamy; p.125 ©Royalty Free/Corbis; p.127 ©isifa Image Service s.r.o./Alamy; p.128 ©epa/Corbis; p.131 StockFood Creative/Getty Images; p.138 ©Steve Allen Travel Photography/Alamy; p.141 ©John Arnold Images/ Alamy; p.142 ©Franck Seguin/Corbis; p.145 ©Alessandra Benedetti/Corbis; p.148 ©Larry Lilac/Alamy; p.150 ©V&A Images/Alamy; p.151 ©Jeff Rotman/Alamy; p.155 ©Jeff Morgan/Alamy; p.158 l ©Anna Peisl/Zefa/Corbis, r ©Jim Craigmyle/ Corbis; p.161 t ©Sipa/Rex Features, b ©Caroline Penn/Corbis; p.168 ©Blend Images/Alamy; p.169 ©PhotoAlto/Alamy; p.170 ©Angelo Cavalli/Zefa/ Corbis; p.173 t ©Image Source/Rex Features, b ©ImageState/Alamy; p.174 ©Photofusion Picture Library/Alamy; p.177 ©Walter Lockwood/Corbis; p.184 ©Stefan Meyers/zefa/Corbis; p.185 ©Ahmed Jallanzo/epa/Corbis; p.187 l ©ImageState/Alamy, r ©BL Images Ltd/Alamy; p.192 ©Holt Studios International Ltd/Alamy; p.193 ©archivberlin Fotoagentur GmbH/Alamy; p.200 ©Max Stuart/ Alamy; p.201 ©Amit Bhargava/Corbis; p.202 ©Gabe Palmer/Alamy; p.204 ©Helene Rogers/Art Directors; p.207 ©Mary Evans Picture Library; p.209 ©J Marshall – Tribaleye Images/Alamy; p.212 ©Oxford University Archives, by permission of the Secretary to the Delegates of Oxford University Press; p.213 ©Westmill Windfarm Co-operation, used with kind permission; p.215 ©Jacek Gancarz (PBN)/Rex Features; p.217 ©Stephen Street/Alamy.

Artwork

Pg.95 Flower illustrations ©Marjorie Blamey, used with kind permission of Domino Books